DA   187722
358
.S2
H39x
1989

Msgr. Wm. Barry Memorial Library
Barry University
Miami, FL   33161

HAYNES

ROBERT CECIL

ROBERT CECIL, EARL OF SALISBURY

ALAN HAYNES

ROBERT CECIL
EARL OF SALISBURY, 1563–1612

Servant of Two Sovereigns

PETER OWEN · LONDON

U.S. DISTRIBUTOR
DUFOUR EDITIONS
CHESTER SPRINGS,
PA 19425-0449
(215) 458-5005

ISBN 0 7206 0716 7

PETER OWEN PUBLISHERS
73 Kenway Road London SW5 ORE

First published 1989
© Alan Haynes 1989

Printed in Great Britain by Billings of Worcester

Men will turn over half a library to make one book.

Samuel Johnson

Subtle craft our sole resource . . .

A Moorish ballad, 1568, Ibn Daoud

Contents

Illustrations

The illustrations in this volume are reproduced by courtesy of the following: Plates 1 and 3, the Marquess of Salisbury; plate 2, Weiss Gallery, London; plate 4, National Portrait Gallery, London; plate 5, Courtauld Institute of Art, London University.

Acknowledgements

Scholars, librarians and archivists in England and the United States, often responding more than dutifully to my requests for information, have made the preparation of this book much easier. I want to thank them again collectively as I have thanked them individually. But still certain people must be mentioned by name: Lynn Hulse, whose paper to the Royal Musical Association on Salisbury's patronage of musicians was invaluable; Julia Merritt; Jane Lingard, who has kindly allowed me to use material from her unpublished MA report for the Courtauld Institute, London University; Dr Pauline Croft; and Dr Robert Evans and Mary Edmond, who sent me an elusive volume. All gave me special guidance and direction. If I have blundered in ways they did not anticipate, the fault rests with me alone. Their generosity is the perfect scholarly rebuke to the slothful and mean-spirited few (happily, very few) who could not even pen a brief reply to an inquiry.

The Authors' Foundation (administered by a panel established by the Society of Authors) provided me with a sum which covered certain expenses in the preparation of the manuscript. This was a great help and most welcome.

My thanks as well to my editor Gillian Beaumont and to Vicki Annis, who typed the book. Above all, I must salute my family who, though slightly bemused by my obsession with Tudor and Jacobean England, supported me through illness and recovery. The book is dedicated to them.

Author's Note

Throughout this book the year is taken to begin on 1 January rather than 25 March.

For the sake of clarity, and because this biography is not completely chronological, I have referred to my subject as Cecil or Salisbury. However, it should be remembered that in 1591 he was knighted; on 13 May 1603 he became Baron Cecil of Essendon (Herts); on 20 August 1604 Viscount Cranborne; and finally on 4 May 1605 Earl of Salisbury.

1

Robert Cecil was the son of Sir William Cecil, later Lord Burghley (1571), and his second wife, the redoubtable Mildred Cooke. At the time of his birth on 1 June 1563, twenty-one years after his half-brother Thomas, his father had been Secretary of State to Elizabeth I for some four years; Nicholas Bacon, his uncle, was Lord Keeper, while his maternal grandfather, Sir Anthony Cooke, had been governor to Edward VI. Born into a Protestant family at the centre of English political life, Robert Cecil spent his entire career in the service of the Crown. Whitehall Palace in particular, with its labyrinthine corridors and enfilades, made the perfect setting for such a brilliantly resourceful man who laboured against a background of threats and bodily infirmity. He achieved and maintained his position of power through fierce attention to the minutiae of public affairs and administration. Few but his intimates ever saw him without a clutch of papers.

Sickly as a baby, a delicate but clever child, he grew up with a definite curvature of the spine which led to the development of a noticeable hump. In adulthood his mere silent presence could disconcert otherwise bold and blustering men; his eyes especially seemed to probe beyond a superficial truth. Yet this was a society that saw many more gross physical imperfections in people through birth traumas and congenital defects, or the calamities of war, than would be seen in England today. The tremor of disgust then could stem from a persistent concern that the deformed exterior betokened a delinquent or dangerous spirit – an unknown miscellany of vices. The deformity that prevented Cecil's mature height ever exceeding about five feet has in the past been routinely blamed on his tumbling as an infant from the arms of a wet-nurse. However, this ignores evidence of a capricious gene in the Cooke line, for his mother was somewhat hunchbacked, and later Cecil's own daughter Frances received treatment at his command to correct her appearance. He had also, like his mother, a shallow declivity on the side of his forehead.

Because Cecil was short, uncomely as a child, contemplative in the way of all junior valetudinarians, and with a splay-footed gait that also precluded sports other than shooting and hawking, his contemporaries were later to give the man a number of cruel nicknames. It was probably a guilt-free (Sir) Anthony Standen, a secret agent in service with Cecil's cousin Anthony Bacon, who coined 'Monsieur de Bossu'. Others were 'Bossive Robin', 'Microgibbous' and 'Roberto il Diavolo', the last two favoured by Antonio Perez.[1] 'Elf' and 'pigmy' were royal choices, and 'bumbasted-legs' and 'St Gobbo' were coined by Francis Davison in a testy mood in 1596.[2] Later still, in medical notes, one of Cecil's many doctors – Theodore de Mayerne-Turquet, Baron d'Aubonne (a Huguenot, born near Geneva, known in England as Sir Theodore de Mayerne) – referred to scoliosis, a clear diagnosis that fits the facts.[3] Whatever the case, William Cecil cannot have observed his son without a twinge of regret that Thomas Cecil, his first-born heir, if not exactly a booby, was unlikely to scale the political heights, although he had a career involving public duties. If Burghley planned for a son to follow him into high office, it surely had to be Robert Cecil. While his general puniness was a serious disadvantage at a time when genuine dwarfs were often court curios, it did mean he was always raised at home.

It is noticeable that the Burghleys declined to follow the well-established contemporary fashion of sending a boy as soon as possible to be educated and nurtured in another nobleman's household. The exchange of children in Tudor

England was a singular, even fossilized phenomenon which had possibly originated in hostage-taking or some other mode of social control during the long agony of the Wars of the Roses. By the 1560s it was to be found at all levels, with the exception of the royal household and amongst the mass of wage-earners. For example, Robert Cecil's contemporary, Thomas Egerton, later Lord Ellesmere, an illegitimate son of a newly squired family, the Egertons of Ridley, was raised in the Ravenscroft family.[4] The Cecil household itself, noted for sobriety and scholarship, became a much sought after home and academy for young aristocrats like the Earls of Essex and Oxford, Rutland and Southampton. But the choice was made by other adults, and the disciplined humanist education they received from tutors, together with the dignified environment, did not always sit well with these effervescent juveniles. So whatever rebukes or discomforts the young Oxford suffered, he more than returned them by his contemptuous treatment of Anne Cecil, whom he had married at the behest of her snobbish parent.

Robert, her brother, may have lacked the physical *élan* of his more robust contemporaries, but since his mother was one of the most learned women of the time, it was as well he proved a willing student. One of his tutors was Dr Richard Howland, later Master of Burghley's old Cambridge College, St John's, and after a period as his chaplain, Bishop of Peterborough. Another tutor was Walter Travers, a Puritan preacher at the Temple from 1581 to 1592, when he spoke for the doctrines of Geneva. He was probably the choice of Mildred Cecil, herself of 'the austerian persuasion'. It has often been suggested that she sent her son's classroom companion Richard Neile (b. 1562) to Westminster School as a generous act of patronage to the fortunate son of a tallow-chandler. But by his own admission later, when Bishop of Durham, he was regularly thrashed at school for his failing to master classical languages, and it may well be that Lady Burghley was simply expressing exasperation at his blockishness – especially if he was holding back her evidently intellectually gifted son. He had, of course, made an early start in Latin and also Greek, in which his mother was fluent. In modern languages he studied French, Italian and Spanish, acquiring a foundation on which he could build in emulation of his father, whose private reading was rarely in his mother tongue. Indeed, the educated, privileged Englishman was then rarely monoglot, though few would have rivalled the author, traveller and politician Laurence Tomson, who mastered twelve languages, or Dr Lancelot Andrewes, said to have commanded fifteen. In English alone he 'was later to enthral King James and Queen Anne in his Easter and Christmas sermons'.

Other subjects to be mastered were cosmography, mathematics, music and calligraphy, and despite pressures in later life he wrote elegantly and recognizably.[5] He was also fortunate to have the run of Burghley's library with its many presentation copies and also illustrated manuscripts. While for sheer size and variety this *bibliotheca instructissima* was inferior to John Dee's, and he assembled his on a fraction of the Lord Treasurer's income, it was a marvellous resource for a bookish boy. Raised as a Protestant by a Puritan mother and tutor, Cecil could have read Calvinist texts from Geneva, as well as psalters. He was certainly thoroughly familiar with the Bible, especially the Old Testament, which later in life he seems to have regarded characteristically as a document giving a revealing slant on power politics. If all this suggests a wearisome little sobersides, there was mirth in his animated friendship with Michael Hickes. The revealing thing about this was that Hickes, Burghley's secretary from 1573, was twenty years older than Robert Cecil, but he was always a teasing, genial man who did much to dispel any tendency in the boy to gloom.

Self-pity might have sat on Cecil's misshapen shoulders if he had too often made a routine comparison of his appearance and aptitudes with those of Robert Devereux, Viscount Hereford from 1572 to 1576 and then 2nd Earl of Essex.* Like

---

* It has recently been established by Michelle Margetts that Essex was born on 10 November 1565.

14

many of this Tudor generation of the 1560s he has recently been identified in a hard-driven thesis as a man of his time – peculiarly driven and ruthless in personal ambition.[6] The two Roberts became court rivals during the lowering 'bottleneck' years of the 1590s. They had probably first met in the mid-1570s when Essex was ten and Cecil twelve. Juveniles will often regard their living antithesis with sour disapproval and it is not hard to imagine the silent resentment of the older boy during the interlude in the Burghley household. Essex went up early to Cambridge (not then a sign of extreme precocity) and there was a court career in prospect. By the time Cecil went to St John's in 1580, Essex's studies at Trinity College were at an end – though he did matriculate in 1579 – because his expenses constantly exceeded his allowance. It was a pattern often repeated in the next twenty years until economic panic, induced by possible bankruptcy, drove him to ruin. In the meantime he left the supervision of the Earl of Hunting-don (the kind brother-in-law of his stepfather, the Earl of Leicester) and withdrew to the family estates in west Wales to spend an apparently fulfilling period consolidating his studies while living at the ancestral mansion at Lamphey.

Nor did Cecil bother to take his degree while a fellow commoner, the most privileged rank of students, with fees paid by their families, so that the Vice-Chancellor, Dr Andrew Perne, mocked by his enemies for his lightning shifts of religious observance during the mid-Tudor crisis, wrote flatteringly that he hoped Robert would return for another year 'for his commendations and encouragement and to the good example and provocations of other scholars'.[7] In fact Cecil was soon admitted to Gray's Inn, where his civility and disciplined disposition again won applause from his elders, but by 1582 he had withdrawn to private study with a recommended tutor called Wilkinson who was still in the Burghley household in 1588. To round off his studies Cecil really needed to go abroad, since as Shakespeare was soon to write, 'He cannot be a perfect man, /Not being try'd and tutor'd in the world.' But for a time Burghley was reluctant to allow this, regarding his son's physique as too delicate, and also because Thomas Cecil's period of travel in Europe years before had been such an expensive failure. The reason was that the eldest son had merely used the opportunity for some mild dissipation away from parental control.

Burghley nurtured better hopes of his tractable younger son who, by Elizabethan standards, seems to have been diffident in such matters, so that he was finally allowed to go to France in 1584. It was shortly after the death of François, Duke of Anjou, whose protracted wooing of Elizabeth several years before had caused such turbulence in the English court. Cecil was surely primed by his father to observe the effect of this demise on the French court factions. Arriving in Paris in late July he was met by the resident English ambassador, Sir Edward Stafford, lately an enemy of Burghley's formidable political rival, the Earl of Leicester.[8] Still, the political neophyte declined to stay with Stafford in order to submerge himself in the French *vie quotidienne*. After a visit to Fontainebleau and with the court still at Blois, he settled to studying, attending daily the public disputations at the Sorbonne, from which he emerged, as he recorded, 'an English-settled Huguenot'.[9] No change there.

Cecil's penchant for doing the correct thing was markedly less discernible in some of the company he kept. His leisure companion was the unruly Dr William Parry, a spendthrift doctor of law once sued for debt and more unusually charged with burglary. Even less routinely, he had nearly killed a creditor.[10] By October 1583 he was in Paris as an agent of Burghley charged with the not too difficult task of keeping an eye on English Catholic exiles who were planning a propaganda offensive against their most hated aristocratic enemy in England – the Earl of Leicester. Since Paris emptied in August, Cecil and Parry did their sightseeing when there was 'little a-doing here, everybody being gone'.

These pleasant days in the city with a companion he clearly liked, visits to Fontainebleau and Orléans, and the lengthy accounts of his observations and meetings written to the

Principal Secretary of State, Sir Francis Walsingham, ended in October 1584: too brief a time for the twenty-one-year-old Cecil, one suspects, but he obeyed his father's call to return to London, where he was elected to Parliament for the first time. He and Thomas Knyvett were returned for Westminster seats, and his cousin Francis Bacon and Dr Parry were also members. It was the latter who, to the consternation of both Cecils, violently attacked anti-Catholic legislation introduced to counter the distribution of *Leicester's Commonwealth*, now being smuggled into England by agents of Fr Robert Persons from his base in Rouen. With the Christmas recess Parry went to ground in order to plot against Elizabeth. Swiftly betrayed, he was tortured; he confessed and was executed. Robert Cecil may have been dismayed by this vile end to a friendship, but it is doubtful if he flinched at it. This was the characteristic demeanour of a man whose loyalty to Elizabeth and James I never faltered at any time. For Cecil, necessity of State overrode all considerations of esteem and affection. Burghley, in the period after this, was surprised by the extent of the dislike felt for his son and political disciple.[11]

Knyvett and Cecil were returned for the same seats in 1586, which was not surprising with Burghley as high steward of the borough. Even so, the young man was not constrained to say anything, although later in his career he would always draw an attentive audience. Also long delayed was his removal to a home of his own, but this also took place at about this time despite his lack of office, and even the reversion of the stewardship of Elsing was only unwillingly granted by the Queen. The reason for her indifference was surely that her attention was focused on the Earl of Essex, the Apollonian stepson of Leicester. Robert Devereux was now twenty – tall, handsome and improvident, a swordsman with a genuine interest in scholarship, a writer of verse. He was poised to take one of the most significant offices of the court, the Mastership of the Horse, from a reluctant Leicester. Essex won his spurs in battle; Cecil's first official duty was to record the meetings of Elizabeth and the House of Commons over the conduct and fate of Mary Queen of Scots.

With Burghley and the Privy Council under a cloud for precipitating the execution in February 1587 of that regally stupid woman, and with Essex boldly pursuing military glory under the generalship of Leicester in the United Provinces, Cecil could only wait for another opportunity. This came with an embassy headed by Henry Stanley, Earl of Derby, who early in 1588 invited him to join a mission for peace talks with Alessandro Farnese, Duke of Parma, Philip II's most successful general. Burghley seems to have been uneasy at the thought of his son undertaking difficult and strenuous journeys in winter but was finally persuaded by Cecil, Mildred Cecil and Sir Francis Walsingham. Moreover, Burghley may have been soothed by Derby inviting the young man to travel in that comparative novelty, a coach, rather than on horseback. The other commissioners were Lord Cobham, Sir James Crofts and Dr Valentine Dale, but it was Cecil whom the Queen asked to write directly to her.[12] Realizing that this might discountenance his elders, he 'sought a means to keep all sweet' while protesting in a letter to his cousin Stanhope (which he knew the Queen would see) that she should condescendingly refer to him as 'pigmy' – a nickname he detested.

On 26 February 1588 the party reached Ostend, a town battered by war and food shortages for which Cecil sought a personal remedy with some nets and a hunting dog. Parma was in Bruges and while efforts were made to resolve the problem of where the two sides would meet, the mission huddled round the inadequate smoking peat fire that set Cecil longing for a real coal-fire blaze that would warm more than his fingertips. Eventually, Dale and a small party including Cecil rode to Ghent, leaving on 8 March and arriving on the 10th, having eaten only an orange each one night. (The bitter Seville orange?) 'It was two days', wrote Dale to Burghley, 'before we had a couple of eggs apiece and then we thought we fared like princes. . . .'[13] In fact, in this land even princes did not live extravagantly, for when they did meet Parma, with Cecil one of those received as a compliment to his father, he

18

remarked that the furnishings of the room were 'small and mean'. He concluded that 'peace is the mother of all honour and state', but there was no peace established by these fruitless negotiations, and he was free to travel again since he had no official part to play in the mission.

After parting from Dale, Cecil went to Antwerp, Bergen op Zoom, Rotterdam, Delft and The Hague. There he met Prince Maurice of Nassau and, being a small man in the company of a boisterous larger individual, felt distinctly uncomfortable. His comment was caustic: 'In my life I never saw worse behaviour except it were one that lately came from school.'[14] By 20 March he was in Brill, where his half-brother had lately been governor, and a week later he was back in Ostend, thinking to observe and report until midsummer. However, towards the middle of April he returned to London to submit a report, and at the same time awaited the expected death of his long-put-upon sister Anne, Countess of Oxford, who died on 5 June.

Private sorrow was all too soon overshadowed by the threat of invasion from Spain. The speed of the developing crisis was such that Cecil's Italian language teacher found his pupil absent so often that he decided to quit the country. This was not a general option. Sir Thomas Cecil, for example, was a gentleman-volunteer at sea, while in contrast Robert struggled with paperwork and for a brief period was Master of the Ordnance of the Army at Tilbury under the command of Leicester, until he was replaced by Sir Francis Knollys. However, when the English and Spanish fleets clashed off Calais on 29 July Cecil was a witness, and if he had any duties at Dover they are not known. The excursion on Sir William Winter's ship was only a short one. Even so, Elizabeth was slowly beginning to appreciate his talents and if Leicester's antagonism had blocked his career development so far, this could not be permanent. In August, when the earl was savouring the annihilation of the Spanish threat and was too tired to think of anything else, the Queen chose Cecil to meet an envoy from Morocco. The Shārif Moulay Ahmad al-Manṣūr sent Marzūq

Ra'is to England in the company of the departing English ambassador to that country, Henry Roberts.[15] The Shārif's intention was to propose a treaty of friendship with England (not in itself so bizarre) as a prelude to participation in an expedition to liberate Portugal from Spanish rule. The prime mover behind Anglo–Moroccan contacts was Leicester, but he was now too exhausted – and latterly ill – to pursue the political possibilities, and on 4 September 1588 he died at Cornbury.

At this time Cecil was also undertaking more private and delicate negotiations. At a court that prized good looks and a fine carriage he was dismayingly deficient, and this surely made him nervous of necessary courtship. A letter to his sister-in-law Dorothy Cecil (*née* Perrot), although not in his hand, indicates his acute nervousness at the possibility of a rebuff from the young woman he had selected as a possible future wife. Yet Elizabeth Brooke, the daughter of Lord Cobham, Lord Warden of the Cinque Ports, surprisingly had no qualms about being wooed by Cecil, for all that he was a younger son and still very much dependent for advancement on the protective advocacy of his father and then the low-key goodwill of the Queen. Plans for the marriage were going ahead when Cecil's mother died – a loss to him since she had been well versed in political arts, and had been constantly about the Queen. Although her demise briefly altered her son's marriage plans, the grieving Burghley gave him in anticipation a property in Edmonton and a farm at Pymmes, not far from the great house at Theobalds, itself bought a year after Robert's birth from the landowner Robert Burbage. Cecil, now a justice of the peace and an MP for Hertfordshire in the 1588/9 Parliament, was appointed Sheriff of the county in August. With this enhancement of his dignity, he and Elizabeth were married on 31 August 1589. It was a happy union, and her £2,000 dowry was more than satisfactory. As Cecil himself once recorded, his wife, a homemaker, could be charmingly naïve, telling everyone she met the price of a particular fabric. He was much less fortunate with his

20

brothers-in-law, Henry and George Brooke.

Cecil and his young bride, who sometimes attended the Queen, had scarcely grown accustomed to their new life together when a political opening suddenly became available. It was the result of the death on 6 April 1590 of Sir Francis Walsingham, whose private papers were immediately stolen. The benefit to Cecil would have been huge and he has long been a suspect. The Elizabethan Secretary of State was a very important man indeed, generally keeper of both the Privy Seal and the Signet, so that all warrants to move the Great Seal passed through his office. Naturally he was frequently besieged by suitors seeking royal approval for such warrants, and in addition he served as a private and public secretary to Elizabeth. He and his clerks drafted and dispatched all the royal correspondence, and since this included diplomatic letters there was an amusing and pointed little acted scene during the Queen's visit to Theobalds in May 1591. It was a dialogue, written by John Davies, between a postman and a gentleman usher concerning the delivery of a clutch of letters, including one from the Emperor of Cathay. The question posed was whether these should go directly to Elizabeth or 'Mr Secretary Cecil'. Blithely ignoring the undoubted fact that the great office was vacant, the postman still insisted that Cecil should deal with them since whatever the Queen's high learning, she was not conversant with Chinese.[16] A good Secretary would oversee a translation, and through his constant contact with the sovereign he was clearly in a position to help in the formulation of foreign policy.

This was of special interest to the Earl of Essex, who since the death of Leicester had espoused the same causes and who the previous year had taken part in a bungled attempt to restore Dom Antonio to the throne of Portugal. Essex was a soldier of outstanding courage, not an administrator, so he had already singled out a candidate for the Secretaryship to block the possible advancement of Robert Cecil if that was in the Queen's mind. With his poignant capacity for choosing the least likely man to appeal to her, the earl again sought the rehabilitation of the languishing William Davison, whom he had defended in the turbulent aftermath of the execution of Mary Queen of Scots. Elizabeth agreed that he had the diplomatic experience required, but she had not the slightest intention of appointing him.

Burghley – now in semi-retirement, melancholy and periodically ailing, already heavily burdened – was now required to undertake the work of Secretary without the title or perquisites. This was meant to be a temporary expedient, but it did nothing to halt the growing rivalry of his son and Essex as alternative names – Henry Killigrew, Edward Wotton and Thomas Wilkes – seemed set but then declined. It was her Lord Treasurer's state of mind rather than body which drew Elizabeth to Theobalds early in May 1591, and his lethargy was eventually dispersed as she intended while he sought his son's promotion to the Secretaryship. As has already been indicated, the entertainments devised for the Queen and court were saturated with blatant hints about the best candidate for the appointment. On arrival she was greeted by Cecil, dressed as a hermit, and to his verse solicitations Elizabeth responded with a mock charter inscribed on vellum.[17] Signed by Sir Christopher Hatton, the Lord Chancellor, the document was addressed to 'the Heremite of Tybole', giving the royal assent to his much-vaunted desire to return to his cave. Three years later on a further visit the hermit routine, always popular, was again played – perhaps for more than it was worth, in view of its familiarity. As it was, the hints and reminders now failed and Cecil's only reward was his knighthood on 20 May. This was essentially a sop to Burghley (Thomas Cecil having been knighted in 1575 during the famous Kenilworth festivities) and was of little significance to the title-holder, who wanted power rather than a mundane honour. When Burghley was ill again during the summer it was thought once more that Cecil might have the office officially, since he was already doing some of the work Burghley could not discharge. But Cecil was still inexperienced, whatever his training for high office, and the most logical – even helpful – policy was not to appoint him prematurely, but to let him work in tandem with his father. In the meantime, giving him a place among the greybeards of the Privy Council was suggestive of his great future.

At this time Essex was in France with a small army sent to aid Henri IV. As usual he scorned economy, though he was teetering on the brink of financial ruin. He had been saved only by the grant of the farm of Sweet Wines, that grand old stand-by of his late stepfather. It was in Essex's absence that Cecil joined the Privy Council on 2 August 1591, a promotion that had so far eluded his charismatic contemporary. At the time of this appointment there were only eight peers and four commoners on the Council, with John Wolley, the Latin Secretary who was knighted in 1592, as the sole possible rival for the Secretaryship. To establish his presence in the highest council of the realm Cecil attended many meetings, while Burghley may also have thought a literary dedication would enhance a growing reputation. It seems very likely that it was he who suggested to William Lambarde, his deputy in the Office of Alienations, that he should dedicate his manuscript called 'Archeion' to Robert Cecil. In October 1591, when it was finished, Lambarde did this, yet much of the recognition the text might have brought the author failed to materialize as it languished in Cecil's hands.[18] He failed to sponsor it, so it remained unprinted, although read by a select group who borrowed the manuscript. The reason for this curious neglect is not known, although it may be correct to attribute it to pressure of work in 1592.

2

Early in 1592 Cecil was appointed to his first conciliar commission – an investigation and trial of Sir John Perrot, whose son's marriage gave him an Essex connection. While serving as Lord Deputy of Ireland Perrot had frequently been drunk and then made ill-judged comments about his sovereign. He supposed this was allowed him because of a claimed relationship to her which did not, however, save him from being convicted of treason. But the death sentence was not carried out and cynics promptly put this down to bribes for the Cecils, which Perrot vehemently denied as he lay dying of natural causes in the Tower.

The second commission required altogether more effort, and the possibility of reward or opprobrium was commensurately greater. In early August 1592 Sir John Borough (or Burgh) in Ralegh's ship the *Roebuck*, supported by the *Dainty* and the *Golden Dragon*, captured, with the late intervention of the ships of the Earl of Cumberland, the great Portuguese carrack correctly known as the *Madre de Deus*, but normally called the *Madre de Dios*. The fighting had been conducted with much ferocity in the year after the destruction of the *Revenge* and the death of Sir Richard Grenville. Certainly the disaster-prone Captain Fernâo de Mendoça (who had been flag-captain to the Duke of Medina Sidonia in the Armada fleet) and his crew resisted more strenuously than was expected of a merchant ship. But when they finally capitulated, the English seamen were able to make a preliminary assessment of their prize, and they were staggered both by the size of the ship – 1,600 tons burden; seven decks – and the variety of its huge cargo. Dropped candles then destroyed a small part of the haul and eager hands began to seize the richest portable booty for stowing away as far as possible from prying eyes. One wonders too about the treatment of the hundreds of black slaves on board since Luanda (Angola). They had been taken aboard in May and could not be held in England as slaves, so presumably they dispersed into the depths of London.

Borough was undoubtedly the luckiest man in the fleet. Frobisher did nothing like as well, taking only a small ship with a cargo of sugar. Then he heard the extraordinary news of the carrack from Captain Robert Crosse of the Queen's ship *Foresight*, and it was Frobisher who gave advance warning of the seizure when he docked in Plymouth. When the news reached London there was an agitated surge of merchants, jewellers, goldsmiths and speculators to virtually every port on the south coast.[1] There was no knowing where Borough would bring his prize, but on 7 September it proved to be Dartmouth, and his major task now was to prevent an orgiastic sacking of the ship.

This was also the principal concern of the shareholders in the voyage, notably Elizabeth, who appointed Burghley and Sir John Fortescue to administer the distribution of appropriate shares of the plunder to the many claimants. A board of commissioners was established of sailors, Customs officials and merchants: Sir Francis Drake, William Killigrew, Richard Carmarden, Henry Billingsley and Sir George Barne, with Thomas Middleton (soon to be clerk of Temple Church) as secretary. To stiffen and underline their authority Robert Cecil was to take charge of proceedings and oversee the unloading – a job made particularly difficult, as was intended, by the provoking filching of the ship's bill of lading.[2] Cecil went first to Exeter, but despite an injunction on movement to the ports plenty of people had already been stirred by greed to make a dash to south-west England. Cecil went on to Dartmouth and Plymouth to set up local commissions to deal with those suspected of pillage, sniffing out the evidence in some cases quite literally, since part of the cargo was a consignment of civet.

To challenge the covetous and sometimes desperate, Cecil needed powerful support from a West Country man, and this he got from Sir Walter Ralegh. Having spent a period in the Tower for his seduction and marriage of Elizabeth (Bess) Throckmorton, Ralegh was now released to overbear the light-fingered. He was also, of course, deeply concerned to see recovery and profit from his own investment, for the enterprise had virtually ransomed him. Since he was popular only in his home territory, he counted on this and the force of his personality to help him recover some of the items already missing. The startling range of these was confirmed by members of the crew: little in bullion, but huge quantities of precious and semi-precious stones; mother-of-pearl; porcelain; pepper; ambergris; elephants' tusks; musk; carpets and jewellery. Crew members thought the material loss so far amounted to some 115,000 crusados or nearly £29,000.[3] Middleton's immediate task was to estimate the value of the remainder, while Ralegh seethed at the vile thought that his release from the 'unsavoury dungeon' (doubtless an exaggeration) might be his only benefit. Within ten days of the ship being docked he was already planning reprisals, and while Cecil remained outwardly calm even he must have stirred inwardly when Middleton, with some trepidation, estimated the remaining cargo's value at £150,000.

This was actually more like an intelligent guess than a real appraisal, with the large items like silks, spices, carpets, and so on being valued eventually at some £141,000 when they were transported to Leadenhall for sale. It was probably the vast quantity of pepper, nearly three-quarters of a million pounds, which caused the greatest problem since selling that quantity quickly would cause a price collapse. Carmarden and Middleton mulled over several schemes to confront this problem, but eventually it was decided to sell it in bulk to a commodity syndicate, with £90,000 being paid in yearly instalments.[4] The men involved outbid the Palavicino group by paying out some £1,300 as *douceurs* to men like Burghley's secretary Henry Maynard, who got £100 for nudging the contract in the appropriate direction.[5] But even £90,000, which was not enough to ward off an Exchequer crisis when the last subsidy payments had been collected, appears paltry when some reports estimated the original worth of the cargo at closer to £1,000,000. Even if this was an exaggeration due to colossal excitement and the figure is reduced to between £375,000 and £500,000, ordinary pilfering had swollen into pillage. The commissioners therefore interrogated anyone with a whiff of salt and tar (if not musk) about them, and Cecil began to take an especial interest in reports of a great uncut diamond. If it existed it had been spirited away in pocket, pouch or orifice, and Cecil set himself the very particular task of tracking it down, 'for prestige as well as money was involved'.[6]

One of Cecil's informants – 'the Frenchman' – was certain that it was genuine and hugely valuable and his story was supported by John Bedford, whom Borough had placed on the carrack for the return to England in the hope of maintaining some discipline. How the story of the stone leaked out is not clear, but Bedford himself received a letter on the subject, which he passed to Cecil, from one Anthony Moon. The letter refers to a great jewel valued at 500,000 ducats. Cecil and Drake had already questioned Alonzo Gomez, one of Cumberland's men who had joined in the looting of lesser precious items, on 1 October, but they got nothing out of him on what was now identified as a diamond. Vicentio de Fonseca thought it had been stolen by an English captain rather than a lowly member of the ship's company, and one possible culprit was Captain Crosse, who had helped himself to stones and pearls valued at 50,000 crusados. Oddly, the accusation does not seem to have harmed his career, for in 1596 he was knighted by Essex for his endeavours in the capture of Cadiz.

Another suspect was William Bradbank of Gravesend, whose stolen treasures were found early in October. He con-

27

fessed to Cecil's agents that he had already sold quantities of jewels and some ambergris for a fraction of their real value.[7] Although he denied any connection with the great diamond, he probably escaped a heavy sentence by desperately dredging up some names: Hugh Merick, captain of the *Prudence*, and a goldsmith called Shory who admitted seeing Bradbank's hoard, although another group of goldsmiths had made a deal to buy the items. Under pressure from Cecil, Shory named them, saying that some had even gone ferreting to Dartmouth in direct contravention of Burghley's prohibition.[8] Cecil would certainly have had these individuals questioned but his investigation stalled until new information in spring 1594, at about the time that the unfortunate Borough was killed in a duel by John Gilbert after a quarrel about spoils from the carrack.

At this time Cecil held as a prisoner a London goldsmith called Bartholomew Gilbert. Although the great diamond was not found, Gilbert was kept in Wood Street Counter for six months until he confessed that he had indeed bought the diamond and now bitterly regretted it.[9] Naturally the stone was expensive; such a price was asked by the unnamed vendor that Gilbert had been forced (despite the dangers) to set up a consortium of other goldsmiths, and through this mesh of contacts the diamond fell into the none-too-safe hands of Robert Brooke of Lombard Street – a name familiar to the tenacious Cecil through his questioning of Shory. With Gilbert's arrest, Brooke had had a powerful attack of nerves, feeling the iron cuffs, and he passed the stone to William Hamore, who claimed to have given it to his wife Alice to hide. When Alice was questioned she revealed a distressing vagueness: she had had the stone, but now could not remember its hidden location.[10] Cecil might be forgiven for wanting to throttle her, but with a wonderful mastery of self he was prepared to wait for the stone to pop up again, knowing that nobody was going to buy it while it was such a 'hot' item. Brooke evidently agreed, for when Alice or William recovered it, Brooke forced one of the original triumvirate of buyers,

Robert Howe, to repossess it.

Once again the diamond vanished – this time for several years, until it figured in Sir Anthony Ashley's persistent campaign to re-establish his credit with Cecil. Late in December 1597 Ashley, Master of the Queen's Jewel-House, detained Gilbert, writing to Cecil: 'I have him at this present in my house till your honour's farther direction.'[11] The newly appointed Secretary did nothing, and by forcing Ashley to proceed it was established that Howe and Terry had given the stone to a cutter who had already worked on it. With the sort of brazen impudence that Elizabethans at their best (or worst) could summon up, they had even sought a sale to Elizabeth, with Sir John Fortescue, the Chancellor of the Exchequer, acting as her agent. She had seen the partially finished gem shaped for a pendant drop and with an advance of £500 had permitted them to proceed. Cecil was by now so close to the throne that none of this escaped him, but he missed the slack end of the affair when absent on diplomatic business in France. Howe and Terry were nervous at dealing with Fortescue and so they required the cutter to nip off a portion of the stone – a fact revealed to Ashley by an indignant craftsman. Howe then boldly promised this fragment, cut and polished, as a gift to Elizabeth if she bought the larger diamond at their asking price. For this temerity Howe and Terry appropriately fetched up in the Marshalsea, but eventually the Queen's desire for the jewel smothered her anger and she promised to pay. Having received it, however, she declined to do anything about such a declaration, and Gilbert, Howe and Terry all began suits against each other. The comedy was almost finished, as in all probability they had to settle out of court.

In 1592–3, when the principal investors in the Ralegh–Cumberland sea venture had received their profits, it was naturally Elizabeth who took the lion's share of some £80,000. Cumberland got £37,000, a glowering Ralegh £24,000, investors in the City of London £12,000 and a handful of others split £8,000. Elizabeth's share and more besides was frittered away on loans, subsidies and even small armies used to prop up Henri IV. Essex, it will be recalled, had gone to France in 1591 when the French monarch was hard pressed in Normandy. It was intended that he should help at the siege of Rouen, but with the arrival of his allies Henri took himself off on other business and Essex followed. On returning to the campaign he was at least partially responsible for the entirely pointless death in action of his younger brother. The flaming Devereux obsession with honour was further underlined when the earl fought alongside his infantrymen like a common soldier. It was the sort of behaviour that won him the enthusiastic plaudits of his men but anxious rebukes from Elizabeth, who did not want him returning to court on a bier like Philip Sidney, or mutilated like Sir John Borough, who had had a finger blown off in a skirmish.

Although Essex defended himself with the Queen and the Cecils, being temporarily on good terms with the younger of the two men, he was recalled. Arriving at court flushed with enthusiasm, he was able to soften the Queen's attitude to such an extent that she even allowed him to return to France. Much of his exuberance then evaporated as a Spanish army advanced from the Netherlands and forced the abandonment of the siege. Essex, ignoring his instructions to return, reflected uneasily on the débâcle, and a further summons for his return to England was forwarded by Cecil to the English ambassador, Sir Henry Unton. Essex snatched the letter from the embarrassed Unton before he could read his instructions, and was mortified at their contents.

In England only Burghley and Cecil of the Privy Council knew of the letter to Essex, with Cecil taking a particularly active part in the background of the Rouen campaign. He had not only Essex's correspondence but also supplementary information from his own agents Thomas D'Arques and Antoine Portman. Moreover, letters from Elizabeth to her favourite – some of which Cecil may actually have drafted as if he already held the Secretaryship – were passing through his hands. He was also her channel for letters to Unton, who was uncomfortable in his difficult job (the Queen was angry with Henri IV). For her 'pigmy' who became her 'elf', however, there were only the preliminaries of power and Burghley himself still exercised the functions of Secretary, failing to write his own letters only when he was ill. Letters – political, personal, sometimes in code – were a crucial aspect of administration and policy-making. It was therefore greatly advantageous for the Cecils to have Thomas Windebank, who had accompanied Thomas Cecil abroad and had later been made a Clerk of the Signet, so close to the Queen as a confidential private secretary. In 1594, for example, he reported to Robert Cecil that a letter sent from the Strand at four o'clock in the afternoon had arrived at Whitehall at one o'clock in the morning – an extraordinary delay, given the distance. In the Queen's declining years Windebank was invaluable in deciding when to place a matter before her, for timing and little deceits could be crucial.[12]

At this time Robert Cecil was his father's adept deputy, not yet an initiator of policy. To assist him to be so he needed to display an independent knowledge of continental politics, and for this he needed to develop an intelligence network of the type employed so successfully by Sir Francis Walsingham. When he died in 1590 his cousin Thomas Walsingham and the Vice-Chamberlain Sir Thomas Heneage had continued with some aspects of the work, but many agents became agitated as their funds dried up, and they tried now to attract the attention of the Cecils. Almost alone in succeeding was Chateau-Martin in La Rochelle, where he was consul of the English merchants.[13] Those cast down by the sweeping poverty of the times found renewed hope only in 1591–2 when another prospect beckoned. The Earl of Essex, as the natural heir of the Walsingham–Leicester alliance, now decided to outflank the Cecils with an intelligence network of his own. Cheerfully using the talents and fortune of Anthony Bacon, the earl outbid his rivals and established a superiority that lasted until 1596 and the treachery of Edmund Palmer. Until then the Cecil nucleus remained at a low ebb, particularly when it was revealed that Chateau-Martin was a double agent (he was executed for intended treachery in Bayonne).

One of Robert Cecil's earliest employees in this shifting morass was the opportunistic Michael Moody, a Catholic recusant* gentleman with at least four aliases and his own cipher.[14] Once employed in Paris by Leicester's old enemy Sir Edward Stafford, he had had a spell in Newgate gaol, but after 1590 he was usually in Antwerp, Brussels or Flushing, apparently to promote a marriage between Arabella Stuart and Ranuccio Farnese, son of the Duke of Parma. This interlaced Moody with English policy, for when Elizabeth became reluctant to send more money and troops to the French King, it was decided that the fifteen-year-old Arabella should be used as a peace pawn. In December 1590 Moody wrote to Heneage that he was in bad odour with the government and wanted employment in France or Spain. In the meantime, London resolved to employ again Thomas Barnes (alias Giles Martin; alias Bartolomeo Rivero; alias M. Chaumont) since he was familiar to Parma from earlier negotiations.

In August 1591 an agent called John Ricroft wrote to Robert Cecil of his conversations with Moody: 'I dare assure your honour he shall not escape the net I will lay for him'.[15] It was a hint of the downward spiral that was to leave Moody (living up to his name) glumly protesting to Cecil that he was 'disgraced by a malicious means'.[16] It is hard to see how when in October of that year he was sending the government information and giving pro-recusant intelligence to the other side. In 1593 he disclaimed any involvement in Sir William Stanley's abortive plot to kill Elizabeth, but he could not escape imprisonment in the Low Countries and by 1596 a report said he was dead.

The major concern of the spy networks of London and the Spanish court in the 1590s was military information, such as numbers of ships in ports and sailings. In May 1593, as the spy Christopher Marlowe was about to be killed, the English

* A recusant was a person who refused to attend church.

were very agitated that the Spanish intended to land on the northern coasts; this fear was so strong that the Earl of Derby, as Lord Lieutenant for Lancashire and Cheshire, was empowered to increase the Queen's forces there. Among those arrested by the Earl of Huntingdon's anti-recusant drive were several known (or suspected) agents of Francis Dacres, self-styled Lord Dacres, who through Anthony Bacon had been putting Catholics on both sides of the Anglo–Scottish border in touch with Essex and even Philip II.[17] Essex was still invulnerable, but Dacres now engineered his own ruin, for having failed with his claims to the family lands he fled to Scotland and thence to Flanders. There he became a Spanish pensioner and planned the conversion of James VI, although by 1595 he was adjudged 'beggarly and without credit'.

Extirpating clandestine Catholics was, in Cecil's view, a policy to be undertaken with the maximum efficiency. In June 1592 Charles Chester was arrested and placed in the Gatehouse while a search of his rooms revealed books, rosaries, a hair shirt and whips. Cecil's embarrassment in this case stemmed from Chester's contacts with the mother of Michael Hickes, Mrs Penne. She had been a friend for years and Cecil had sought her help in October 1588 when he coveted a silver bell that had once belonged to the shipwrecked General of the Andalusian squadron of the Armada, Don Pedro de Valdes. The bell had passed to Lady Gorges and Cecil had no wish to be beholden to her.[18] As far as Chester was concerned he warned Mrs Penne to clear out anything pernicious the man might have left in her home. Her lack of response led to an even sharper letter and then she hastened to reply: 'I will not wittingly conceal anything of his, nor will be found I hope, to have fostered him to any ill purpose.'[19] Cecil relaxed a little and wrote that he never thought she had been an accomplice of Chester. The friendship was briefly renewed, although the ailing old lady died in November. Did Cecil pause then to consider that his pressure might have hastened her end? Did he regret it?

3

Until 1593 it is reasonable to see Robert Cecil as a political
novice, albeit one with particular advantages of birth, education, tutelage and, above all, inclination. Early in that year
he received an opportunity to assume another responsibility
often associated with the office of Secretary. A Parliament was
called for February and he was one of the five Privy Councillors deputed with the delicate task of piloting the Queen's
business through the House of Commons. Elected again as
senior knight for Hertfordshire, he was no longer to be the
silent onlooker, and the business was money since, as indicated, the profits from the *Madre de Dios* were not enough to
ward off a financial crisis. Elizabeth's obvious hope of a quick
response was dashed by the intervention of Peter Wentworth,
who sought to raise the taboo topic of the succession. His
sincerity was unquestionable, but his arguments merely
buzzed in the air and he was put in the Tower to live out a
moderately comfortable last few years.

Cecil's maiden speech was delayed until 26 February when
he rose to give that grand parliamentary stand-by – the
nation in peril. With further speeches along these lines by
Wolley, Fortescue and the confident Francis Bacon, who
declared the whole matter to be one of supply, the House
decided to set up a committee on supply with Cecil as a
member. The following day, however, members veered into
controversial territory, not necessarily intentionally, by intro-
ducing a bill to restrict the functions of ecclesiastical courts.

Elizabeth's proprietary interest in the Church led to her sharp rebuke of the Commons, who were told to give their attention solely to supply. This the Commons did, only to find themselves at odds with the Lords, who were demanding three subsidies when the counter-offer was two. In this tangle the want of supply gave the Commons the advantage and the Lords found their discussions limited to the dangers to the realm. The Commons debated the matter on 7 March, and now a succession of speakers indicated their approval of a triple subsidy until in the afternoon there was a disagreement about the speed of payment. The government wanted all speed, while others argued about the precedent this would create. One of the latter voices expressing this view was that of Francis Bacon who, with a spirited disregard for the impression he was making, effectively wrecked his court career for years by voicing his disapproval. To save the day Cecil intervened again: stressing the country's jeopardy, dismissing fears of a precedent to the Queen's advantage, and proposing that the triple subsidy be paid over four years. Agreement was reached and the bill went through its third reading on 22 March.

To have achieved this with a House of Commons that was increasingly less inclined simply to acquiesce to government legislation was a tribute to Cecil's growing skills and confidence. Without having held a major government office he had become, with remarkable speed, its voice in the Commons. Yet with the opposition of Essex still to surmount, Elizabeth did not yet feel inclined to appoint him Secretary. She had routinely balanced Leicester and Burghley as courtier-statesmen, and now it seems she hankered again for the mechanism that had served her well for thirty years until the untimely death of Leicester. If it was indeed a conscious act of policy rather than nostalgia she had dreadfully misjudged Essex, who had returned from France in 1592 in an aristocratic high dudgeon. To maintain his dignity as a patron like his stepfather, Essex was forever pestering the Queen for offices for his clients and himself. When Hatton died late in 1591 Essex wanted to be Chancellor of Oxford University, as

Leicester had been, but Elizabeth saw to it that Lord Buck-hurst was elected instead. This was a particular blow, since Cecil was already High Steward of Cambridge and even gave his support to Essex's application.[1]

Very possibly it was this rebuff that convinced Francis Bacon that if his patron was to thrive against the Cecils, he needed fresh advice. The consequence was the introduction to the earl of Anthony Bacon – a much-travelled though ailing man whose very individuality made him suspect to more conventional minds, even that of his own mother. The Bacon brothers were then joined by the peerless cryptographer Phe-lippes, and within a short period Essex had an intelligence network that outdid those of Burghley and Cecil. It was given some sort of boost when Antonio Perez arrived in England. Once the Italian Secretary for Philip II and sometime con-troller of his intelligence service, Perez fled from an imbroglio with enough state secrets and papers to be interesting to Henri IV. He entered his service and in April 1593 the King sent him on a mission to England, where after a brief period in the French Embassy he became an intimate of the Essex circle. Moving from one residence to another to avoid the worst outbreak of plague for many years, in midsummer he stayed at Gaynes Park, a Sidney house in Epping, and then he moved to Sunbury, where he met Dom Antonio of Portugal and the Queen's physician, a Portuguese Jew called Dr Lopez.[2] By January 1594 he was back in London at Gray's Inn staying with Francis Bacon, and then after a short spell with the High Master of St Paul's, John Harrison, he finally came to rest at Essex House, maintaining 'a small but costly household, including a priest for mass'.[3]

Such extravagant behaviour required high protection and Perez got it as a leading figure in Essex's growing spy net-work. To give validity to their operations spies need plots, so it comes as no surprise that Essex was informed of one six months after the arrival of Perez. The starting point for this may have been rivalry between Lopez, who gathered information for Elizabeth, and the newcomer, whose movements were watched for Lopez by another Jew. Whether by accident or some obscure design, Lopez revealed some intimate medical secrets about Essex and incurred his powerful displeasure. Further, it was revealed that Esteban Ferreira da Gama, in the service of Dom Antonio, was also in the pay of Philip II. Nothing could as yet be proved, so da Gama remained in the custody of the Portuguese pretender. Then, shortly afterwards, Gomez d'Avila was arrested by Essex's men as he returned from Flanders with crucial letters. These linked da Gama with Esteban de Ibarra, the Secretary of War there. But da Gama had friends in England still, including Lopez, whose spying activities were probably stimulated by simple greed. He had always lived beyond his means, petitioning the Queen and Leicester for gifts and being granted a monopoly for the importation of aniseed and shumac.

Yet somehow da Gama came to be convinced that Lopez had betrayed him, and possibly this conversion was achieved by the garrulous 'cagey old Spanish rogue' Perez.[4] Da Gama now claimed that Lopez was a Spanish agent planning to kill Dom Antonio. All this was rather scratchy and circumstantial, and Elizabeth, who had turned a blind eye to her doctor's Spanish dealings, remained as sceptical as the Cecils about the meaning of all this. Lopez had burnt all his papers when d'Avila was arrested, so when he was examined at Burghley's house on 21 January 1594 he simply brushed aside da Gama's accusations – even when confronted with him. Unwilling to concede that Essex had uncovered a real plot, Cecil told Elizabeth on the basis of this first interview that Lopez had nothing to answer. When the earl next appeared at court she rebuked him as a 'rash and temerarious youth' for hounding Lopez. The earl responded as if to embody her comment: he went into a retreat, refusing to speak to anyone but Lord Howard of Effingham for two days, Indeed, he ceased to sulk only when Howard joined the commission of investigation.

The pressure on Lopez was mounting. Da Gama held on to his story and the doctor finally admitted that he knew the contents of the letters between da Gama and the government in Flanders. The discovery that he had accepted a ring from Philip II put Lopez in the Tower. Then the capture of another agent, Manuel Luis Tinoco, set a further nacreous layer on the initial piece of grit. Tinoco confessed that he and da Gama were to join in arranging a great service to Spain – and they planned to use none other than Dr Lopez. By now Essex was totally convinced that the 'point of the conspiracy was her Majesty's death' with Lopez living up to his whispered reputation by choosing poison.[5] Cecil too now began to shift with the collective agitation emanating from Essex House, and so jointly they begged Elizabeth to exercise caution. Still probably unwillingly, she agreed that Lopez should be continually interrogated, and gradually he admitted small services to Spain so that he might pocket some payment from these contacts.

In the meantime da Gama and Tinoco allowed the doctor's activities to seep out as they were closely questioned. Eventually da Gama admitted that he had written a letter to Spanish officials in Flanders, with the approval of Lopez, offering the elimination of Elizabeth for 50,000 crowns. Then in February Tinoco confessed another dangerous supplement to the story; in this Ibarra had told him that Lopez had himself offered to kill her. The threat stemmed in particular from the separation of da Gama and Tinoco because they had no opportunity to manufacture a story, and Lopez sensed the ground slipping from under him. Thoroughly alarmed, he admitted a plot launched with the benign agreement of the government in Flanders but vehemently denied any intention of going through with it. His delay had been 'for fear of jealousy her Majesty might have conceived thereby'.[6]

The fumbled defence and the slow accretion of 'evidence' led to a trial by special commission at Guildhall on 28 February. Essex and Cecil were commissioners with Lord Rich, the Lord Mayor, Lord Howard of Effingham and Sir Thomas Heneage. The testimony of da Gama and Tinoco not surprisingly meant the prompt conviction of 'the vile Jew', a ghastly echo of Marlowe's famous play *The Jew of Malta*. Two weeks later

38

Tinoco and da Gama were convicted, but then there was a pause until Lopez was finally executed on 7 June, a victim of Essex and a stern-faced Egerton, for a time Attorney-General. One curiosity of the episode is that da Gama was apparently released and several years later he wrote to Essex from Morocco. Cecil's involvement in the disturbing business was not quite ended, since he was commissioned to write a report on the case after a sour comment from the Archduke Ernst. The published account that appeared in 1594 was the work of Charles Yetswiert, one of Elizabeth's secretaries.

Cecil and Essex were now able to take the measure of each other in the Privy Council, with the earl joining it in February 1593. Certainly for a time he seemed to take his cue from Cecil, whose family motto was *prudens qui patiens*. Anthony Bagot commented on a newly acquired poise, 'clean forsaking all his former youthful tricks, carrying himself with honourable gravity' [7] Essex told Egerton that he wanted an active public life because his esteem for the contemplative, studious existence had plummeted. This being so, it is not surprising that he decided to press the merits of Francis Bacon for the vacancy of Attorney-General when Sir John Popham became Lord Chief Justice. Unfortunately for patron and protégé, Elizabeth was maintaining her hearty antipathy to Bacon, refusing to allow him to attend the court. Essex worked solemnly to dissipate these feelings, and Bacon himself turned to his uncle and cousin for additional support. In this he was wasting his time, for Burghley wanted promotion for Sir Edward Coke.

Late in September Bacon heard that Coke had been summoned to court. With the matter apparently in the balance he wrote to Burghley's patronage secretary, Michael Hickes, urging the latter to tilt things in his direction. Cecil, who had no particular esteem for his cousin, did say he would help by putting Bacon's case to Burghley. The Lord Treasurer was not to be won over entirely, though he agreed to support Bacon for the lesser office of Solicitor-General which Coke would leave vacant if promoted. In the following month Essex

left his sick-bed when told that Elizabeth was about to pronounce, but he only succeeded in delaying the matter. Some of
the bitterness of rivalry and of hopes deferred burst out late in
January 1594. Cecil and Essex, after an examination of
Lopez, travelled together from court. Cecil asked Essex about
his choice of a candidate for Attorney-General, and the earl
apparently snapped his response. What is missing from the
report of the conversation is the tone of Cecil's next comment
about Bacon being a young man. Even so, it seems clear that
Essex's temper was rather fragile: 'I could name to you, Sir
Robert, a man younger than Francis, less learned and equally
inexperienced, who is suing and striving with all his might, for
an office of far greater weight.'[8] The thrust of this was clear
enough. Cecil then urged the lesser office of Solicitor-General
for Bacon, since he opined it 'might be of easier digestion to
Her Majesty'. Essex spat out his response, ending: 'I think
strange both of my Lord Treasurer and you, that can have the
mind to seek preference of a stranger before so near a
kinsman. . . .'[9]

The report of this was enough to convince Burghley that he
must again broach the matter with the Queen. In fact he had
a dual purpose for hurrying to court: not only the appointment
of Coke, but the office of Secretary for his son, with Stafford as
his colleague. The last element failed, but in April 1594 Coke
did become Attorney-General. This left the vacancy nominated by Cecil and he declared his support for Bacon's candi-
dacy without reservation. He wrote to Sir Thomas Egerton,
now Master of the Rolls, 'that I have no kinsman living (my
brother excepted) whom I hold so dear'.[10] Perhaps he meant it
at the time, or he intended a neutral figure like Egerton to
convey it to the other side.

A curious alliance was briefly formed. Burghley and Essex
lobbied Elizabeth together on Bacon's behalf, with the earl
getting a brusque command that he should go to bed if he
could find no other topic of conversation. Immoderate in everything, even friendship, Essex could not follow the example of the
late Earl of Leicester, who had the priceless gift of being able to

'put his pride in his pocket'. The wearying submissions and protestations went on, with Bacon ruefully claiming 'that no man ever received a more exquisite disgrace'. Not until early November 1595 did Elizabeth appoint Thomas Fleming. All Essex could do at this point was to compensate Bacon with a gift that allowed him to pay off some of his many creditors. It was characteristic of the earl that he should be so open-handed, and of Bacon that he should need it. Sir Thomas Bodley probably expressed it best when he wrote: 'She hated his [Essex's] ambition and would give little countenance to any of his followers.'

The sometimes gentlemanly, sometimes raw pursuit of rivalry for power was far from being confined to the court. Both sides maintained a powerful interest in the north of England, with its strategic border and local hurly-burlies. The principal agencies for government control beyond the Trent were the Northern circuit of judges and the Council in the North. Cecil's appointment as Secretary, when it eventually came, seems to have prompted greater scrutiny of the circuit bench when a clutch of the older judges appeared vague about government intentions. To help them to focus their under-standing the Star Chamber charge was reintroduced – an address to judges that seems to have been aimed, particularly in 1595 and the following year, at four elderly judges.[11] It was also intended, in part at least, to bring about a closer super-vision of men who seemed partial, wayward or simply inef-ficient. Among those curbed for his impertinent opposition to the Council of the North was Sergeant Yelverton, who in 1602 was forced to change his circuit.[12] Another judge under Cecil's regard that year was Sergeant Heale, who rode with Judge Gawdy on the Home Circuit. A noted drinker, 'he played such pranks, and so demeaned himself that he is become both odious and ridiculous.'[13]

Initially, Essex had an advantage with the Council in the North because several of the more important members had been allies and followers of the Earl of Leicester, and they transferred their loyalty. Moreover, despite his private esteem

41

for Puritanism Essex, as has been noted, had links with local Catholics and prevented the penal laws being too strictly enforced aginst recusants. In this he was helped by the comparatively mild attitude of the Lord President, Huntingdon, a relation by marriage who, although also a Puritan, was not by inclination a persecutor. Even Archbishop Hutton of York declined to pursue a vigorous policy of compulsion. Thus one of the Wright brothers of the Gunpowder Plot was allowed to live openly in his father's house in York while busying himself in seeking converts to Rome. It was also through Essex's associate Edward Stanhope, one of the legal members of the Council, that Thomas Percy kept in touch with the earl. So Cecil had pertinent reasons for seeking to place some of his kinsmen and supporters on the Council.

His first success was the appointment of Charles Hales, followed in 1595 by John Ferne and then little Sir Thomas Posthumous Hoby, a hunchback cousin of Cecil. Ferne was a relative of Cecil's friend Lord Sheffield, and he became Secretary of the Council. A month later Ralph, 3rd Lord Eure, was appointed warden of the Middle Marches to succeed Sir John Foster, then well into his nineties and grown increasingly slack in his administration. Although Eure was a patron of Puritan preachers he had many Catholic sympathizers among his allies in Northumberland, a fact that Bishop Matthew of Durham found perturbing. In 1600, when Eure was Vice-President of the Council, he was publicly snubbed by Yelverton. The following year the Sergeant made the error of doing much the same to the Lord President, and since by then it was Thomas Cecil, Lord Burghley, he paid the price for this peculiar indiscretion by a summons to the Star Chamber followed by demotion.

Years before this Robert Cecil had been greatly exercised by the compelling question of a successor to Huntingdon, whose office as Lord President was the key to real strength in the north of England. When the earl died in December 1595 Essex supposedly tore his hair in dismay and popped his buttons with the swelling up of his stomach, 'as if some great design had been frustrated thereby'. In February 1596 he was less agitated, for he secured the rule of the north for Archbishop Hutton, but the churchman became only head of the Council, and in theory the great office of Lord President was still vacant. When Essex went to Ireland in April 1599 Cecil was able to push Hutton aside, ostensibly on the grounds of age and ill-health, and in August Thomas Cecil became Lord President.

Huntingdon's death was not the only significant demise at the end of 1595. From then and through the following spring promotion or death left a number of high offices vacant, so Essex's extravagant anxiety state did at least have some cause. One of the fatalities was Sir Thomas Heneage, latterly Vice-Chamberlain, Treasurer of the Chamber and Chancellor of the Duchy of Lancaster. But again Elizabeth stalled matters: the Duchy was placed in commission and its seals were handed over to Burghley. Keyed up to provide something that would convince his clients of his power, Essex joined the indecorous scramble over the mortal remains with a campaign for the appointment of Thomas Bodley as Secretary – still the most contentious prize of all. It seemed inevitable that Elizabeth should soon make an appointment, for in February Sir John Wolley died. As Secretary for the Latin tongue he had done much of the routine work that would normally have fallen to the Secretary of State. His assistant in this effort was Thomas Windebank, a Clerk of the Signet since 1577. For several years Wolley and Robert Cecil had been writing jointly upon various matters that fell within the scope of the office, and with Wolley gone and Burghley fading, Elizabeth had very little option other than a formal decision between Bodley and Cecil. There was another Clerk of the Signet – her 'swiftsure', as she called Thomas Lake – but he lacked the depth of experience, although he was speedy and accurate in secretarial work.[14]

In this case Essex had certainly picked a candidate of high quality (albeit, as it proved, a somewhat fragile ego). Bodley was the son of an Exeter merchant and had underwritten his diplomatic career by a judicious marriage to Anne Ball (*née* Carew), a wealthy widow whose late husband had made a fortune from pilchard fishing. Essex urged Bodley's appointment with a frank zeal that led him to disparage Cecil in the same sentence. But Bodley advanced no further, despite a decade of experience, and he eventually became so disenchanted with his treatment at court that he threw up his career to avoid the buffeting, and retired to a life of private scholarship. Despite the sneers of some of his contemporaries that he used his wife's money Bodley achieved a kind of immortality in Oxford and beyond by the maintenance of the Bodleian Library. All Essex could offer a little later was a consolation prize of a small collection of books plundered from the home of Bishop Mascarenhas in Faro during that summer's Cadiz expedition. Cecil was alerted to their arrival in the country by his agent William Stallenge, who looked on Catholic literature with a baleful eye.

Essex was thwarted over Bodley, but for the office Wolley had left vacant he notched up a needed success. It went to his candidate Henry Savile, a scholar and later one of the translators of the Bible for James I. Cecil may have been disposed to accept Savile quietly because of his obvious gifts, or more routinely because the previous year, when Savile had a suit to present, he had promised Cecil 300 angels for satisfaction. In this case the disappointed client for office was not a Cecilian but another follower of Essex, his secretary Arthur Atey. Once secretary to the Earl of Leicester, the translator of a book by Perez, Atey was compensated in 1597 with a seat for Dunwich in the Commons. But Bacon was still excluded, even when Egerton (the employer of the poet John Donne) became Lord Keeper of the Great Seal (an office combined with that of Lord Chancellor under Elizabeth) and left the Mastership of the Rolls.

4

In the 1570s and 1580s English foreign policy had been shaped by the two contrasting views of Burghley and Leicester, with Elizabeth as adjudicator. In broad terms the earl had been the court spokesman for the adventurous war party, while Burghley took a far more cautious, defensive line. Elizabeth, tethered by fears of pitiless expenditure, veered between these views as circumstances dictated. Lacking the deeper convictions of Leicester, she broached intervention in the struggle of the United Provinces against Spain only with great reluctance. In the event the tribulations arising out of it suggest that her policy fell short in many ways, not least because Leicester's expeditionary force, mounted at great public and personal expense, achieved so little. However, he did stall the Spaniards and when Philip II made the cardinal error of seeking to defeat the English on their own territory, he was defiantly repulsed in 1588. But the possibility of further Spanish armadas remained, and there was continual anxiety in England about another threat – that to the energetic but unsteady throne of Henri IV. His political conversion to Catholicism in 1593 caused disgust in England but no rupture. The Cecils put forward the view that he should be aided only if it was unavoidable. Essex regarded this with disdain, wanting the weightiest possible intervention in France as the spearhead of an active war against Spain. This view was later endorsed by Antonio Perez when he arrived in England, while the notion of supporting the man with the best title to the throne certainly chimed with the Queen's royalist conscience.[1] The campaigning by the French and English was inconclusive for years despite the disbursements of cash to Henri IV, who remained, as Sir Henry Unton wrote, 'a king . . . who maketh wars without money'.[2] By 1595 English forces had also gone and he was forced to stand alone.

Late in July of that year a new Spanish army moved from Flanders to lay siege to Cambrai. A succession of French envoys sought fresh aid from England when loans had already cost Elizabeth some £200,000. With a quaint glance back at history she agreed to more help if Henri allowed Calais to pass again into English control. In view of today's problem with our Common Market partner Spain over Gibraltar, it was just as well Henri refused and Cambrai fell. The King's response was brisk, if unsubtle – he threatened to make peace when Spain had just landed men in Cornwall. Four Spanish galleys, driven off course while *en route* to Brittany, put men ashore to devastate the countryside and burn Penzance. Unton was the carrier of soothing messages – that was the intention – but their contents were undermined by a bellicose Essex. He backed Henri and urged him to clamour for assistance. The further withdrawal of some English troops from the United Provinces for a frontal attack on\Spain, agreed in the Privy Council in March, then made the situation immediately worse for Henri since the Spanish were able to besiege Calais. At this time Essex was in Dover preparing for a major naval expedition against a Spanish target, and naturally he wanted some means to deliver the French town, but it fell on 20 April.

The most significant soldier-statesman in England after Essex, and certainly his senior in age, was Ralegh. He was pressing for an attack on Cadiz, and in this he was strongly supported by Perez. The Spaniard had returned to Paris in autumn 1595 'accompanied by a bodyguard and secretaries supplied by the Earl of Essex and wearing his livery'.[3] Godfrey Aleyn had been an aide but forfeited the trust placed in him by copying confidential letters; this cost him a spell in the Clink and Essex's employment. So the essential link between the earl and Perez was now provided by Robert Naunton, a Cambridge MA who was sent to France in February 1596 ostensibly as tutor to Robert Vernon, the younger brother of Elizabeth Vernon. She was later the bride of Essex's friend, the Earl of Southampton, and Naunton himself married into the Essex clan. He found his service in Paris most wearing; even so, his bride was Penelope Perrot, a niece of Essex. In Naunton's case this did not exclude a saving Cecil connection and years later he became one of the Secretary of State's personal assistants.[4]

In the meantime the loss of Calais proved to be the irritant that clarified Anglo–French options. In May 1596 there were negotiations between Elizabeth and Henri out of which came the Treaty of Greenwich, and among those who came from France was Perez, now shunned by Essex, who was busy with the preparations for the Cadiz expedition. By the treaty Elizabeth agreed to limited help for Henri, who was bound not to make peace unilaterally. To signify the accord the Earl of Shrewsbury, accompanied by the Garter King of Arms, was in Rouen in the autumn to present Henri with the Garter that had been given him in 1590. Cecil very probably knew about Essex's extended dealings with Henri – either through his agents or, failing that, through Unton until his death in March 1596. For the time being, however, there was nothing to be done and his letters to the earl at this time show no hint of animosity or rancour.

In fact placing clients created fewer problems because Essex was so preoccupied, and it was Cecil who drew up the commissions for the earl and Lord Howard of Effingham as they bickered over status and hence wrangled over the leadership of the expedition. Cecil, in conjunction with his ally Howard, also put up the *Truelove* for the force which, when it sailed in June, owed a significant amount to his particular achievements at the planning stage. His reward for service, somewhat unflatteringly delayed, came just a month later when Elizabeth conferred on him the office for which he had prepared himself – an office coveted as an essential prelude to real power. As Secretary Cecil held his position at the Queen's pleasure, while the annual fee of £100 was for life. Clearly at this juncture, with Essex absent, her long-standing unease about allowing Cecil a major office while Burghley lived was curbed. Not so the incensed scorn of Francis Davison, still smarting at the disgrace of his father, who wrote from Lucca to refer with heavy sarcasm to 'the late instalment and canonization of the venerable saint'.

In the weeks following Cecil's step up to office, many conflicting news reports reached London about the events at Cadiz. The fighting for the town was certainly fierce; the destruction of the Apostolic galleons horrifying; and in English eyes the failure to capture a great treasure ship almost equally distressing. By mid-July Cecil had more accurate reports than most from George Carey of Cockington.[5] It was now apparent that once again undisciplined pillaging of the town and the failure to capture significant prizes had savagely reduced the prospects of a strong profit. Even so, learning from the past, Burghley established a commission to be ready in Plymouth for the returning fleet. One of its members was again the luckless Richard Carmarden, who at about this time consulted the famous astrologer and healer Simon Forman about melancholy and depression.[6] It is not surprising that he felt so afflicted when the whole wearisome business of separating looters from their loot began early in August and lasted through the autumn 'in an atmosphere of recriminations and hostility'.[7]

One of those who stumbled at this time was Sir Anthony Ashley, who had been with the fleet. Even so, he was still twirling about trying to restore his credit with Cecil, and failing. The cause was his cupidity, and hearing of his arrival in London the new Secretary had him spied on.[8] Richard Drake found a vantage point in a shoemaker's premises next door to Ashley's house in Holborn, and his surveillance was rewarded with evidence of trunks being delivered in the middle of the night. To Ashley's chagrin these were promptly seized, but it was only part of a consignment. The *Lion's Whelp* had arrived in Plymouth with more, but as Sir Ferdinando Gorges reported to Cecil on seeing the commissioners, she stood off without unloading.[9] Ashley decided to broach all this by confessing to the Privy Council, hoping to save the day with candour. He might have saved his breath, and his situation was further undermined by Sir Gelly Meyrick, a confidant of Essex. Cecil knew that his listing of Ashley's peculations was to screen Essex, but he was still not inclined to overlook Ashley's preposterous behaviour. Despite the latter's protestations he ended up in the Fleet prison and was only released early in October, giving the appearance of being thoroughly chastened. Cecil, as we know, wanted the great diamond from the *Madre de Dios* and for a time Ashley was to be his stalking horse.[10]

The gem would have made a startling Christmas gift to Elizabeth, for whom the Cecils gave a party. It was the last great family occasion for Lady Cecil, for after giving birth to a second daughter she died in late January 1597. Cecil was stricken and gossip had it that while in mourning for the sweet-tempered woman who saw past his deformed body, his hair went grey. He remained in his house and attended no meetings of the Privy Council for the whole of February. His distress was intensified because his children – William, Frances and the baby Catherine – were motherless. Six months after his loss he was warned by his aunt, Lady Russell, to come out of his melancholy or he was likely to become 'a surly, sharp, sour plum'.[11] No doubt his feelings of sorrow were intensified early in March when his father-in-law, the Lord Chamberlain Cobham, also succumbed. As he declined it was widely believed that Ralegh had achieved an unexpected , though welcome, *rapprochement* between Cecil and Essex. He had generally been on good terms with the former, certainly since 1592, and although his relations with Essex were turbulent, in policy and ideals they had much in common. In fact the easing of relations between Cecil and Essex more probably stemmed from their joint absence from the Privy Council. Essex too had retired to his home, either because of ill-health or because of fatigue combined with pique following his return from Cadiz. Communications between the two men were couched in soothing or consoling phrases.

Cecil and Burghley were merely 'overseers' of Cobham's will; the executors were Sir John Leveson, Sir Thomas Fane and William Lambarde, the jurist and author.[12] Much more important than Cobham's private resources and who got what was his office as Lord Chamberlain, which would immediately test the quality of the accord between Cecil and Essex. George Carey, Lord Hunsdon, was appointed and as a consequence he vacated the Wardenship of the Cinque Ports, so Essex swiftly nominated Sir Robert Sidney. It took Elizabeth just two days to settle that the new Warden would be the new Lord Cobham, Cecil's brother-in-law Henry Brooke, whom Essex detested. To placate the earl a little she took up a suggestion, probably made by Cecil, that he should be made Master of the Ordnance, and he was more than a little distracted by preparations for another blow against Spain. On 22 May 'Great England's glory and the world's wide wonder', in Edmund Spenser's phrase, was given sole command of the venture.

The concord was such a flimsy thing that its chances of real growth were always low, 'but in outward form it continued unabated'.[13] Thus Essex withdrew his opposition to a grant to Burghley's secretary Henry Maynard, and Cecil undertook a suit on behalf of Anthony Bacon. Even Ralegh benefited – restored to his functions in June as Captain of the Guard, he was to be Rear Admiral to Essex on the 'Islands Voyage'. With Essex away from court it was Cecil who procured the renewal for him of the Sweet Wine farm, and also promised that Parliament would be stalled until the earl's return. Clearly by now Cecil was becoming indispensable as a member of the government, taking on a good deal of the burden of routine work as Burghley, still alert but old, fatigued and ailing, waited for the end of his duties. It was a situation that teased supplicants and diplomats alike, since the old man's wrath, if he was slighted, could still make them tremble. But the power was shifting inexorably to the man who was 'a courtier from his cradle', and in spring 1597 rumour had it that he was to be appointed Chancellor of the Duchy of Lancaster. On 18 April Cecil, Ralegh and Essex dined cheerfully together without discord. It was allowed that Cecil should indeed have the Duchy, and Ralegh a valuable contract to feed 6,000 men mobilized for the summer campaign. The warrant was prepared, with a remarkable alacrity, within three days. For Cecil things were not so speedily effected, and it was not until early October that Elizabeth handed the seals held by Burghley to his son. The patronage attached to the office was substantial, and hence lucrative. It also added a significant clutch of boroughs to those where he could wield influence during elections.

The principal elements of the plan to strike again at Spain were that Philip II's fleet at El Ferrol should be destroyed, and that Terceira in the Azores should be seized as a base for an attack on the Indies fleet. But in difficult circumstances Essex failed to carry out his commission, and the only beneficiaries of such an expensive failure were Cecil and Henri IV. The latter recaptured Amiens and declared that the delay in the sailing of the Spanish treasure fleet had had a noticeable effect on the operations of his enemies.[14] When the new session of Parliament opened on 24 October Essex was landing at Plymouth, his fleet having been battered by the same October gales which broke up the new Spanish Armada. Arriving in London he found himself rebuked for his expensive failure, while Lord Howard of Effingham, who had stayed at home, was elevated to Earl of Nottingham. Essex was predictably galled by this and shut himself up at home in Wanstead, refusing to attend meetings of the Privy Council or the House of Lords, where Nottingham would have seniority as Lord Steward. This was the office once held by the Earl of Leicester, and its transmission to Nottingham seems temporarily to have unhinged a man still suffering from the effects of months of a marine diet, as well as consciousness of military failure – the one strand in his struggle with Cecil in which he was supposed to be pre-eminent. Essex even went as far as to seek a duel with his elderly rival or one of his sons.

Various compromises were aired as the entire court was taken up with the affair. Important decisions were delayed or jeopardized as Essex would not attend the Council and Elizabeth declined to do anything without him. Burghley wrote pleading for his return, while Cecil pondered the necessary emollient manoeuvre that would lure him back. Either he or Ralegh eventually devised it: Essex would be made Earl Marshal to restore his precedence and his temper, the patent being drawn up by Cecil, who even consulted the earl on such amendments as he thought necessary. There was also the sweetener of the appointment of an Essex client, Thomas Smith, as Clerk of the Parliament. Adroitly, Cecil even managed to manufacture a certain cordiality in his dealings with Anthony Bacon, at a time when Nottingham and he stood to benefit from a little venture of their own. The *Truelove* had been sent to the Barbary coast on a privateering venture and the ageing Lord Admiral and young Secretary of State profited from a simple, if dubious, ruse. Ostensibly the vessel was in royal service, so the record of the ship's company was doubted, while supplies at royal expense for six months' service doubled the length of time the *Truelove* was actually at sea.[15] Cecil was also now able to draw on £800 allotted to secret service funds in pursuit of public advantage and private gain.[16] It was a happy, if not altogether necessary, coincidence if the two meshed. With official salaries held at levels that verged on the miserly it was inevitable that men should seek other rewards for services to the Crown, and do so without blushing. Gifts in cash or kind were rarely refused, although later in his career Cecil occasionally balked at a naked bribe when it was offered by one of his countrymen for benign attention to their wants.

In the House of Commons of 1597 Cecil served with his half-brother, a nephew, seven first cousins and various other relatives.[17] Throughout the session he led those with court attachments and his management showed increasingly how adept he had grown, with business smoothly dispatched, notably the question of subsidy. What he could not resolve he postponed, including the defiantly contentious matter of patents and monopolies. For the time being the government promise of reform was enough. As for Burghley, although he took breaks increasingly for illness and recuperation, he still pondered foreign and domestic affairs. He had enough strength in autumn 1597 to take his seat in the Lords, with a rebuke for peers who absented themselves. In December he met delegates from Henri IV, who now wanted English participation in peace talks, despite the fact that he had recaptured Amiens. De Maisse, who looked at the ageing Queen of England with an unsparing eye for wrinkles and decayed teeth, was the new French ambassador to London. His task was to convince the English that peace could be achieved, when Burghley had doubts. He thought the Dutch had to be included in a general pacification of western Europe, and there were real doubts about whether Spain would ever agree to good terms. Moreover, the Dutch stoically held the view that their great enemy was weakening and that a year could see the long-sought victory. The challenge to Elizabeth was whether she lost an ally in Henri or continued to shovel money into his struggle at a time when the English economy was troubled.

De Maisse noted her deliberate hesitations. He could, however, apply pressure, for there was a distinct concern in London that Henri might just be able to spatchcock an arrangement with the United Provinces. When he told Elizabeth late in December that the Dutch were sending envoys to France, she angrily announced that she wanted English representatives at any negotiations, fearing now for her loan repayments from both France and the United Provinces. This was at a time when she was pouring out treasure on a colonial war in Ireland. Early in January 1598 the French envoy returned home, carrying with him a promise that English representatives would follow almost immediately.

As England's premier soldier and leader of the war party

Essex felt bound to refuse the leadership of a special embassy, but the significance of the business to be conducted would not allow for the dispatch of some minor courtier or official. Hence Cecil was appointed for the last time to a mission that would take him abroad, with John Herbert and Sir Thomas Wilkes as his colleagues. It was rumoured that being out of the country made Cecil uneasy and the consequence was an *ad hoc* arrangement, with Essex agreeing to do nothing of startling consequence in the interim period. Cecil wrote placatingly: 'I shall labour nothing more . . . than the conservation and requital of your true friendship, from which nothing shall divide me but separation of body and soul.'[18]

The writer of these plangent words was about to sail from Dover to Dieppe when a Spanish fleet bound for Calais came into the Narrows and caused a flurry of consternation in London. The Earl of Cumberland was ordered into the Channel with all available ships and the Spanish were harried into their intended destination. With their dispersal Cecil was able to cross to France, though Elizabeth had nervously thought to recall him. Then the English delegation sustained a further shock when their expert on French affairs, Wilkes, suddenly died. When Cecil finally arrived in Paris he found that Henri had deserted the city for supposedly early campaigning in Brittany. When he did face the King in late March he was constrained to listen to a lecture on how badly France needed peace. Inconclusive talks went on for days, with the additional factor that the Dutch envoys were outraged at the thought of a peace constructed on their much-vaunted years of sacrifice, wherein their commitment was more spasmodic than they liked to admit.

Then news of great significance arrived from London. 'Our hearts so boiled as we held ourselves accursed to tread upon this soil' – so fulminated Cecil (and Herbert) when they learned that Spanish and French envoys had opened negotiations at Vervins. Once again crucial letters had been intercepted by Elizabeth's agents – this time the correspondence between Archduke Albrecht of Flanders (Spanish Netherlands) and Philip II. The English negotiators went to beard Henri IV about this perfidy, but he temporized and invited Cecil to join the conference. He would not consider this without the consent of the Dutch and they remained belligerent, so that by early April it was clear that Henri alone was being wooed into a settlement. Cecil could do nothing but unfurl his arguments while applying for the passports of the English party. The peace between France and Spain was concluded later in the month.

Not dismayed but certainly perturbed, Cecil landed back in England on 29 April and his first action was revealing: he went to the ailing Burghley's bedside, leaving Elizabeth to wait her turn. The great attachment between father and son seemed all the greater as the old man's health failed during the summer. Coached by a brilliant political realist, Cecil had little to fear in the future except the final extinction of the two great figures who had commanded the political stage as a duo since the death of the Earl of Leicester a decade before. On 10 July Burghley wrote his last letter to his son and disciple in his own hand, while as late as 21 July he could summon the energy to dictate a letter on official business. Realizing the gravity of his decline, Elizabeth went to his bedside and fed him some soup, but even that sovereign presence had no power to shackle time and the Lord Treasurer died on 4 August 1598. A little more than a month later he was followed by Philip II.

5

Affairs of state did not falter simply because 'the great helmsman' had died. It was almost immediately necessary to give sustained reflection to the problem of Ireland, where English armies suffered a major reverse at the Battle of the Yellow Ford. The victory of Hugh O'Neill, Earl of Tyrone, 'was the greatest military disaster the English ever suffered in Ireland'[1] – so much of a calamity that with the benefit of hindsight it is possible to regret that the English presence was not eliminated. But the settlers took refuge in towns or in England, while Tyrone was beseeched for an armistice. Elizabeth, however, had no inclination to surrender to force, for all that she 'grew weary with reading the Irish dispatches'.[2] Essex too showed a growing interest in the fate of the English in the towns and peat bogs, responding to Francis Bacon's suggestion that he should pay greater attention to events there, especially since the Devereux estates in Ireland had been half ruined by incursions and were further threatened by Tyrone.

One very particular problem was finding a Lord Deputy to stem the losses, a matter the Queen discussed with Essex, Nottingham and Cecil. At first she favoured giving the poison chalice to Essex's uncle, Sir William Knollys, while the earl's candidate was Cecil's good friend Sir George Carew, Treasurer-at-War in Ireland. The Queen remained adamant for Knollys and the result was a shouting match in her privy chamber, with Essex turning his back on her in high dudgeon and Elizabeth responding by slapping his face. With his usual animation in such a situation Essex was so incensed that he began to draw his sword – whether to lunge at her or break it over his knee, if such a thing was possible, is not clear. Having been bundled aside by an aghast Lord Admiral Nottingham, Essex stormed out of Whitehall for a bout of melancholic sulking. His petulant rage was not easily displaced this time and a letter from Egerton urging him to submit, an admonition of no great severity, failed in its intention. Essex did now seem to believe in the paranoid notion that his enemies were abundant and triumphant: 'I had rather they should triumph alone, than they should have me attendant on their chariots.' Cecil does not seem to have done anything to prompt this baleful view, and in August Sir Henry Lee wrote to Essex that 'Mr Secretary did you good service in council, and the Queen liked it well. . . .'[3]

In September 1598 Essex was ill again with physical symptoms of a wretched mental state. As usual it was this that allowed for a reconciliation with Elizabeth, so that by the middle of the month he was again admitted to her presence. This gave him the opportunity to sue for the office of Master of the Court of Wards, vacant since Burghley's death and a prop to anyone's finances. But like the office of Lord Treasurer, the matter was too delicate to be settled when beset with clamour. It may be that Elizabeth had already in principle decided it should go to Cecil, who in June the following year, and with some grumbling, gave up the Chancellorship of the Duchy of Lancaster. But still the problem of Ireland had to be confronted and even someone as unflustered by danger as Ralegh, busy with remodelling Sherborne Abbey in Dorset, showed no interest. Elizabeth then veered towards the bookish Charles Blount, Lord Mountjoy, whom Essex thought lacking in real experience of war. This was somewhat ironic, since Blount, very probably the subject of Hilliard's most famous and puzzling portrait miniature *Young Man among Roses*, had been wounded in battle as early as 1586 while serving in the United Provinces with the army of the Earl of Leicester.

Sir William Russell refused to go to Ireland and Sir Richard

Bingham, an experienced soldier knowledgeable about Irish conditions, was ill and soon to die. By some manipulation and his own self-seeking Essex gradually manoeuvred himself into the appointment. Although he had misgivings he felt that if he lost the leadership of the military faction in the country his entire position at court would be undermined. Moreover, he and the Queen knew that his reputation would attract men to his service; this was confirmed when rumours of the appointment in October brought a flood of letters seeking commissions. Even so, the actual appointment came only in January 1599.

When the new Lord Deputy left London on 27 March, he took with him the largest army assembled during the entire reign. In addition, his powers exceeded those of any of his predecessors. Yet even before he left for what he recognized as a venture full of perils, he made a personal decision that seemed calculated to wreck the tentatively restored and still fragile unity with Elizabeth. Essex required his friend the Earl of Southampton to be his Master of the Horse, which the Queen flatly rejected – first on the perfectly sound grounds that Southampton lacked military experience; secondly, less objectively, because he had married against her very pronounced wishes. The obvious man for the post was Lord Grey, but Essex simply waited to get to Ireland before following his own inclination. His campaigning there proved undirected, sluggish and hideously expensive in men, horses and equipment. To mount it Cecil had probed every financial avenue, finally going to City of London financiers for a loan at 10 per cent interest.[4] And if the provision of horses and wagons was not speedy enough for Essex, it is doubtful if Cecil was behind it. Indeed, the earl was advancing crabwise to ruin while Cecil thrived in London, being sworn Master of the Court of Wards on 20 May, just as his rival was heading into Munster and Leinster. This effort was grotesquely misplaced since the strategy established before Essex left London was that he was to march north to Ulster, the heart of Tyrone country. The main Irish force was there and, given the size of Essex's army when he arrived, he should have been able to fight a pitched battle successfully. As usual, though, he could not easily accept that a woman in London could have a clearer idea of military strategy than the man on the spot. All he now saw was that his enemies swarmed, the Queen was hostile, and he was mired in a land where it is hard to distinguish summer from winter.

One critical fact in Essex's perturbations was that in his absence Cecil had edged out Archbishop Hutton as head of the Council in the North. He was replaced by Thomas Cecil, 2nd Lord Burghley, to do what was necessary to undermine any possible rising or Scottish inroad. Robert Cecil was well aware that Essex was not only corresponding with James VI, but had a number of northern Catholic contacts. With the Queen manifestly ageing, Cecil was disturbed by the thought of a recusant rising in the north to secure the succession of James and toleration. To prevent this Burghley had to mount a campaign against recusancy that made no distinction between the followers of the pro-Spanish Jesuits and the followers of the Seculars, who were willing to take the oath of allegiance as the price of toleration. The measures then were harsh but successful: upwards of 150 Northumbrians were convicted of recusancy at the Newcastle assize held in August 1600.[5] There was no rising to break the peace of the north of England in 1601.[6]

In the meantime, in Ireland, Essex was contemplating a most dangerous sortie back to England. When Elizabeth got wind of his possible return after appointing a deputy, she forbade him to do so without her express commission. Fear in England about another Spanish fleet (a tradition that had not died with Philip II) was more than matched by the shiver induced by the notion of Essex shipping the remnant of his army back to England. That was the fevered possibility he was trailing before Blount and Southampton, and even the latter saw that this was courting disaster. The Lord Deputy was dissuaded from the grand gesture, but the other strand in his thought could not be smothered. So he sailed from Ireland with a small personal cohort, and arrived at Nonsuch Palace in Surrey early in the morning of 28 September. Cecil was warned by Lord Grey of this freakish turn of events, but before the Secretary could alert Elizabeth, Essex had virtually stormed her bedroom, to find her still preparing for the day. It is difficult to imagine who was more disconcerted by this strange encounter. One must suppose the Queen, since she could not know if the travel-stained man before her had set in motion a plan to seize her. However, having established that his speed precluded more than a handful of followers, she maintained her welcoming tone until the afternoon.

After dinner 'he again went into her presence', according to Rowland Whyte, and this time her attitude was much stiffer, 'for she began to call him to question for his return, and was not satisfied in the manner of his coming away and leaving all things at so great hazard.'[7] The next day Cecil and other Privy Councillors held a hastily convened meeting, with Knollys and the Earl of Worcester seeking to exculpate Essex. After a dinner held in two chambers for the two factions Essex was required to defend himself before the Council, and on 1 October he was placed in the custody of the Lord Keeper Egerton at his London residence, York House. With hindsight such a prominent dwelling may have been an error, since Essex had wide popular support in the city. If he was to be held under restraint somewhere the Reigate home of the Lord Admiral might have been better, especially since it was this strain of defiant popularity that kept the Queen from instituting proceedings in the Star Chamber. Even so, his release was not talked of and on 29 November the Council presented the sovereign's case against Essex in a series of speeches there. It was Egerton who led the proceedings, with Buckhurst and Cecil following, and finally Popham speaking to denounce those who spread malicious rumours. Obviously they were not sufficiently chastened by this, since on 22 December the bells of the city tolled when it was rumoured that Essex was dead of dysentery. Once again Elizabeth was moved by his infirmity and sent her own doctors as well as a supply of the royal *potage*.

The recovery he made in the New Year was not matched by a sustained lightening of Elizabeth's sense of grievance and her policy of distancing herself from her erstwhile favourite. In mid-February 1600 the rumour was that he was indeed going to stand trial in the Star Chamber, but Cecil persuaded him to write submissively to Elizabeth and she finally put the idea aside. Despite this Cecil and Essex were not reconciled, for all Cecil's 'mild courses' so strongly disparaged by Ralegh, who made no effort now to hide his antipathy to Essex. There was little likelihood they ever would be, though Cecil was 'not unappreciative of Essex's winning qualities of candour and generosity, gallantry and courage'.[8] True, the passing of years had taken some of the shine from these attributes, but the notion that Cecil was a vindictive and malevolent plotter against Essex cannot be sustained. Further, the rumour at court that Bacon was stirring the Queen against his patron led Cecil to write from his house at the Savoy: 'Cousin, I hear it, but I believe it not, that you should do some ill office to my Lord of Essex: for my part I am merely passive, and not active, in this action; and I follow the Queen, and that heavily, and I lead her not. The same course I would wish you to take.'

On 20 March 1600 Essex was allowed to return to his town house, but he was still in a form of custody maintained by Sir Richard Berkeley, and in theory was not allowed contact with his family or friends. There he remained until 5 June and a specially convened court held at York House, where the charges were very similar to those made previously. The special commission of judges and councillors heard him finally admit his errors, begging for mercy in a tone that moved many of the two hundred specially invited audience. No doubt Francis Bacon, one of the four Crown lawyers, was affected, particularly when he heard Coke denouncing the earl in his customary abusive mode. But Elizabeth's aim of fracturing the Essexites had been achieved, and since he was to remain in his London home without power, stripped of his offices of Earl Marshal and Master of the Ordnance, she could risk being magnanimous, and late in August he was given his freedom. Bacon had deserted; Mountjoy, the lover of Essex's sister Penelope, was disengaging; but still others remained loyal including Lord Henry Howard, Southampton, Rutland and a clutch of impoverished would-be courtiers like Sir Robert Crosse and Sir Griffin Markham. The failure of the ambiguous Howard to defect is interesting, although as his political biographer has pointed out, he did seek to protect himself from ruin by maintaining friendly relations with Cecil.[9] By nature a 'trimmer', Howard had a certain amount of influence with Cecil and he was the mediator between the two rival factions on behalf of James VI, whose interest in the throne of England was reaching fever pitch.

Within a very short time Essex was once again over-wrought. This time the cause was money and the necessity of renewing the Sweet Wine farm, which Leicester and he had used to underpin their court careers. Negotiations on this and other matters were undertaken by a lawyer the earl employed, Henry Lindley,[10] but this time Essex himself took over the campaign, since he had nothing else to do and his financial situation was desperate. Fiscal ruin as well as political ruin was now a dreadful possibility. The immediate requirement of £5,000 to stave off bankruptcy could scarcely be met by borrowing from friends, who were all in debt. Elizabeth read his honeyed pleas but delayed a decision until the end of October, when she declared that no one would benefit from the licence except the Crown – she would administer it herself.

To Essex this was a calamity, a vile confirmation of his psychotic fears that his enemies controlled the Queen. He ignored the evidence of her passionate inclination to make her own choices and his brief period of mild demeanour was cast off. All that 'military dependence' Bacon had warned against began to cluster at Essex House, keeping odd company with a number of Puritan ministers. None of the picturesque ruffians lured to London by a fistful of angels and Devereux family retainers had any time for politics, and so they found a villain in the supreme politician Cecil. His intelligence network alerted him, by interfering with all correspondence between England and Scotland, that there were many exchanges between Essex and James VI; these had been going on for years and latterly were in terms that might broadly be considered treasonable. By 1598 James was entrusting to Essex all aspects of policy he wanted negotiated in England, and later the earl suggested joint action between James's forces and the English army in Ireland as a way of compelling Elizabeth to make a formal declaration that James was to be her successor. Essex had no dynastic ambitions for himself; his first aim was to eject the Cecils and his second to fill his empty coffers.

The notorious special performance of Shakespeare's *Richard II* was played for the Essex faction after dinner on 7 February 1601. It seems that Essex had seen many performances of this drama of compelling reverberations and found it haunting.[11] Cecil too seems to have known it, though the idea that he saw a performance at the London home of his cousin in 1595 is an oft-repeated error. Sir Edward Hoby's invitation may have been to show Cecil a picture, or a manuscript (now lost) on King Richard III by the bishop of Ely. There was no notion or possibility of a performance of a play by Shakespeare or anyone else. Even so, with its abdication scene the play was certainly saturated with meaning for Essex and his heterogeneous cluster of followers, and there is the additional point that before he inherited his earldom Essex had been styled Viscount Hereford, as had the Bolingbroke of the text. Nor was Elizabeth unaware of the freight of significance attached to it. The same evening she requested the Privy Council to take action, and some months later was reported as saying that she was Richard II.

Preferring to meet at the Lord Treasurer Buckhurst's house instead of Cecil's or in Whitehall, the Privy Council chose John Herbert (regarded as expendable, perhaps?) to go to Essex with a demand that he should appear before them to explain his actions. Herbert managed this and returned with the message that the earl declined to comply because he feared for his life. The following day the stuttering treason flared up, only to be extinguished – in good measure by the organizational skills of the Cecils. The fiasco drove Essex to retreat to his town house to destroy papers, including incriminating letters from James VI, one of which he is supposed to have worn in a small bag hanging from a cord round his neck. With his friends scattered and deserting, he had no choice but to surrender if he eschewed suicide. He and Southampton were arrested and taken to Lambeth Palace before a brief river trip to the Tower.[12] A wonderfully unflustered sovereign might have left them there but for the threat from Captain Thomas Lee, who eluded capture until taken while making his way to seize her, intending to force her to release Essex. Swiftly tried, he was equally swiftly beheaded – a fitting end for a man who had once sent Elizabeth the head of Fiach McHugh.[13] Lee's dangerous excursion led to an army of royal officials investigating the plot, and as the confessions mounted up there was more than enough evidence of treason. Even so, no one would admit to anything heinous planned against Elizabeth; the main thrust of the confessions was that Essex's enemies were to be removed from the court. The principal enemy was Robert Cecil, and this was the line taken by the earl at his trial in Westminster Hall. There he launched the accusation that the Secretary favoured the claim of Philip II's daughter, the Infanta-Archduke Isabella, to succeed the Queen: a claim derived from Isabella's descent from John of Gaunt.

Cecil was not yet a peer, so he was not sitting in judgement on his rival. But he was listening to the presentation of evidence and defence from behind a tapestry, and when attacked he made a dramatic interjection. Falling on his knees before the peers, he claimed the right to speak in his own defence. This agreed, he challenged Essex to name the courtier who had told him Cecil's thinking on the crucial matter of succession. When the earl named Southampton, he was produced and coaxed into naming another source – Sir William Knollys, no less. So, without being told exactly why he was summoned, Essex's uncle was called for examination and promptly cleared Cecil. The conversation had in fact been about a book by Fr Robert Persons on the succession in which the Infanta's claim was advanced. Cecil had said nothing more than that he wondered at it being taken so seriously. Essex's accusation was worthless and he could only stammer in consternation that in being reported to him the words had taken on another sense. Beside the gravity of the original charge this was a lightweight excuse, and after further exchanges with Cecil the expected verdict of guilty was pronounced. The death sentence was mandatory but Essex managed to leave the court with a smile. His bravado soon faded when the full enormity of his fall engulfed him.

There followed an unhappy episode when, realizing that Elizabeth did not intend to be merciful this time, he summoned Cecil and other councillors to his cell. He had decided to proclaim his guilt and to apologize, but the effort was tainted by his desperate attempts to devolve some of the blame on to others including his sister, Penelope Rich. Her earlier interrogation had been conducted by Buckhurst after the Star Chamber examination of Essex. A beauty, clever and resourceful, she had impressed James VI in her correspondence begun over a decade before. These 'Rialta' letters* in a modest code were of course meant to be secret, but Burghley had access to them, since Thomas Fowler, a former employee of the late Earl of Leicester, kept him well informed.[14] Acting on instructions from Robert Cecil, Buckhurst had first to find Penelope, who had quickly withdrawn to Barn Elms to keep company with her sister-in-law Frances, Countess of Essex. When he did meet her Penelope charmed away the serious tenor of his questioning so that Cecil, on Elizabeth's behalf, rebuked him for being 'so apt to excuse my Lady's course'. She remained a problem because of her very open conduct of an affair with Lord Mountjoy, whom Elizabeth had every reason to gratify as the new and invaluable Lord Deputy of Ireland. The victor over the Spanish at Kinsale could accept

* Penelope Rich = Rialta = the Exchange.

the punishment of his kinsman Sir Christopher Blount, but to expect him to acquiesce in the punishment of his lover might have been too much.[15]

Penelope Rich had many saving connections. So did the Earl of Southampton, whose spell in the Tower did not end in execution. Essex, Christopher Blount and others were beheaded there on 25 February; but Southampton was reprieved. Until the executions there was still a danger of a rising to release Essex. Such an exploit was planned by a group of London apprentices led by one Alexander, but they were discovered by Cecil's spy network and remained in prison until at least July.[16] This was mild indeed, and for someone like Southampton there were reasons to be guardedly optimistic, with Nottingham and Cecil working with 'all our wits and power' to save him. With his mother and wife addressing pleas to Cecil, Southampton was fortunate that the Queen's own misery chimed with the Secretary's efforts. The earl therefore lived to become a friend of the man who had done so much for him.[17]

A number of Essex's northern associates paid moderate fines for their indiscretion. This was a calculatedly merciful punishment occasioned by the government's determination to render northern Catholics powerless while not driving them into a revolt stemming from despair. Their hopes rested on James VI, since they had supported his claim to the English throne after the execution of Mary Queen of Scots, and James had wooed them with hints of toleration. But they knew nothing of the tentative moves made in Scotland and England to bring Robert Cecil and the King closer for a mutually beneficial arrangement. The arrival in London of James's ambassadors, the Earl of Mar and Edward Bruce, shortly after the execution of Essex, led to a meeting in Cecil's Strand home. This set in motion another secret correspondence from several sources. James (who had once loathed Cecils) quickly excised old memories of their involvement in the execution of Mary, and in his replies Cecil offered analysis, clarity and deference, in the belief that if England was to escape a civil war after Elizabeth's death, the country needed a king to preserve the changes dating from the Reformation and the Elizabethan settlement. Lord Henry Howard also joined in the correspondence with James; this was accepted by Cecil as a means of reducing the amount of writing to be done. Howard's deployment of satire and insult when writing about certain court contemporaries meant that Cecil could be more fastidious.

6

Lord Burghley's deliberate choice of his second son as his political heir did not alter the requirement of primogeniture. Burghley House, near Stamford (even today with a park twice the size of Monaco); the principal landholdings; and the great London home on the north side of the Strand – all passed to Thomas Cecil. Over the years the genial young man had matured into a responsible parent himself, and a sustained supporter of his more gifted younger half-brother. Most of the lands and property earmarked for Robert Cecil were his by the marriage settlement of 1589, but during his decline in spring 1598 Burghley revised his will to increase the share. Robert Cecil (now thirty-five years old) would receive all the family holdings, including Theobalds, in Hertfordshire and Middlesex, as well as the manor of Essendon. The Secretary also inherited a part of his father's papers and books, but despite these careful provisions the old patriarch could not prevent some family acrimony because Robert Cecil inherited the guardianship of Lady Bridget and Lady Susan Vere. Together with these daughters of his late sister and the Earl of Oxford, he was to share in the goods, money, plate and valuables which remained in Burghley's bedchamber. The executors of the will – Thomas Bellott, steward of the household, and Gabriel Goodman, the Dean of Westminster – were to divide these items, and Thomas Cecil was angered at not receiving any of the jewels.[1] There was also some trouble with Oxford, who now sought the custody of his daughters after years of neglect. Cecil soon grew weary of the pirouettes of greed and, depressed and irritable, turned for support to Michael Hickes, who offered a temporary home to William, Frances and Catherine – an offer refused because one of the girls was ill.[2]

Cecil was then living either in a Savoy apartment, a perquisite of the Duchy of Lancaster, or in a house which he may have built adjacent to Burghley House on the eastern side. His passion for building and land purchases intensified with Burghley's death and his own appointment to the Mastership of the Court of Wards. He could now emulate his father without appearing to rival him. His inheritance brought in something around £1,800 a year at this time, much of which would have been devoted to the maintenance of Theobalds (pronounced 'Tibbles').[3] Hitherto his property activities had been spasmodic, directed towards a quick-fire profit which could then be reinvested in something like privateering. In 1594, for example, he acquired a house in Holborn which he sold to Sir Matthew Arundell. In the same year he raised the very substantial sum of £1,750 for land purchases in Lancashire, sold four years later for a fine profit to Nicholas Mosley, a future Lord Mayor of London. In 1597 he paid a sort of homage to his forebears with his first permanent purchase. In a deal saturated with family significance he acquired for £200 from a cousin, William, the farm at Alltyrynys on the Welsh border in Herefordshire where the Cecils had originated.[4]

Another country dwelling, though much closer to London, was the Great House down the Thames in Chelsea, later known as Beaumont House. This had come to Burghley as a gift from Lady Dacres (sister of Lord Buckhurst), who bequeathed it to him, with remainder to Robert and Elizabeth Cecil, in her will dated 20 December 1594. After her death in May 1595 the house was surveyed and plans were drawn up by a Mr Torrington.[5] Nothing seems to have been done until Robert received the property some time later. Then proposals for alterations were made by John Symonds and William Spicer, the latter having made his reputation in renovating

Kenilworth Castle for the Earl of Leicester many years before.[6] However, it was the submission of John Thorpe of the Office of Works that was carried out.[7] The renovations included a new front, yet with the work done, to exacting specifications, Cecil lost interest in the house. The Countess of Huntingdon had paid £700 for a smaller house in the same area, and in deciding to sell Cecil hoped for a hefty return on his investment. It was offered to Sir John Fortescue, who declined to buy it, but Cecil found another victim in Henry Clinton, Earl of Lincoln, and his daughter and son-in-law, Lady Elizabeth and Sir Arthur Gorges. The price was a monstrous £6,000, and not surprisingly payment was dragged out for years.[8]

Lincoln's eventual weary offer of another property in London, or even pearls, was rejected because Cecil needed cash to buy land on the fashionable south side of the Strand. Burghley had been content to live on the north side, but Cecil was hankering after a spot abutting on to the river for easier access to Whitehall. The palaces that lined the bank had once been the London homes of bishops but were now rapidly passing into secular ownership. The transfer from bishop to nobleman had been the fate of one property Cecil could afford. Once the town house of the bishops of Carlisle, it had been sold to Lord Henry Herbert, and since it was in a prime position between Russell House and Ivy Bridge Lane, Cecil was enthralled at the prospect of acquiring it. The owner was persuaded to accept £1,000, and once Cecil had obtained the building he had it demolished and replaced by one apparently designed by Simon Basil.

The first part of Salisbury House, known as Great Salisbury House, was put up on the site of the present Shell-Mex building. To squeeze it in Basil had to build across the Lane, a narrow thoroughfare leading down to the river; the Lane was removed further to the west. Jutting a little into the Strand, the new building was a three-storey courtyard house with four-storey corner towers on three projecting angles.[9] These martial echoes in the design may have stemmed from Basil's work on fortifications, though Essex and Northampton

House had much the same appearance. The latter was actually a palace, which according to contemporary opinion rivalled the finest residences in Europe. When Northampton acquired land in Greenwich for expanding his country house it was at the expense of Basil himself, who was induced to take down the upper garret and second storey of his home. When Northampton pressed him to demolish a wing a pained Basil took the matter up with Salisbury in October 1611, just before the earl became a martyr to rheumatism in his right arm.[10]

The chapel at Salisbury House probably kept Cecil from having to worship under public scrutiny at nearby St Martin-in-the-Fields. He did, however, provide a yearly benevolence of £16 for the poor of the parish, when by contrast Basil's contribution was five shillings.[11] Among those more prosperous individuals who did worship in church was John Thorpe, a vestryman and member of the Court of Burgesses who was employed by Cecil and the parish as a land surveyor.[12] In June 1600, when the parishioners of St Martin's were seeking a preaching minister, they asked Cecil to refer the matter to the archdeacon, as well as Cecil's friend Walter Cope and the pious Thomas Bellott, a brother of the Bishop of Chester, Hugh Bellott, and the Receiver General to the Dean and Chapter of Westminster, George Bellott. Although Thomas Bellott lavished attention on the Abbey Church of Bath, he did manage a loan of £100 for the rebuilding of St Martin's in 1607.[13] Other contributors then were Cecil, the Earl of Bedford and the Earl of Northampton. Raphe Dobbinson, who was instrumental in the rebuilding, was a bailiff of Westminster, as well as vestryman of the church. Some of his correspondence with Salisbury survives at Hatfield, and among them is the less benign request for the payment of 23s. 6d. – the cost of the commissioned ironwork on which were set the heads of the Gunpowder conspirators Thomas Percy and Robert Catesby.

Among the parishioners of St Martin's in the 1590s were the Colt brothers, Huguenot immigrants from Arras in France. John and Maximilien were both sculptors, and years later it

71

was Maximilien who carved Salisbury's elaborate tomb for St Etheldreda's, Hatfield. As an artist from a family of artists, it was natural that he should marry into another. On 31 January 1604 at the Dutch church in Austin Friars he married Susanna, daughter of the elder Marcus Gheeraerts, one of whose landscapes has recently been rediscovered at Burghley, and his widow Susanna, a sister of John de Critz, the serjeant-painter. Susanna Colt was also a sister of Sara Gheeraerts, who married Isaac Oliver, the portrait-miniaturist who was a pupil of Nicholas Hilliard.[14] By this complicated conjugal route we arrive at the career of one of the greatest English Renaissance artists, whose early progress was so stimulated by the Earl of Leicester and then by Burghley. He was limner, goldsmith, jeweller, calligrapher and engraver, and his reputation for excellence as a painter was underlined in a rather quaint fashion by a petition to Burghley in 1593 from two painter-stainers.[15] Samuel Thompson and Hugh Bennett sought a monopoly of painting arms for funerary escutcheons under the control of Clarenceux King of Arms. When they sought an answer from Robert Cecil a year later they added that they were content that Hilliard should join them in the work, for he was 'so well known for his sufficiency and care in his works'. Whether he did so is open to doubt, though the money would always have been useful.

The first of Hilliard's six surviving letters to Cecil was written in March 1594. It was a petition on behalf of a young immigrant engraver, Abel Feckman.[16] Two months later his plea was endorsed by Alderman Richard Martin, the long-serving Master of the Mint. Feckman's criminal activity was a dangerous involvement in faking coins for a man called Webb and his employee, Morgan. The young man was lured into this enterprise because he was newly married and desperate for a little extra money. Hilliard had been urged by the Earl of Cumberland to accompany Feckman's brother-in-law with the petition, but his gout was so painful he could not ride his horse.

As it was, money problems were not solely the province of

junior employees. Hilliard, with a large family, injudicious investments and refined, expensive skills, seems to have had difficulties over many years, much to the irritation of his father-in-law, Robert Brandon. A warrant dated 11 December 1591 to the Treasurer and Chamberlains of the Exchequer authorized payment to Hilliard of £400. But it was to be an indirect reward, taken from monies or goods forfeited in the Exchequer Court, and eight years later Hilliard complained with some dismay to Cecil that he had received only £40.[17] A decade later he was writing to him that having taught English and foreign apprentices who pleased 'the common sort exceeding well . . . I am myself unable by my art, any longer to keep house in London, without some further help of Her Majesty.'[18] He added that an annuity of £40 recently granted at Cecil's prompting was a great help, allowing him to move from London to stay with friends in the country, free from rent payments and living expenses. Even so, there were still outstanding debts to be met. He hoped in vain for Cecil's aid in getting the Queen's permission to move abroad 'for a year or two at the most', which he must have known would not be granted. His other hope was that Cecil would take Hilliard's son Laurence into his service. The young man spoke Spanish (whereas his father was fluent in French), could write well and draw, but Cecil ignored the request and four years later Laurence became a freeman of the Goldsmith's Company by virtue of his father's membership.[19]

Cecil's interest in painting was sustained and he became a cultivated collector. But architecture and its application to his envisaged building projects became a passion, and he once remarked that he would 'show himself a good architectour'.[20] The last word is in itself revealing, showing that the profession of architect had yet to emerge. This meant that men like Burghley and Cecil could take an uninhibited interest in their own projects, using expert advice and consulting European, not just parochial, sources – evidence of Hendrik van Paesschen's work on Burghley House has now emerged. The senior Cecil set the example of owning a number of books on the subject, including Philibert de L'Orme's *Novels Invention pour bien bastir* – which is rather like finding a senior British politician today having the writings of Frank Lloyd Wright in his library.[21] One publication that went into Robert Cecil's library was Jacques Perret's *Des fortification et artifice architecture et perspective*, published in Paris in 1601. Yet it has to be said that this interest did not lead to innovative commissions, and Cecil's suite in his new town house consisted of a bedroom and study with elaborate panelling by John de Beeke (or Booke).* He chose to move in during October 1602, though the plaster-work was still damp and the rooms smelt 'moist and musty'. Early in December he gave a party that was also a house-warming in the most genuine sense – it had been delayed for some days by cold and bad weather.

Elizabeth, one of the marvels of her age, was one of his guests who saw several entertainments. One was a skittish piece called *A Contention betwixt a wife, a widow and a Maide*, written by the Middle Temple lawyer and poet John Davies. Accepting the commission to write for the occasion was a way for Davies to thank Cecil for his efforts to rehabilitate him – in 1598 he had fallen out dramatically with his witty friend Richard Martin. The cause was nonsensical, a past Christmas revels entertainment to which Davies had taken such exception that he had appeared in the Great Hall of Middle Temple to attack Martin. Not surprisingly Martin and his fellow-Templars took exception to this outrageous bullying, and Davies was expelled.[22] Before Cecil had joined Sir John Popham, the Lord Chief Justice, to have him reinstated in 1601, Martin may have got his revenge by cheerfully conflating two men called John Davies (or Davis) in a rumour about the Judas who had betrayed Essex's intentions. Was it just coincidence that Burghley was in London in February of that year?

* Or even Bucke. Originally probably Van der Beck, indicating Dutch ancestry. A 'widow Beeke' was buried in St Anne, Blackfriars, in 1600; his mother, perhaps?

This time the evening's entertainments were given without trouble, and the only blemish was when Elizabeth hurt her leg or ankle on leaving. With the party over, the household went back to its ordinary routines, while work on the house and garden continued. For an expert opinion on the latter Cecil was able to consult Sir Walter Cope, who used a hydraulics system in his own garden.[23] Cope, a sometime gentleman usher to Burghley, had a passion for collecting extraordinarily disparate objects, or what the Elizabethans and Jacobeans called 'toyes' – manufactured exotic objects or bizarre items found in nature which, when augmented by rare coins or jewels or clocks, might constitute a collection to be placed in cabinets in a special room: the so-called *Wunderkammer*. Burghley had had such a room, and one of the items that went into it was a *Handsteine* sent from Germany by John Dee's notorious medium, Edward Kelley.[24] Cope and his contemporary Richard Garth had the collecting passion and probably copied their employer. When the Swiss writer and traveller Thomas Platter was in England in 1599 he visited Cope's house in the Strand and recorded an amazing list of items.[25] It is not clear if any had been the gift of Burghley in his will, or what happened to the *Wunderkammer*. Since Cope was a guest at Cecil's December house-warming and was allowed to present Elizabeth with a 'toye', it may have been something Cecil himself inherited but felt it was appropriate for Cope to give away. Cope was also a member of the Elizabethan Society of Antiquaries.[26]

It was not only mechanical or manufactured rarities that intrigued Cecil. Like James I he took an interest in the breeding of lions kept in the Tower, and his own dinner table was enlivened by a parrot which stalked it looking for morsels. It was presented to Cecil by Sir John Gilbert, who had supplied clear, if limited, details for looking after it:

He will eat all kinds of meat, and nothing will hurt him except it be very salt. If you put him on the table at mealtime he will make choice of his meat. He must be kept very warm and after he hath filled himself he will set in a gentlewoman's ruff all day. In the afternoon he will eat bread or oatmeal groats, drink water or claret wine: every night he is put in the cage and covered warm.

Rare birds, monkeys and hunting dogs were kept or given as presents, and it seems possible that those featured in a portrait of Princess Elizabeth, who was passionately fond of parrots, came from Salisbury's own collector in the Far East.[27]

Cecil's opportunities to buy land outside the capital coincided with the mounting pressure of expenditure on the Crown of the war in Ireland. In the decade up to 1603 nearly £2 million had been used, and to allow this Elizabeth, against her inclinations, was forced to sell Crown lands. Cecil was perfectly placed to anticipate the richest items. The badgering of Lincoln for payments on the Chelsea house had underwritten his town purchases; now Cecil launched into a whirl of buying in the country. He began by spending over £4,500 on a clutch of properties in the west of England, including the famous St Michael's Mount in Cornwall. Cranborne estates in Dorset made him a neighbour of Sir Walter Ralegh at Sherborne, and Warnborough manor in Wiltshire enhanced the sequence of purchases, so that to register his pleasure he gave Elizabeth a ruby and topaz jewel. He was right to be exultant, since in the next few years he took £2,900 from fines alone.[28]

Cranborne was a key purchase, the kernel for others like Cranborne rectory and priory bought for £2,000 from Sir Ralph Horsey. In achieving this consolidation he flattened the prior claim of Sir Anthony Ashley, still smarting from his imprisonment and cringing before Cecil in the hope of regaining royal favour.[29] In 1605 Salisbury engaged John Norden – then surveyor for the Duchy of Cornwall – to survey Cranborne Manor, though for several years he held back on demolition and rebuilding.[30] When he did decide to go ahead in 1608 it was after James had paid a first visit to Cranborne

Chase, where it was possible to hunt bustards, pine martens and fallow deer. There was a follow-up visit in 1609 and by then William Cecil was also showing an interest in the property that gave him his title.[31]

The house was a very old one even then and Hatfield accounts record a payment in December 1609 of £5 to William Arnold for 'drawing a plot for Cranborne House'.[32] Even during the struggle for the Great Contract, it was noted in March 1610 that Arnold 'spends every day a whole hour in private with my Lord Treasurer about his buildings'. In fact, that year Arnold was mainly engaged on the construction of Wadham College, Oxford, but in November he received £40 as part of a £250 fee for constructing a terrace and kitchen.[33] Features of the old hunting lodge were retained, but an extra floor was inserted, while at the south-west corner of the house, where there was a projection forming a low tower, Salisbury increased the height and for balance a south-east tower was added.[34] Lattice windows, loggias and tall brick chimneys were included in the new design, which took in ornament derived from pattern books like *Architectura* by Hans Vredeman de Vries.[35] Through such manuals he became 'one of the foremost popularizers of Mannerist models'.[36] Any house today subjected to such wilful hybridizing would certainly look appalling (compare the ignorant stupidity of replacing sash windows with modern metal window frames). Happily, Cranborne had a mason of whom it was said he was 'the absolutest and honestest workman in England'; the romantic charm of the house is testimony to his talent, and to the taste of his employer.

In January 1602 Cecil bought, for some £5,000, a bran tub of Crown properties spread over counties from East Anglia to Cornwall.[37] Three months later he was seized by the buying frenzy again, acquiring for about the same amount six Cornish manors which when surveyed promised little chance of improvement. The recommendation of his steward Roger Houghton, in Cecil's service for forty-two years, was that they should be sold back to the Crown at once. This was done just before Elizabeth died, but two months after their purchase Cecil paid over £6,800 for properties closer to London, and in December 1602 he had to find a hefty sum for the Brigstock Parks in Northamptonshire.[38] His notions of improvement there were greeted with fury by the poorer inhabitants of Rockingham Forest. In an area of over 2,000 acres that made up the big and little parks, there were many deer for them to hunt with bows and arrows. They also grazed animals and took fuel, so that the whole fabric of their lives depended on access. After a survey by Israel Amyce, a procedure the people knew often came before a disastrous threat to their livelihood, Cecil's plan was to cut down the trees on 900 acres, and reduce the deer herd from about one thousand animals to six hundred. The land freed would then be turned over to pasture for sheep or cattle. Not surprisingly 'the bare sort' rioted, and the disorders were ended only when Cecil distributed alms.[39]

This did not put an end to his difficulties, for he had obtained the parks by sharp practice, elbowing aside Sir Francis Carew, who wanted the reversion of them when the lessee, Lord Hunsdon, died.[40] Success was actually less important to the elderly bachelor Carew than to Nicholas Throckmorton, his nephew and heir and brother of Arthur Throckmorton, who saw an opportunity to get back at Cecil when James I arrived in England. A fanatical hunter of animals for so-called sport, James was naturally perturbed that the 'noble art of venery' should be ousted by utilitarian and plebeian sheep. His immediate response to a petition to halt improvements was a command to Cecil to cease this activity. The latter's response was to protest his title to what was private property. However, to win James's confirmation of this very important holding he agreed that deer should remain in the little park, although to the understandable fury of the peasants the great park was enclosed.[41] Arthur Throckmorton himself raised sheep, but his flock remained at about 1,200 animals and he seems to have been an easy-going landlord.[42] His unease at crossing Cecil soon became clear, and in the summer of 1604 he wrote emolliently (he hoped):

'My fortune is not so favourable as to make me wanton, nor my folly so great as to forget your force; my wishes are that in so unequal a rank we might right one another. . . . For Brigstock, it never entered my thoughts to mislike therewith, much less to complot any complaint.' Clearly Cecil had not been pleased.

In three years Cecil had spent over £35,000 on land purchases. This was a startling burst of activity and raises questions about how he managed to finance this colossal expenditure. The answers, as is usual with most things about the man, are not a little complicated. First, he had the means because he had the business instincts a twentieth-century capitalist would recognize and salute. Cecil was prepared to take risks in buying and selling, if necessary squeezing friends, suitors and rivals in an uncompromising manner. Not even his family was immune; his brother-in-law Lord Cobham's political ruin only preceded his financial dismemberment by interested parties including Salisbury (as he then was), and a number of his associates: Alexander Prescott, the goldsmith and money-lender; Roger Houghton and John Daccombe. Anyone seeking the renewal of a lease found how expensive it could be, so between 1598 and 1601 £4,400 was raised from fines for renewal. Money also came from timber and stock sales from the estates in Hertfordshire and Middlesex inherited from Burghley.[43] The starch patent was another source of profit stemming from the comparatively new Elizabethan fashion. Burghley had given the manufacturing monopoly to Sir John Packington and others in 1588.[44] A decade later this was passed to Buckhurst and Cecil; it was revoked in 1601 as Elizabeth sought to placate Parliament.

As Master of the Court of Wards Cecil was, of course, following in Burghley's footsteps, and the profits were satisfactory. There was also the grant in 1601 of the farm of the customs on imported satins, silks, velvets, cambrics and other luxury materials. These were all coveted by wealthy people of fashion and came mostly from Venice, textiles having figured prominently in the city-state's economy for hundreds of years.

79

Venice was also an entrepôt for Eastern silks, as well as an outlet for Tuscan and Lombard wools. The opulent materials made in the city were imported into England from the Low Countries, and there was no doubt that demand was rising, so when figures for the late 1590s showed a sharp fall in Customs receipts the inescapable conclusion was that this was caused by smuggling. To reduce this Exchequer officials opted for the lease to be given to a contractor paying a fixed rent. Since Vincent Skinner, one of the auditors of receipt at the Exchequer, had until the 1590s been one of Burghley's secretaries, it is not surprising that Cecil was selected. Although the fixed rent was nearly £9,000 a year, he had only to stifle some of the highly profitable smuggling to make a substantial sum.[45]

When Elizabeth died the farm lapsed and there was a great deal of rumour-mongering and jockeying for position. This was partly caused by Cecil's muscular administration so far, for he thought the initial profit too low, stiffened his patent with the connivance of royal officials and increased vigilance at the Customs House in London, so that receipts blossomed – so much so that importers like mercer Baptist Hickes, the brother of Michael, sent up a chorus of wails. This was not surprising when the payment for April–November 1601 was £189, while for May–December the following year it was £569.[46] In 1603 it was whispered that Cecil's under-farmers intended to seek a lease directly from James I, but Cecil was far too well situated for there to be much likelihood of success for them.

William Massam, a prominent member of the Cranfield–Ingram financial clique, was aware of all this. In his approach to Cecil he proposed that the minister should either 'retain the patent wholly to yourself, placing honest men to see the execution thereof, or farm it out unto any man of account'.[47] Massam had calculated that Cecil would surely sublet. Good advice and the contacts between Ingram and Cecil might then lead the latter to favour the Ingram–Massam syndicate. However, Cecil followed the old route of finding a Customs officer, and even when he changed his mind there was competition from a rival block headed by Samuel Hare and Richard Venn.[48] Remarkably, the new lease from James I was for fifteen years with no increase in rent, a surrender of royal advantage that marked a number of the new monarch's open-handed dealings with courtiers. Cecil sublet the farm for six years only to an amalgamated group including Ingram, Massam, Hare, Venn and the Customs official Francis Jones. His income from the lease was 2,000 marks or almost £1,400 a year. Cranfield's calculations showed that the merchants themselves were also making a profit from the enterprise. After the increase in the rates on imported silk in 1604, Cecil left the old lease intact, with the same merchants paying cash for the increased value of the farm – £3,286. 4s. 7d.[49] The profits total from this farm must have been huge, for when the unexpired lease was surrendered by William Cecil, 2nd Earl of Salisbury, in 1615 his pension was set at £3,000 a year for twenty one years in compensation. The King's profit from the farm rent was a reliable but modest £8,900 in 1604, and following the new Book of Rates some £15,900 a year.

The other minor farms on the duties on wines, gold and silver thread, tobacco, coal and currants prepared the way for the endeavour known as the Great Farm. Negotiations began on this in 1604 and were finally sealed on 6 February 1605. Cecil's association with the syndicate revealingly headed by Francis Jones was primarily *pour encourager les autres*. Two rival groups existed.[50] The first was under the leadership of Sir John Swinnerton; the second was headed by the wealthy Levant merchants William Garway and Nicholas Salter, who eventually absorbed the Jones group. Their triumph in pursuit of the Great Farm left Cecil (now briefly Lord Cranborne) £6,000 richer as he withdrew – it was a gift from them which probably helped to underwrite two land purchases: a manor bought from the Earl of Nottingham and the South Mimms estate bought from the executors of Lord Windsor for over £5,000.[51]

The last elements of Cecil's capital accumulation for consideration here were privateering and exploration – different

81

activities, but often intertwined. Cecil took an interest in them from the mid-1590s, dipping his toe first in Ralegh's Guiana enterprise of dazzling promise but little substance. For all that, on his return Ralegh wrote a book, dedicated to an unimpressed Cecil and Lord Admiral Howard, called *The Discoverie of the Large, Rich and Bewtiful Empyre of Guiana*. Both the dedicatees were also well acquainted with Charles Leigh, the pioneer of English settlement in that area in 1602–6.[52] The discretion of the two men has so far obscured their activities, but there seems little doubt that they existed.[53] Beyond any spasmodic private profit there was a deeper interest in extracting from Spain real trading concessions in any further general peace – a free-floating option that seems to have been around at the turn of the century.

In the Mediterranean privateering was flourishing, not only in Muslim Algiers and Tunis but also in Valetta, Pisa, Palma, Naples and Leghorn. Individual Englishmen were determined not to miss out on the profits of the sea-robbers. In December 1600, for example, Cecil and Buckhurst underwrote a special mission by Richard Gifford to the coast of Spain, with a commission of reprisal obtained from Dr Julius Caesar, then judge of the Admiralty court and a subordinate of Notting-ham. The legitimate project was swiftly set aside by Gifford, who in conjunction with a proclaimed pirate, Captain Hugh Griffith, seized a Valencia-bound Ragusan grain ship loaded with Sicilian wheat. Since there is plenty of evidence that given the opportunity Ragusan vessels could be equally ruth-less, it is not necessary to feel too deeply for the seized vessel and her crew. The prize was taken to Tunis, where the ship and cargo were offered to ransom. There were many networks of intermediaries and when Griffith was paid off, Gifford boldly went with the vessel to Leghorn. This was an open port, but for whose complicity 'stolen goods would have rotted in the ports of Barbary'.[54] When he got there, however, Gifford was arrested by officers of the Grand Duke of Tuscany. This was an irate response to the great success of John Troughton in the *Lioness*, who near Majorca captured the

White Greyhound out of Middelburg, which was carrying sugar to Leghorn. This seizure threatened the future of Gifford, and it was his good fortune that Cecil and Buckhurst persuaded Elizabeth to write soothingly to the Grand Duke. Thus it was that his naughty career continued for several more years. As for Cecil, he had invested £700 in the *Lioness* and he got back something over £7,000.[55]

One or two Englishmen were apparently uneasy at this borderline activity. Greville, the Treasurer of the Navy, regarded with some suspicion after the Essex episode, and Vice-Admiral Sir Richard Leveson, son-in-law of the Lord Admiral, declared that 'for subjects to make wars as it were in fellowship with their sovereign must needs be dishonourable and prejudicial in all manner of respects'.[56] Yet this did not prevent Leveson from capturing a rich Portuguese carrack in June 1602 in an exploit which recalled the famous one a decade earlier.[57]

7

The Treaty of Vervins in 1598 underlined the dangerous thinness of the foreign policy options open to Elizabeth and her advisers. Once again the only allies were the Dutch, who were manifestly set against a general pacification. Although the Queen's relationship with the United Provinces had been turbulent since the days of the Earl of Leicester's intervention in their affairs in the mid-1580s, she felt no sustained inclination at this time to desert them.[1] Years of propping them up with loans and men could not be cast aside if there was a possibility they might succumb to Spain or even fall under French influence, as had once been threatened. But peace was highly desirable given the huge burden of the struggle against Tyrone, and so Thomas Edmondes was sent to France with the aim of finding out through the French what Spanish conditions would be. In the meantime, Elizabeth had no option but to sign a new treaty with the Dutch with financial clauses that affected both sides. More important was the clause (hitherto unthinkable) that would allow her to make a separate peace with Spain. However, the prospect of this dimmed when the ruler of the supposedly independent Spanish Netherlands (Flanders), the Archduke Albrecht, went on a long visit to Spain, following his marriage to Isabella.

In mid-January 1599 one of the Archduke's councillors, Geronimo Coemans, arrived in London for an interview with Cecil. His claim was that he had been sent over to initiate and conduct peace talks by the interim ruler, Cardinal Andreas.

Cecil discussed his arrival with Elizabeth, who read the letters Coemans had brought only after her gallant Secretary had rubbed them over his own face in a check for poison.[2] He, Buckhurst and Hunsdon then talked to Coemans, whom Elizabeth found impressive. He was therefore required to return home to obtain full authority from both the Archduke and the government in Spain. Very little regard was given to the notion of the independence of the Archduke's territories.

Coemans returned to England from Brussels in mid-March. He stated that Philip III had been consulted and favoured peace, but he failed to produce documents to support this claim and Elizabeth felt she had no option but to ignore him. Cecil and some of the Privy Council were slightly more optimistic than others like Essex, but his objections were set aside and the Queen allowed that this somewhat dubious envoy should return again to Brussels with a letter urging the cardinal this time to get full authority for a conference. It was some weeks later, in May, that Cecil heard that the mission was delayed by the absence of Cardinal Andreas in Germany. Shortly after this it was revealed that Coemans had gone to Spain in pursuit of the necessary authority, and to maintain the thaw Elizabeth and the cardinal in the meantime exchanged letters that were polite but inconsequential.

In July 1599 these modest activities seemed likely to collapse. The reason was the almost inevitable summer flap in the south-east when news reached England of yet another Armada. Essex was then in Ireland, about to make his armistice arrangement with Tyrone at a meeting conducted bizarrely in the middle of the river, but in his absence the country seemed notably at risk, and the Spanish held back only because of a large Dutch fleet cruising off the Spanish coast. Here was a powerful suggestion that Leicester's marine reforms in the United Provinces had proved thoroughly useful.[3] However, when the Dutch sailed on to Madeira there was a further bout of panic in England on a report that the governor of Brest had been asked by Spain for anchorage there. The alarm was dispelled only when an English fleet was put into commission, and then in August news arrived that in giving chase to the Dutch, the Spanish had as usual been crippled by adverse weather.

At this time Coemans reappeared. In an interview with Cecil he claimed that authority from Spain had been granted and could be expected at any moment. Given the high uncertainties of that summer and the fact that it had been Cecil's first crisis since the death of Burghley, Coemans was now not especially popular and 'that justly moved [me] to be very dry unto him'. Once again the lone envoy was sent back to Brussels, and this time he was also asked to arrange for the widening of any talks to take in France and the United Provinces.[4]

The strain in Anglo–French relations was particularly marked at this time because Henri IV owed Elizabeth over £400,000, and showed no inclination to pay. There was an additional problem in administration in England because no one at the Exchequer could immediately lay hands on the bonds given by the King, although four were later found in a search.[5] Meanwhile, Sir Henry Neville was appointed resident ambassador to France, arriving in Paris on 8 May 1599. In many ways he was an obvious choice: well educated and a travelled man of the world, he had private wealth (a definite advantage), a knowledge of the language, and was related by marriage to Cecil. Before his departure a year later Neville briskly pursued all the matters of concern to his monarch, such as the repayment of loans and the restoration of sales of English cloth at Rouen, where they were now arbitrarily excluded in that characteristic Gallic mode. Indeed, Neville's robust conversation in audience with Henri IV led to shorter and shorter meetings.[6] But this did not depress the bustling envoy, who wrote a stream of dispatches to Cecil, not only about the French court, but about the dynamic range of English policy. As for Henri, he was well aware of the peregrinations of Coemans, and felt distinctly nervous because the Franco–Spanish peace was definitely shaky. He was also suspicious that Coemans was achieving more than was being acknowledged in London, or in the Spanish Netherlands by the French envoy.

In August Coemans was back in London; he declared that Philip III had agreed to negotiations between the Archduke and England. It was with this in mind that Albrecht was returning to Brussels. In September Coemans delivered letters from Albrecht and Isabella, which called for peace talks and suggested that a meeting place be chosen. The events surrounding the eruption of Essex from Ireland delayed this, but when he was disgraced at least one obstacle to peace was removed. Coemans travelled back to Brussels with the message that an English envoy would soon follow, and as the Dutch stood back from the proposed conference it was Thomas Edmondes who was sent to the Spanish Netherlands at the end of the year. He put up the proposal that the meeting should be in England, but when this was rejected he settled for Boulogne. Then he went to Paris to get Henri IV to send representatives.

Back in London in February 1600, Edmondes was very quickly followed by the Archduke's envoy, Audiencier Verreyken. When what he set out proved unacceptable he wrote to the Archduke for further instructions, only to find that Brussels deemed everything on hold until the approaching conference. It was now that Henri's resident ambassador in London, Boissise, decided that the moment had come for intervention, with the King contemplating overtures for the renewal of the Treaty of Blois. As it happened, his anxiety over the conference was redundant. Sir Henry Neville, England's First Commissioner, John Herbert (newly made a Secretary of State, but clearly Cecil's subordinate and so called 'Mr Secondary' by the wits), Robert Beale, and Edmondes arrived in Boulogne in May 1600, and were soon locked in a preposterous struggle for precedence with the Spanish. This farce continued for two months until in late July the conference simply sagged to a halt. No formal opening meeting was ever held. The only Spanish concession was that in any future dealings Elizabeth would have precedence if the meetings were being held in the

United Provinces in the presence of their representatives.

Neville returned to London in August 1600, but stumbled into an error of judgement that would cost him dear, notably with Cecil.[7] In France Henri was relieved and pleased by the débâcle since he was involved in a serious dispute with Savoy that threatened another round of fighting with the exhausted giant, Spain. When he concluded peace with Savoy he effectively nullified the only leverage England had in the struggle to secure his co-operation over debts and trade. Nothing would bring him back into the war, not even the Spanish-inspired conspiracy of the Duc de Biron in 1602. Henri's aim became increasingly to avoid doing anything until Elizabeth's successor was known. She was variously regarded in Europe; clearly a phenomenon, she was not, however, immortal and it was her good fortune to have Cecil to rely on increasingly after Essex in the formulation of English foreign policy. Even so, it is worth bearing in mind the importance of Buckhurst and the Howards in the Privy Council, and the fact, acknowledged by Cecil, that Elizabeth still ruled. Moreover, since all the problems of the period required a change of direction and personality, it is not surprising that there was yet no comprehensive peace. The missing element was James VI, who feared that Anglo–Spanish contacts would allow Spain to build up a party to support the claim of the Infanta to the English throne. James might be gnawing his knuckles, but since Cecil had no particular liking for Spain it was no hardship not to make peace for the time being. Only when power in England had been safely transferred could the larger problem be solved.

That this was the grand achievement of Cecil and James VI must be a cause of some surprise today, as it would have been a cause of wonder then if it had been in the public domain. James was an Essexite and regarded Essex as a martyr. For many years the King loathed Burghley and then Cecil as the prime movers behind Elizabeth's Scottish policy. Cecil was, of course, the son of the man whom James held responsible for 'cutting his mother's throat', and was still suspected of favouring Edward Seymour, Lord Beauchamp, for the succession. Nottingham and Cecil together were linked with the claim. A Catholic letter deciphered in November 1600 noted that Beauchamp was related by marriage to Sir John Stanhope, a friend of the two men and a favourite of Elizabeth. Indeed, the Lord Admiral's sister was the second wife of Beauchamp's father, the Earl of Hertford. Beauchamp's claim, like that of William Stanley, Earl of Derby, came from their line of descent from the younger daughter of Henry VII. James VI and his first cousin Lady Arabella Stuart were the claimants representing the line from the elder daughter. Henry VIII had settled the succession on the younger line, but the legality of his will was in doubt. James's claim, the best lineally, was also at risk because of his alien birth, which by English law excluded him. Fringe claimants were the Earls of Huntingdon, Rutland and even Essex. Catholics had to look beyond all the Protestants to the Infanta Isabella, while anti-Spanish Catholics had to cast about and so often fixed on Alessandro Farnese, Duke of Parma – who, genealogists declared, with tiresome detailing, had a slightly stronger lineal claim than the Infanta.

In the 1590s James's passion to inherit had been so acute that it was fortunate he was beyond Elizabeth's chastising reach. He had no desire that she should proclaim a successor under his provocation but he engaged ceaselessly in intrigues, even in Rome, as if it was an essential element in statecraft. No wonder Elizabeth's letters to him often have a minatory tone. Two letters from Cecil to George Nicholson, the English agent in Edinburgh, also sought to revise the King's notions.[8] Cecil significantly denied supporting Beauchamp, and when James's ambassadors, the Earl of Mar and Edward Bruce, arrived in London in early March 1601, they had contacts with the Secretary. They must have been relieved, even elated, when they found he was willing to underwrite the Stuart succession in the male line: Arabella was the candidate of the most wishful thinkers. A simple cypher was worked out and the ambassadors returned to Scotland in May. It was left to James to nominate Lord Henry Howard as a mechanism for the correspondence on the English side. Secrecy was of greater concern to Cecil than to the King, and it was for this reason that one of his secretariat, Simon Willis, was discharged. The employer was unwilling to risk an injudicious word from an employee who had until then been primarily concerned with intelligence matters.[9] When Willis failed to win back his place he went to Rome and became an ardent Catholic convert.

Howard was an important letter-writer in this bundle of correspondence which was not simply limited to Cecil and James. Howard also wrote directly to the King, and Mar and Bruce – letters famous for their invective and length, his particular targets being Ralegh, Northumberland and Cobham. This 'diabolical triplicity' was also the subject of some of the letters Cecil wrote warning James that they, especially Ralegh, tried to appear favourably disposed to his accession out of self-interest. One can almost hear Ralegh's scoffing derision at this piece of cheek. As a commentator has noted, there was still a general unease that some or any of this material could fall into the Queen's hands, and it appears that Cecil made them general rather than particular in the hope that discovery would not disturb her. The 'secrecy meant to assure their safety rather affirms her power'.[10]

The power was evinced during the conduct of parliamentary business in 1601 when the dominating question was money – how it was raised and from whom. This was understood beforehand by Cecil, who seems to have anticipated some difficulties and hence secured nominations to a number of seats in the Commons, his secretariat being represented by Levyn de Munck (Levinus Munck), who assisted the Secretary in foreign affairs. Originally from Ghent, he had received papers of denization before taking his seat for Great Bedwin in Essex. In the spring Cecil and Buckhurst had been considering what steps should be taken to deal with controversial patents and monopolies. Elizabeth had promised reforms years before but nothing significant had been done, and although a commission of Privy Councillors was now established, the inertia was not dissipated. The landing of Spanish troops in Ireland meant that the Commons were willing to come up with an extraordinary grant; a fourfold subsidy was voted. But their attack on monopolies was not blunted and the failure of the commission 'required very considerable effort and skill on the part of the Crown's spokesmen led by Cecil, to contain the issue'.[11] At this time Cecil's caution in debate was understandable but Elizabeth was uninhibited, scything down a bill for the reform of Exchequer abuses as well as bills to control bullion and armaments exports. When Cecil reported the clamour against monopolies Elizabeth promised the Speaker a proclamation to revoke a large number of them. The printed copy of this was in the hands of MPs three days later.[12] The stone sealing the tomb had been rolled away and excitement was great. The pleasure of the members then deepened when Elizabeth agreed to see the whole Lower House crammed into the Council Chamber at Whitehall. There she delivered what became known as her 'Golden Speech', a verbal apotheosis and rhapsodic statement of the cluster of principles that had underpinned her long, defiant reign.

In 1602 Cecil had a period of illness before the house-warming party. Pressure of work and fears for the future combined to cause this physical setback. Fortunately, he had recovered when the decline of Elizabeth early in 1603 became noticeable, not long after the forty-fourth anniversary of her succession. When the court moved to Richmond in late January a period of extreme cold set in, yet the Queen's bizarre whim was to wear 'summer-like garments' when furs would have been more suitable. Thomas Cecil was concerned and wrote to his half-brother that, being old, she ought to take more care of herself. Nearly sixty-one himself, Burghley knew something of the aches and random pains of old age. By March it was clear that Elizabeth was sinking and she was overcome by a kind of torpor made all the more obvious by the contrast with her previous energy. Since continuity was a special consideration for the government, even without her selection of an heir, Cecil sent a draft proclamation to James VI on 19 March for his approval. He prepared memoranda dealing with royal valuables and also copies of accounts, but apart from noting the great offices that were vacant, he left no evidence of preparing any of his clients or dependants for James's accession. Burghley actually inquired 'to know what is to be looked for', and the answer for Robert Cecil was 'no change' in so far as this was possible. When Elizabeth died at Richmond early on the morning of 24 March the authority of the Privy Council lapsed, and it may have been this that encouraged Robert Carey and his brother Lord Hunsdon, the Lord Chamberlain, to tangle with Cecil at a crucial time.

A fable has attached itself to Robert Carey – that on a signal from his sister Philadelphia, Lady Scrope, herself addicted to gambling,* a ring with a blue stone dropped from a window on Elizabeth's last breath, he galloped north immediately, exhausting horses in his careering effort to be first with the news at the Scottish court. This version of the events has rather obscured the account given in Carey's *Memoirs*. He wrote that during Elizabeth's last illness he had communicated with James warning him not to stir from Edinburgh until he heard from him. According to Carey, on the night Elizabeth lay dying he went to his lodgings, leaving word in the Cofferer's office that if she died he was to be called. To guarantee entry a porter was sweetened with an angel, and when the news arrived Carey left his bed to hasten to the gate. By then the Privy Council had halted all movement without a warrant and it was only through contact with the Comptroller, Sir Edward Wotton, that Carey was allowed in. When taken before the Council he was told he would not go to Scotland until they permitted the journey, and when they all went off to Cecil's room Carey decided to seek out his brother. Although he was tired and ailing Hunsdon got his brother out, and Carey rode to Charing Cross and the lodgings of Sir

* She tried once to borrow £300 from Robert Cecil to meet her gambling debts.

92

Thomas Gerard, the Knight Marshal. There he stayed until 9 a.m. when, hearing that the Council were gathering in Whitehall's old orchard, he sent a message by Gerard declaring his availability. The *togati* were apparently pleased and Gerard sent Sir Arthur Savage, a friend of Ralegh, to fetch him. As Savage and Carey hastened to the Council Gerard, now friendly with Cecil, appeared with a warning from Sir William Knollys that if Carey put in an appearance he would be restrained.

Taking horse at about 10 a.m. as Cecil prepared for the first public proclamation, Carey galloped north. Somewhere on the border he gave command that James should be proclaimed king, and according to Stow this was done at Berwick by Sir John Carey.[13] Robert Carey was kicked in the head by his horse but reached James on the third evening, and although it has been suggested that one George Marshall beat him, the favour the King showed Carey makes his claim most likely.

In London, the public proclamation read aloud by Cecil to a gathering of citizens was made before Whitehall. Then he and an escort rode to the Bar of the City, where there was a little flurry of civic pomposity from the Lord Mayor, who asked Buckhurst to surrender his collar of office as a security that the correct claimant would be proclaimed at St Paul's. Later that night the Council's 'Letter of Allegiance', signed also by the Lord Mayor, a clutch of courtiers and leading churchmen, was sent by Sir Charles Percy, brother of Northumberland and Thomas Somerset, son of the Earl of Worcester. Once deeply involved in Essex's treason, Percy had escaped reasonably lightly, and he wrote later in a most effusive manner to Cecil acknowledging him as 'a chief cause of my living at this hour'.[14] Reaching Holyroodhouse on 28 March, Percy and Somerset delivered a letter which included a complaint about Carey's headlong dash. The principal area of ambiguity is why did the Careys act so freely? Was it because of the rumour reported by Sir John of the marriage of Arabella, combined with distrust of Cecil? Lord Hunsdon cannot have known of the secret correspondence between

Cecil and James, and if he believed a delay was meant to put Beauchamp on the throne, then he was behaving logically. His brother not only carried the news, but had James proclaimed king of England while still in the north. In doing this he exceeded all authority, but gave James a time advantage if he had to assert his right by force.[15]

There is another possibility which strongly suggests a Cecil finesse. By it Hunsdon was made to appear to act against Cecil's wishes, either consciously or unawares. The necessity for this continued juggling was that he had played both sides, and if the Seymours and Talbots and their many friends found out, it might have embroiled England in the turmoil he was desperate to avoid, making the country intensely vulnerable. If the choice of Percy was deliberate, so was the stumble over Robert Carey. He was trying to keep back the news only until certain steps made the throne safe for the king he intended. If Arabella Stuart, then at Wrest House, had married Beauchamp, the rumour of him being in the field might have become self-fulfilling. An advance on London by the couple and the seizing of the initiative in the north by her friends could have undermined James.

Naturally the navy could be secured if the Lord Admiral joined Cecil in his grand design, and there can never have been much doubt of this. Now (if not before) Cecil surely revealed his secret correspondence with James to his old friend, and Howard joined him in urging the other councillors and courtiers that it was too late to exclude a man poised on his side of the border. The proclamation in London had to be made even though Cecil's draft had not yet been acknowledged, and as it happened, the actions of the Careys were a useful bonus. By these tactics Cecil and his Howard adherents subdued any possible English claimants, none of whom was noted for exceptional courage in adversity. In fact the declarations of loyalty flowed in, with Hertford's so generous as to be almost hysterical.[16] The general pull for James became so powerful that Northumberland and Ralegh, both of whom had wanted for different reasons to hold out for concessions, were left stranded. Events proved this to be lamentable for them, notably for Ralegh in the early days of the reign. In the 1601 Parliament he had been Cecil's provoking main rival; and sprawling on the same bench (to ease his leg wound?) had blamed the latter when Elizabeth ignored his claim to be a Privy Councillor.[17] This was lop-sided thinking, and for him to allow the gap to widen over the transition of the Crown was disastrous. It was, after all, an event Cecil regarded as crucial to the country and himself, and it was always his inclination to conflate the two. No longer trusting Ralegh, especially when the soldier was bound to attack any peace with Spain, meant that Cecil now had no inclination to restrain the vituperative efforts of Lord Henry Howard.

So the triumph of self-promotion of Sir Robert Carey was in this reading not really his at all, but Cecil's. An interesting question that remains is whether James was fully conversant with the deft strategy of his greatest ally. Certainly the King showed a high unease, vibrant with the thought that some act of cunning policy might sweep the prize away. Harington among others had nurtured this fear with the thought that Arabella and Beauchamp might (as it were) be shoehorned in before James could do anything. When this did not transpire Stuart gratitude to Cecil was virtually inexhaustible, never to be totally eroded. As Thomas Lake, Clerk of the Signet, reported to the Secretary from Edinburgh, the news was excellent, the King deeply gratified by the wise service he had received.

As for Carey, his full-blooded effort was rewarded by James making him a Gentleman of the Bedchamber (though he was discharged from the post under English pressure when the King reached England). Other rewards of land, property and a life pension of £100 were more permanent, and later he became Chamberlain to Prince Charles. Lord Hunsdon, soon to die (possibly of syphilis), received a token that was far more oblique and curious. Within ten days of James's arrival in London, the Lord Chamberlain's acting company became the King's Men. Shakespeare and his gifted colleagues became

Grooms of the Chamber, each receiving a measure of scarlet cloth for a livery. This change was effected under the Great Seal with Letters Patent prepared for Cecil as Lord Keeper of the Great Seal. It was a mark of royal favour significantly beyond what their quality and previous Essex sympathies might usually have elicited. All this surely stemmed from the services of the Careys, since James had only a slender interest in theatre. His preference was for low clowning.

To the generality of Englishmen who had heard of him (and in remoter areas few had), James was a little-known personality made more interesting because he brought to England a family. What was known (or believed) was favourable: he had a reputation for learning, piety, good nature and liberality. There was at all levels wonder and hearty relief that the whole matter of the succession had been routinely concluded when 'for years all Christendom held for certain that it must be attended with trouble and confusion'. Shakespeare himself, with a pleasing paradoxical flourish of melancholy overset with anticipation, gave the collective sigh of relief expression in Sonnet 107:

> The mortal moon hath her eclipse endur'd
>   And the sad augurs mock their own presage;
> Incertainties now crown themselves assur'd,
>   And peace proclaims olives of endless age.

Peace was indeed the absolute guiding principle, and that was what was to follow. With hindsight alone is it possible to regret that the dynasty was flawed – but where in contemporary Europe fared better? Cecil had achieved the change brilliantly, with exemplary application.

8

The long-established King of Scotland was now ruler of England. It was at once advantageous and disadvantageous to have had such a background. The principal advantage was that James was thoroughly versed in kingcraft and indeed was the first ruler of Britain to publish his own account of the position and duties of a monarch. *The True Lawe of Free Monarchies* appeared in 1598 and set out his ideas of divine right so that anyone in England who had read it knew what was in store. The principal disadvantage was that James had been King of Scotland, for many years a turbulent faction-ridden independent nation, and his survival there had required luck, guile and political instincts that appeared warped in the English context. The countries were profoundly different and it was a lurking thread of idealism in James that made him inclined to ignore this. His deep misunderstandings of so many matters had the result of undermining Scotland's culture, and he ambiguously yoked together two countries that might have better remained apart.

James was at least thoroughly educated in the humanist fashion of the Renaissance by George Buchanan and then Peter Young, who had tempered some of the severity of the former. Taught Latin and Greek, French and Italian, he was of course utterly deficient in simple arithmetic and economics. On the other hand he was vastly confident and well read in Calvinist theology, and the Bible and the bottle remained two potent sources of comfort. Indeed, he 'was never happier than when engaging in religious controversies and confounding his opponents with quotations from Scripture and abstruse Latin commentaries.'[1] Once a writer of verse and then of prose, notably as a polemicist, he revelled in debate for its own sake and was sufficiently proud of his writings to have them published in folio in 1616. His patronage of writers in Scotland, especially poets, had enriched the nation's literature, but he was much more diffident, even idle, in England because as he grew older his enthusiasm waned. Ben Jonson collaborated with Inigo Jones on the famous, ephemeral court masques which have recently received a good deal of attention from scholars. Queen Anne adored them; they bored James. John Donne was lured into the Church to achieve the sort of advancement he had seen snatched away after a hasty love match, but it was not satires James wanted now, only sermons. Shakespeare may have noted the new king and been made a Groom of the Chamber, but it was a passing phase; soon he was politely ignored. Other writers found such indifference painful: Michael Drayton's hopes evaporated and by 1606 he was attacking James and Salisbury in his verse.[2]

The coincidence of attaining the English Crown with its many attendant problems, and a growing if spasmodic indolence, was partially obscured by James's active passion for hunting. This was principally a male pursuit and his ardour for it never dimmed, for all its violence and gore. Those who joined him in the field usually flourished, and Cecil's own son William was one of them, quitting his studies at Cambridge to go as often as possible to Royston. Cecil's rather desperate requirement that William should practise his Latin at a gallop with his tutor Morrell was, however, a flop. As Morrell reported, 'The sound of Latin was so harsh mid the cry of dogs that it came not oft.'

If James could not eliminate his enemies in combat, then symbolically he could exultantly massacre fur and feather substitutes. It was a trait quickly noted and while none in England was anti-blood sports, some did think that a private pleasure was being grossly indulged. Hutton, the elderly

Archbishop of York, wrote with polite candour to Robert Cecil as early as December 1604 calling for 'less wasting of the treasure of the realm, and more moderation of the lawful exercise of hunting'. Cecil's reply was that of a man who liked hawking and shooting – a rebuke to the churchman and a compliment to the apolaustic King, who took 'such manlike and active recreations'. Even if this does lean excessively to James's side, the notion that hunting displaced government detrimentally is not borne out. True, James lived up to his breezy declaration to Cecil that 'we shall surely load your shoulders with business', but government decisions did not fold because James was reluctant to quit the field. There was killing and carousing, but the correspondence with Whitehall was heavy. Moreover, James could claim health reasons for his addiction. His ailments (like those of his chief minister), suffered at various times, would require a paragraph, so exercise and fresh air were counted as vital, even if they did little for his haemorrhoids. Nothing was going to stop his headlong gallops, and to serve his pleasure fallow deer were imported from Norway!

The English nation not only got a king to replace Elizabeth, but also a dynasty with a number of his blemishes. James himself was stubborn, grubby, ungainly and coarse-grained, for all his humanist education. He had married Anne, the blonde daughter of Frederik II of Denmark and Sophie of Mecklenburg. Perhaps the most that can be said about her was that she liked art and was fertile over many years at considerable cost to her body and emotions. James was a misogynist with a powerful preference for other men; women were contemptuously held to be 'no other thing else but irritamenta libidinis'.[3] But Anne was required to bear his children and there was already an heir apparent in Prince Henry, so James's infatuations for other men were simply noted and exploited. Once he had been deeply attached to a French kinsman, Esmé Stuart, a product of the French court where the tantalizing question had been whether Henri III had been a 'male-female' or a 'female-male'. Not surprisingly, English courtiers who preferred men fared well at James's court: notably Lord Henry Howard, made Earl of Northampton, and the Earl of Southampton, twice blessed because he had also been close to Essex. Later, after Salisbury's death, Sir Francis Bacon would achieve high office for a brief golden period in his career. As a parent himself James naturally accepted marriage and procreation for some of his male favourites, so clearly he would have revelled in the muscular, changing-room atmosphere of a sports club today, though he would have skipped the shower. He flourished when surrounded by inebriated cronies and lavished favours and slobbering attentions on them even as he reviled actual sodomy.

If these handsome, greedy, self-promoting young men were less continuously and infuriatingly meddlesome in politics than was once thought, with James sometimes able to resist their more ridiculous notions, still he wanted their flattering attention. Actually not all were good-looking; some attracted his paternal indulgence through charm and wit. James Hay was called 'camelface' by Princess Elizabeth, but he was the only Scot regularly employed as a diplomat after 1603. He was made Master of the Robes in 1605 and his conduct of the office was grotesquely inept and extravagant, without a rebuke from James. Yet despite these permissive infatuations with men James longed to improve and polish like any pederastic schoolmaster of any age, wincing at their genial ignorance, he managed to establish a moderately cordial relationship with Anne, and after some disputes over the raising of the children – especially Prince Henry – and whatever the distortions in their marriage, he never failed to treat her as a queen.[4] His relationship with his eldest son was somewhat more bumpy, for Prince Henry as he grew older was always polite, but in a rather stiff manner that may have cloaked a certain contempt. They shared a passion for horses and hunting, but unlike his father the prince was fastidious (in sexual matters perhaps even a little prudish). Homosexuality and swearing were aspects of daily life he regarded with strong disapproval, as if on the former inclination he had taken his father's public moral and didactic tone in the *Basilikon Doron* (1599) seriously.

Exultant at his succession, James was moved by an almost frantic desire to quit his birthplace. Even now he was apprehensive that the *hortus paradisus* might be snatched from his eager grasp. It was also a major concern that he and Anne should make their mark instantly with a triumphant entry that all would remember. To achieve this, new clothes and jewels would be necessary – literally so, because with a regal flourish, as the Venetian envoy Scaramelli noted, Anne gave away 'among the ladies who remained behind all her jewels, dresses, the hangings of her rooms everything she had without exception'.[5] James asked the Privy Council in London to forward 'such jewels and stuff with other furniture as coaches, horses, and litters . . . and all things which they might deem fit for the use of Queen Anne'.[6] The Council had the temerity to refuse on the grounds that it was illegal to send any of the Crown jewels out of England and James had to expand on his original request, indicating that he did not expect the state regalia, merely 'such jewels and other furniture which did appertain to the late queen as you think meet for her estate', with the added proviso in a later letter: 'the rest may come when she shall be nearer home'.[7]

Although the royal couple were ill matched, James enjoyed indulging their joint passion for jewellery now that he had the opportunity. One of those who moved south to profit from this was the royal jeweller George Heriot, who in ten years sold the Queen items valued at £40,000.[8] Other purchases were made from Sir John Spilman,* one of Elizabeth's jewellers; Hugh Middleton, Peter Van Lore,† John Acton and Abraham Hardret. The latter's appointment as a royal jeweller did not begin very satisfactorily for him and he was soon pleading his position to Cecil.[9] This changed dramatically when James embarked on his policy of spending large sums to bolster belief in his status as God's vicegerent. The divine right of

---

* Originally John Spielmann from Lindau am Bodensee.
† Van Lore came originally from Utrecht.

kings and queens required plenty of sparkle, so another jeweller to benefit was William Herrick, a man of great abilities and good looks. By a patent he became the King's principal jeweller and was knighted on 2 April 1605 for making a hole in the Sancy diamond. This allowed James to wear the fifty-three-carat jewel, which he had bought the previous year for 60,000 crowns from the French ambassador. The royal pleasure in pearls, surely referred to obliquely in Webster's tragedy *The Duchess of Malfi*, seems never to have abated. In 1605 Anne paid £740 for a rope of pearls; £900 for a single pearl; and Van Lore received £3,000 for certain pearls pendant.[10]

James I and Queen Anne began the journey south on 5 April. At Berwick the King fired a piece of ordnance himself, a measure of the rapture he felt which for the moment raised him above his constitutional timidity. The audience from the town would have watched with mixed emotions, since peace and unity flowing across the border meant that Berwick was doomed to become a backwater. There was also a flow – threatening to become a torrent – of honours, the sort of largesse that did not immediately empty his pockets, even if it debased the titles. Cecil for a time had to remain in London, steadying affairs, so that while James and his entourage chatted incomprehensibly, the burden of entertaining them fell on Burghley. It was only on 18 April that the newly reappointed Secretary of State met James at York, followed by further encounters as the King was entertained on the route to London. After six days Cecil pronounced himself satisfied that the kingdom had a promise of 'greater felicity' than ever before, and when the monarch was received at Theobalds for ten days this enthusiasm seems to have transmitted itself to the crowds, who thronged to catch a glimpse. James himself was also prepared to make a public affirmation of his confidence in Cecil by making him Baron Cecil of Essendon. The ceremony was held on 13 May 1603.

For the time being, though, Cecil was not yet 'the Alpha and Omega of the Council'. The King began by paying off debts to the Essexites by three peerages out of his first four creations. Mountjoy, now the Earl of Devonshire, also joined the Council.[11] Lord Henry Howard, now Earl of Northampton, embarked on a late flourish in his political career, forming with his nephew Thomas Howard Earl of Suffolk and Cecil 'the trinity of knaves', James's genial phrase for the group within the Council who dealt with routine state matters. The alliance between Cecil and the rancorous, rapacious Northampton actually survived, not without strains, for longer than might have been expected, but Northampton's patronage did not have the scope of Cecil's, and the senior partner in political terms kept a watchful eye on his ageing associate, including his correspondence. The Earl of Worcester also took part in deliberations, but undoubtedly Cecil was the principal figure, and part of his strength derived from his Mastership of the Court of Wards which he had taken on in May 1599.

Cecil's response to this was a curious one, since it would inevitably increase his patronage and personal wealth. On 23 May, just two days after the appointment, he was telling Sir Henry Neville of his reservations, saying with apparent regret that he had 'resigned a better Place', the Chancellorship of the Duchy of Lancaster, in order to take his father's old office. He would surely have been stung if the office had fallen to anyone else, but he proclaimed himself hedged about by 'new orders, as in the office I am a ward myself'.[12] If this accurately reflects the state of affairs then the orders can only have come from Elizabeth, and may explain why Sir John Fortescue had declined the office. Cecil's correspondence dealing with the transactions of the court, which had a tiny London staff but over forty representatives (feodaries) in the counties, reveals the anxiety and urgency that could be generated. It was regarded by the gentry in particular with a mixture of fear and powerful self-interest, since it provided revenue for the Crown in such an arbitrary and ungovernable way. A long-lived family might escape its attentions, while several minorities might seriously undermine or even ruin a hitherto wealthy one. Not surprisingly a family threatened by the jurisdiction of the court could feel driven to deception, concealing an heir.

It was the death of a tenant-in-chief of the Crown that made the age of an heir or heiress significant. If that person was a minor (a male under twenty-one or a female under fourteen) and even a fraction of their inheritance was land held *in capite* from the Crown, then the entire estate fell under the jurisdiction of the court. This then leased out their lands for an annual rent paid to the Crown, and the minor was sold off to a guardian who could determine such things as their marriage. Lessees and guardians could be different people and the predatory guardian was much feared, especially by those who lacked the power to protect themselves from what today would be called asset-stripping. Even before he became Master Cecil had often been approached with offers of money or goods by a supplicant hoping for a wardship at Burghley's direction.

As Master himself he was a thorough administrator, reaping increased rewards for the Crown from an ageing financial mechanism, while lining his own pockets. The work of the court was highly detailed and the feodaries found him exacting: 'a flood of orders poured from the Court, tightening up central control over them and setting out their responsibilities.'[13] They did not always respond, and the Deputy Feodary to Michael Hickes in Essex, John Meade, was either corrupt or idle. This was at a time when Cecil was pressing to increase the Crown's revenue from wardship, cutting down on the profits snuffled up by middlemen and seeking 'to protect the interests of the ward and his family'.[14] His achievement of the former aim can be seen by the rise in revenue to the Crown: from some £17,000 in 1599 to over £22,000 in 1601–2.[15] To a certain extent he was undermined by the quixotic attitude of the Queen, who liked to reward her oldest and closest friends.[16] Fortunately for her, what she gave away was balanced or submerged by fines for leases and the annual rents.

Cecil's official fees for the office of Master were £200 a year with a diet of 200 marks (the equivalent of luncheon vouchers, with one mark equalling 13s. 4d.). On top of this there were casual fees for the use of the court seal and the passing of liveries (the process involving an heir who had come of age) which came to nearly £500 a year.[17] The value of the office went far beyond these comparatively paltry amounts, as Scaramelli pointed out, for the Master could arrange private sales of wards which must have made Cecil several thousands of pounds a year. It has been estimated that his total annual income as Master was about £3,000.[18] Nor was he the only one to benefit, for friends and dependants also picked up valuable wardships they could sell for a profit. But this was not always the case: Hickes asked for one wardship in 1602 after he had ceased to be a feodary and before he was appointed Receiver-General of Crown lands in the City of London and three surrounding counties – request refused. Cecil said he was submerged by courtiers wanting it as well, but without appearing to do so he intended to benefit from the competition.[19]

The tussles for subordinate offices in the court could be sustained. In 1603 Edward Curle petitioned for the reversion of his father's office of Auditor, one of two, held by William Curle since 1589 with Walter Tooke as his colleague. Both families kept a ferocious grip on this office, while the Hare family maintained a monopoly of the two clerkships; Edward failed in his submission, but his brother Francis was successful in 1615 and followed his father in 1618. Since William had enjoyed the favour of the Cecils it seems appropriate that he should have found his last resting place beside Salisbury in Hatfield church.* Salisbury's tomb is grand and eye-catching (see Chapter 16); Curle's low and modest. In 1605, when the court attorney died, there were two candidates for the post and James allowed the Master to make the selection between Serjeants Hobart and Foster. Both were eventually knighted and became Judges of the Common Pleas, but on this occasion Salisbury advanced the Hertfordshire man Thomas Foster. It is impossible to believe that they did not freshen matters with a gift to the Master, although he does seem to have felt a

* But only on the whim of Victorian restorers in 1871–2.

105

certain unease about routinely accepting presents for favour. A Mr Proby acknowledged with surprise that Sir John Stanhope 'told me it was your practice not to take anything of charge from those you like best of.'[20]

A testimonial like this from a tainted source need not be taken too seriously. Gifts were taken, and so were the customary New Year offerings ranging from the spectacular to the trivial. At the beginning of 1603 Cecil got plate from his half-brother, a small casket from Sir Robert Crosse, who had thrived; the Merchant Adventurers sent him 'a great standing bowl' which, together with Sir John Roper's and Mr Nicholson's, was sold to the goldsmith and money-lender Alexander Prescott. However, Cecil kept a fire shovel, tongs and door lock from the Comptroller of Works, as well as two barrels of figs from Mr Savage.[21] Even so, he was not implacably set against fiscal reforms providing he could protect his position, and his conservatism in such matters can be overstated. Almost immediately after James's arrival in England the Lord Treasurer Buckhurst (soon to be Earl of Dorset), no miser himself, was looking for methods to underpin the winning but costly generosity of the new monarch, and Cecil proposed reforms of fiscal feudalism to include the abolition of wardship for a fixed annual rent agreed in Parliament. Thus at the opening of the session in 1604 Sir Robert Wroth proposed composition for wardship. Probably he was acting as the mouthpiece of Cecil, who by this time (March) had gone to the Lords.[22] Wroth's motion was discussed and the Commons decided to ask the Lords for a conference on wardship, a means of promoting business that required agreement by both houses. The conference, governed by certain rules of parliamentary etiquette, was held on 27 March and several of Wroth's grievances were touched on, though wardship and Dorset's plan to accept composition for respite of homage received most attention.[23] Then Cecil muddled the issue by asking the conference to consider the 'Goodwin election' and when the Commons committee declined, the conference, the first of many, broke up.

Wardship was dormant then for some weeks as other issues such as the royal project for union took up much parliamentary time. Discussion of purveyance also went on, with Cecil supporting composition of £50,000 a year to replace it. If this could be done for purveyance (and the Commons were unconvinced), then why not a similar scheme for wardship? At least two MPs tried to effect a union between the two schemes, but after debating wardship again it was decided to keep it as a singleton. However, in picking up negotiations with the Lords, the Lower House asked that the second chamber should join a petition for the abolition of feudal tenures. This would end wardship, respite of homage, licences of alienation and *primer seisin*. Composition would have to make a suitable sum available to the Crown in recompense for all of them.[24] Until late May Lords and Commons were working in tandem on the matter, but then on 24 May the conference proposed for the following day was postponed until the day after, and on the 26th things fell apart. The proposals of the Commons' committee were quite wide-ranging, not only arguing strongly for the abolition of wardship but anticipating a number of problems such as the need to compensate the redundant officers of the Court of Wards.[25]

Between 22 and 26 May Cecil had looked at the proposal again and had decided to abandon it. Since Wroth had proposed the matter it was perhaps inevitable (if uncomfortable) that he should shoot it down. All the conclusions of the committee on wardship of which he had been a member he now opposed as the agent of Cecil. In the void left by his volte-face he put forward a suggestion that every man should dispose of an underage heir in his own will and that a fine should be paid on this. The Lords completed the demolition during the afternoon conference, saying that the idea of buying out feudal tenures should be dropped. A startled Sir Edwin Sandys had to report this back to a bemused Lower House, where there must have been a stir of anger. There is the possibility that Cecil himself was only responding to pressure from James, who had decided to throttle any scheme that had the support of the Commons while they proved so sullen about his grand proposals for the union of England and Scotland. But thrusting the blame on to James does not seem to chime with the feelings of the Commons that they had been seriously misled by the Lords, where Cecil was such an important figure.

In fact it was the suddenness of Cecil's change of tack that makes it so teasingly peculiar, and one reason that may be adduced is that the officials of the court had gone on the counter-offensive. The Commons had named a committee on 16 May for its forthcoming conferences with the Lords.[26] Among the members were Sir Edward Lewkenor, MP for Maldon, a lawyer with much experience of the court's workings, and John Hare, Inner Temple bencher and, in conjunction with his brother Hugh, the Chief Clerk of the Court. His new patent of the grant of the clerkship named his son Nicholas Hare as his successor and he was a pugnacious man, thoroughly discountenanced by the attacks on wardship, and by implication on the officers of the court. Since he had such a significant interest in the preservation of the institution it would not be in the least surprising if it was he who drafted a defence of the court and its officers presented to Cecil.[27] As has been pointed out by expert scrutiny the text is not written in his hand, but the arguments are Hare's.[28] Add to that the probable date of presentation to Cecil – 24 May: the fact that he read it, and annotations in his hand, bear this out; James's lack of warmth to the scheme, the potential loss of patronage and income, and above all the fact that his subordinates were fiercely opposed to it – all this caused Cecil to think again. He even used a number of Hare's citations in his own speech to the conference on 26 May. On reflection he had decided that an internal realignment rather than a structural reform was necessary; hence the prodding of the aged parliamentarian Wroth to put forward the alternative motion 'that every man by his last will and testament might dispose of his child'.

This was only a rather flimsy reminder of a recent reform of the court which allowed 'tenants-in-chief to buy out the wardships of their heirs during their own lifetimes'.[29] This provision, though not entirely novel, had hitherto been reserved as a privilege for a mere handful of Crown servants. If tenants-in-chief pursued the matter or were required to by law, opposition to the court might be very much diminished. Parents would have a clear advantage and need not be stricken by the horrible snares that otherwise lurked for their children; royal revenue would not be lost. Indeed, there might actually be a real gain since concealing a wardship would be pointless. Wroth thought 'some bill to that purpose might be thought on', a statement that underlines the prevailing ignorance of the reform. Cecil had tried to nudge an understanding among tenants-in-chief by writing to the feodaries whose task it was to spread the word. He also replied to the question put by several tenants-in-chief about what would happen if they purchased the wardship of an eldest son, only to have him die first. He answered that the payment to the court applied to the wardship of an heir – not necessarily an older son, not any particular child. He saw it as a genuine benefit, and must have been rather baffled at the sluggish response. But he was wrong to imagine that the controversy over wardship would evaporate; he misjudged seriously the mood of the Commons, not in itself surprising when he could gauge it only by report.

Although he had been in the House for years and was generally well regarded, he was above all a minister of the Crown and his dispassionate, rational approach did not find comprehensive support. When Sandys reported to the Commons on the lamentable conference with the Lords, the result was a decision 'to justify their proceedings on wardship directly to the king himself, a decision which gave birth to the Commons Apology'.[30] Many months later, in the late 1606 debates on esuage, a variety of land tenure on the Borders, Nicholas Fuller reverted to the special matter of wardship and was widely supported; though not by Salisbury. He was still ruminating on the possibilities of change, and in 1610 made the boldest push for wide-ranging reforms based on a new principle of taxation. His notions, if not bogus, stemmed from

pressing political and financial requirements, not moral outrage of the kind that animated Fuller, who in 1606 described
wardship as 'against the laws of God and nature'.[31]

John Hare saw no merit in the abolition of his livelihood,
but by a nice irony he was one of those who had been
provocatively active against purveyance for many years. The
provisioning of the court, with all its waste and graft, was
conducted by purveyors who were empowered to compel
ordinary traders to sell their items at low prices at a time when
the cost of living was rising painfully. Counties could exclude
the hated purveyors only by composition, and many had
chosen that only after the purveyance crisis of 1589. The
sponsor of the bill to curb purveyors then was Hare, and
among those prominent in the debate were Francis Bacon,
George More and Robert Wroth.[32] These men were again
prominent in the debates of 1604 which were given particular
meaning by the Queen and Prince Henry having their own
households. The bill produced in the Commons, followed by
their petition to James, showed how serious matters had
become, and in response at a conference on 8 May Cecil
proposed that for £50,000 a year purveyance would be abolished. This figure deflated any sense of urgency, and apart
from debate nothing happened.

When Parliament met again in 1606 there were still chal-
lenges to purveyance, but with Salisbury seeking abolition in
return for composition the bill was smothered in the Lords.
Thus there is evidence here that far from being a dull, even
reactionary administrator, a politician only able to ape his
father, Salisbury was flexible and innovative, greater in the
range and courage of his thinking than most of his contemporaries. The sour strictures of Francis Bacon on his cousin are
not merely tendentious but misleading. As it was, it took only
another four years of royal extravagance for Salisbury to
conclude that the financial crisis confronting the country
required a bold scheme 'to place royal finance on a new basis
of permanent direct taxation'.[33] Two key elements in the effort
to find the way out of the straitjacket of debt were proposals

for the abolition of anachronistic purveyance and wardship, but Salisbury had stirred real antagonism for the government in 1604 by his dramatic reversal of direction. Years later the memory of this proved a significant burden.

9

Beyond the requirements of a foreign policy to deal routinely with France, Spain, Scotland and the Low Countries Elizabeth chose to strengthen Anglo–Ottoman contacts. These, generally on a reasonable footing, were unfavourably regarded in Scotland and Europe, where she was looked on as an ally of the Turks. In 1597, by an imperial mandate, all Englishmen were ordered to quit German territories within three months. Elizabeth replied in January 1598 by expelling the Hanseatic merchants based in the Steelyard (now covered by Blackfriars station). After various delays the command was repeated and early in August the Germans filed out under protest, reporting to the Hanseatic Diet: 'We left because it could not be otherwise . . . Alderman Heinrich Langermann leading the way.' When the organ-clock commissioned by the Queen and Cecil as a somewhat belated gift to mark the accession of Mehmed III was completed by Thomas Dallam, someone noted: 'Here is a great and curious present going to the great Turk which no doubt will . . . be very scandalous among other nations specially the Germans.'

Even so, Anglo–Imperial contacts were not wholly obliterated. In 1598 Elizabeth received Vilém Slavata, and Jan Diviš, younger brother of Karel Žerotín, who had been in England ten years before, had links with the Essex circle.[1] According to one of Cecil's correspondents, Slavata was a cousin german of the same Žerotín with letters for Elizabeth, 'whose hand he desires to kiss'. Presumably he was sent by

1 Robert Cecil, 1st Earl of Salisbury, by Marcus Gheeraerts (II)

2 Elizabeth I *c.* 1570

3 James I by John de Critz, after a portrait by
Paul van Somer

4 The Commissioners at the Somerset House Conference, 1604. *Left* (from the window end): Juan de Velasco, Duke of Frias and Constable of Castile; Juan de Tassis, Count of Villa Mediana, Spanish Ambassador in London; Alessandro Robida, Senator of Milan; Charles de Ligne, Count of Aremberg; Jean Richardot, President of the Council of State; Louis Verreyken, Audiencer of Brussels. *Right* (from the window end): Thomas Sackville, Earl of Dorset; Charles Howard, Earl of Nottingham; Charles Blount, Earl of Devonshire; Henry Howard, Earl of Northampton; Robert Cecil, Lord Cecil of Essendon (later Earl of Salisbury).

5 Monument to Robert Cecil, Earl of Salisbury, in St Etheldreda's, Hatfield, sculpted by Maximilien Colt.

Rudolf II to try to resolve the merchant dispute.

Scraps of evidence and a handful of names suggest concern in London about the simultaneous and wayward activities of (Sir) Anthony Sherley.[2] A man of grandiose political ambitions and raging conceit, he contrived a pseudo-diplomatic career based on the exotic notion of an alliance between Shah 'Abbās of Persia and the Christian rulers of Europe, headed by Rudolf II. Travelling with Hussain 'Ali Beg, the envoy of the Shah, Sherley made his way to Prague, where the party was showered with imperial ceremony and enthusiasm. The news of this reached England to distress the merchants of the Levant Company, who had already given Cecil two coveted Turkey carpets for his diplomatic efforts in Constantinople on their behalf. They feared that Sherley, already a secret agent for Spain and Scotland, would wreck everything, and they implored Elizabeth to halt his progress through Europe. Rudolf embraced Sherley's spiralling notions with surprising alacrity for a man supposedly beset by terrifying mental disturbance. To win over Elizabeth he may have sent Jaroslav z Donína to England as his envoy. The Doníns were the Bohemian branch of the extensive German clan of the Burgraves of Dohna.[3] Jaroslav z Donína, the son of Jindřich, had succeeded to his father's title in 1597, and two years later sold the family estate at Benátky to Rudolf II, who made it over to Tycho Brahe. The mission began in England during late spring 1601 and the envoy's diplomatic aide and contact here was Stephen Le Sieur, who had himself been to Prague as a representative of the Merchant Adventurers and maintained contacts there with the English Catholic poet in exile, Elizabeth Jane Weston, a resident since 1598.[4] Le Sieur was certainly chosen by Cecil, to whom he later wrote to point out that having kissed Elizabeth's hand on arrival, the Czech envoy wanted to do the same before he left. In the interim – summer 1601 – Donína's party left London for Scotland, and possibly it was his presence that stirred James VI to write on Sherley's behalf to Shah 'Abbās.

Then the party travelled to the north of Ireland to see the

Earl of Tyrone, and also visited Donnell O'Cahan. The encounter with a host of scantily clad women at the door of O'Cahan's house was a mighty surprise. Even more startling was the appearance of the Irish chief himself, who joined his Czech guest by the open fire. Casting off his loose mantle and shoes, O'Cahan sprawled naked while chatting in a relaxed manner in Latin.[5] The distinguished visitor was cheerfully invited to throw off his heavy garments, but he hastily declined out of embarrassment at the hitherto well-concealed sign of male sexual arousal caused by the nonchalant display of the women.

Back in England by September, Donína was very anxious to see Elizabeth again before he left for Prague. Le Sieur wrote to Cecil on the 11th of that month that if she wanted to hear a report of what the Czech had seen in Scotland and Ireland, 'I am persuaded he will, with due respect, observe her commandment and conceal nothing.' From the second phrase it is obvious that Le Sieur realized the reasonable limits of candour before the Queen. However, because he omitted to write to the newly appointed Vice-Chamberlain, Sir John Stanhope, making an appointment for Donína (because he thought Cecil would do it), the Czech's plans ground to a halt. On 16 September, when he kept his appointment with Cecil to be presented, he found that the Secretary had gone to the country 'without leaving any commands regarding me'. One curious fact links Slavata and Donína beyond their desire to kiss Elizabeth's hand. Born Protestants, both became Catholic converts at about this time, and Donína seems to have ended his days in the South Tyrol as abbot of the monastery of Nova-cella.

However, one of his brothers remained a diplomat and went on the ill-fated imperial mission to Persia in 1602, hoping to enhance the dramatic scheme floated by Sherley and Hussain 'Ali Beg. It was led by István Kakas of Zalánkemény, who died before reaching Ispahan, and it was left to Georg Tectander von der Jabel to complete the journey. The volatile Englishman and the equally tempestuous Persian spent a good deal of time on efforts in Prague and in Rome, where they met the Pope. After they had literally fought over who took precedence, their negotiations with Clement VII achieved little despite the intervention of the ubiquitous Father Robert Persons. Outside the papal apartments Sherley managed to get into a violent argument with Cecil's agent Thomas Wilson, whom he indignantly accused of having attempted his murder. Wilson denied the charge angrily but expressed his willingness to apprehend Sherley if Cecil desired to bring him back to England for examination before the Privy Council.

For all his epistolary support of Sherley, a crusade in the East was not the main concern of James I. He came from a kingdom at peace with Spain and the key element early in the reign was the speedy ending of Anglo–Spanish hostilities. This was put in hand with a cease-fire, a source of relief to both sides in a struggle that had sagged into a bellicose non-peace. The Spanish had been defeated at Kinsale (1601) and had been unable to put together another invasion fleet since the so-called 'Invisible Armada' of 1599. The only area for English exploitation of crumbling Spanish strength was at sea, and even there the level of successful privateering had tapered off. James detested it and its twin, piracy. Even before the signing of any treaty he cancelled all letters of marque and summoned home all ships at sea that carried them. This was bound to mean a painful loss of income to Cecil's elderly colleague, the Lord Admiral Nottingham. His life of princely consumption had hitherto been supported by his collection of a tenth of all enemy goods and ships brought home to England.[6] His calculated response was to marry a Scottish heiress aged nineteen, the sister of the Earl of Moray. The Spanish responded to James's overtures in a general way by granting English ships access to Spanish ports, and although the English alliance with the Dutch remained and English troops still served with them in the war against the autonomous provinces of the Archdukes Albrecht and Isabella, Philip III of Spain, like his brother-in-law, had to send a delegation to England to offer congratulations to the new monarch.

At the first intimation of the arrival of foreign ambassadors James appointed Sir Lewis Lewkenor as Master of Ceremonies to receive and entertain them. First to arrive from the United Provinces was Prince Frederick of Nassau, with Valcke, Oldenbarnevelt and Brederode. James, however, with his highly charged ideas of royal prerogative, had no relish for promptly meeting men he cast as rebels and traitors owing large capital sums to the English Crown. His ploy was to give various excuses to delay any audience with them until the arrival of Charles de Ligne, Count of Aremberg, who brought the agreeable news that the Archduke had liberated all English prisoners as a gesture of goodwill. Two days later Henri IV's envoy Maximilien de Bethune, Marquis de Rosny (and later Duc de Sully) arrived, hoping for a treaty of alliance against Spain if there was a Spanish attack on France.[7] It was he who was responsible for that famous clinging quip about James I being 'the wisest fool in Christendom', which despite the best efforts of revisionist historians today is probably not far from the truth.

Henri IV was undoubtedly worried about the possibility of harmony being retrieved for Anglo–Spanish relations. Personalities had a modest part to play here, for his dislike of James was matched by the latter's disapproval of him. For the time being James maintained a friendlier stance towards the Archduke, even as French hopes for peace relied on keeping the Dutch and English embroiled with Spain. It was the permanent French ambassador in London – Christoph de Harlay, Comte de Beaumont, sometime owner of the Sancy diamond – who suggested that James should be warned that if he ceased to help the Dutch they would be forced to make links with France. Cecil countered this by making it clear that there was no intention to abandon the Dutch. He had already taken this line with their envoys, while declining to offer any particular aid for the relief of Ostend. This had been under siege by the Archduke's forces since 1601, and the situation there was now desperate, but Cecil refused to believe that it was as grave as was made out, and in an interview on 27 May with the Dutch he spoke in such a way that they could not avoid the view that England's purpose was peace. This was so detestable to them that they did pause to wonder if James was angling for the offer of a protectorate over them, and the thought of Anglo-Danish pressure on Dutch trade in the Baltic further distressed them. Yet Cecil's attitude at the same time convinced Aremberg that he really favoured war, and the Dutch had bought him. He reported that the Estates-General had distributed £30,000, with Cecil getting a hefty slice.[8] But then Aremberg thought everyone had been bought, and certainly Archdukes Albrecht and Isabella were not best served by a man in ill-health who became enmeshed in the curious, ill-conceived manoeuvrings of Ralegh, Cobham and others against Cecil.

Perhaps de Rosny heard the same rumours as Aremberg, for the 'diabolical triplicity' before Northumberland's withdrawal began with the French envoy. He did his best to inspire James with distrust of Cecil at their prompting, aided by Beaumont. But on this matter, since it went against the grain, his attention lapsed, and very soon de Rosny and Oldenbarnevelt were swapping views on how to keep England at war while France was at peace. Oldenbarnevelt might have been excluded from the King's chamber, but he would not easily give up, and had himself smuggled into a gallery at Greenwich in order to confront James.[9] The King was sufficiently impressed by his arguments to ask that he repeat them for the benefit of the Habsburg ambassadors, but the size of Dutch requirements in further loans drained an inclination to do anything else.

De Rosny, as expected, failed to square the circle. With Henri IV seriously ill and France liable to collapse in chaos if he died, the special envoy wanted to return home, albeit without having won over Cecil or James. He needed something tangible and since England could not afford a rupture with France before any peace with Spain, he got the signing of the Treaty of Hampton Court, which was ratified by both kings.[10] It commited James to the Dutch in such a way that after a peace with Spain 'James's neutrality would be pro-Dutch rather than pro-Spanish'. It is doubtful if de Rosny could have got anything more from Cecil, even with a larger pension – if there was one. Northampton, not always to be trusted in these matters, told Sir Robert Cotton that Cecil received one; further, the French statesman later admitted in a book that Henri IV had instructed him to *obliger au service de sa Majesté* some of James's leading courtiers, and it is difficult to see how he could have achieved this without gold.[11]

To head the Spanish Embassy in London Philip III chose Juan de Tassis, later Count of Villa Mediana, a middle-aged career civil servant with no experience of princely politics. When he arrived in England Tassis found that the King was (not for the last time) away hunting, with the perfect excuse of a particularly bad outbreak of plague. The envoy therefore sensibly spent some time meeting and trying to assess, beyond the instincts of his prejudices, various important people, while wondering if a peace treaty was indeed possible. He was helped, as Arabella Stuart noted, by his 'great store of Spanish gloves, hawks' hoods, leather for jerkins', as well as the services of a perfumer. Of Cecil the new envoy wrote that he was 'the sage of the realm', albeit one who 'is as heretical as Satan'. He was astute enough, however, to recognize that Cecil was a crucial figure, even if he suspected that the King relied on him 'more from necessity than liking'.[12]

The first meeting of a somewhat nervous envoy with James at Winchester was delayed until early October. There was a certain nip in the air then, probably because the credentials Tassis presented to the monarch omitted his title 'King of Ireland', an omission stemming from the Spanish desire not to offend the Pope, who claimed Ireland, 'like Naples, [is] a papal fief'. The second encounter on 11 October, a private meeting, was more cordial as James received a gift of horses and jewels were given to Anne. Since James had put his prestige behind a peace initiative and given it considerable exposure, he was somewhat disappointed that Tassis did not have full powers to negotiate. These went instead to Juan de Velasco, Constable of Castile and Duke of Frias, on 1 October as full reports of the reception of Tassis were still being awaited at the Spanish court in Valladolid (it moved to Madrid in 1606). Clearly nothing was going to be done with unseemly alacrity, for de Velasco did not leave the court until 30 October and took two months to reach Brussels. Dignity and Spanish prestige were his principal considerations, although he certainly wanted a treaty. Unlike Cecil he did not feel that England and Spain were natural enemies, and although moderately concerned for the fate of English Catholics, he could see that Spain could do little for them without diverting urgently needed resources from their continental aims.

On reaching the court of the Archdukes, Velasco wrote to Tassis that he would prefer peace negotiations to be held on neutral territory. James was not pleased at the delay, but the Constable's excuses for staying put (approved by the Council of State) flowed – gout, personally agonizing but diplomatically useful, and the necessity of further deliberations with Philip III.[13] His belief that haste would show an excessive desire for agreement may have been an important card in his hand, but it did not make life any easier for Tassis.[14] He had to keep meeting the Privy Council, and in March 1604 he expressed the polite hope that de Velasco would now stir. Still throughout April he had to continue the preliminary negotiations without the knowledge of support from Philip III and the Council of State – their letters had failed to arrive.

In that cold mid-May, when furs were still being worn in London, the Archdukes' commissioners arrived: Jean Richardot (a veteran of Vervins as well as the failed Boulogne meetings), Audiencier Louis Verreyken and Count Aremberg. But still the Constable remained in the Spanish Netherlands, reasonably pleading infirmity and delegating his powers to Tassis and Alessandro Robida, a trusted Milanese lawyer. This manoeuvre caused a flutter in London because Tassis had already sought from James the use of Somerset House. This was a bold choice because it was considered second only to Whitehall for grandeur, and it was a dower house of Anne for her personal use. She agreed that the Constable should have it for his visit and on the King's orders it was lavishly equipped and redecorated. There was a further unusual concession that the negotiations would be held there, and James also decreed that during the whole time of the Constable's stay in England he and all his entourage would be entertained at the Crown's expense – a typically expansive gesture that cost in the region of £300 a day, much to the dismay of the Lord Treasurer. However, for the time being Tassis was the principal commissioner and on the day before negotiations opened James announced the names (or titles) of his five representatives: Cecil, Northampton, Nottingham, Dorset and Mountjoy, now Earl of Devonshire, on whom the Protestant cloak of Essex had in part descended.

The negotiations over the Anatolian-carpeted table in the chamber of Somerset House lasted from 20 May to 6 July in eighteen sessions. At the opening meeting Northampton, ever loquacious, spoke first in Latin, followed by Robida and then Richardot in French. At later meetings it became apparent that he was becoming increasingly hostile to the Spanish envoys, complaining that Spanish requirements were swamping those of the Archdukes. Richardot himself squirmed when the English commissioners privately mocked the autonomy granted in 1598 to the Spanish Netherlands by implying that it was hollow,[15] but he probably remained unaware of the residual strength of pro-Dutch attitudes in the House of Commons – something well known to the English negotiators. Not surprisingly, over half the sessions dealt with various aspects of the Dutch rebellion. The rest covered trading relations between England and Spain, the Low Countries and the West Indies. The fourteenth session had one topic that then stirred English blood in anger, just as bullfighting does today. Robida, Tassis, Northampton and Cecil looked at the Inquisition and gave particular scrutiny to its dealings with

English traders and seafarers. Since this would have raised questions of law, two gifted Englishmen in Spanish employ were surely consulted. The principal figure was Dr Robert Taylor, a Yorkshireman trained in law at Douai. His subordinate was Francis Fowler, of an exiled Catholic family, also a lawyer and Taylor's brother-in-law. Like so many other highly educated Englishmen of the period they were excellent linguists, Fowler being fluent in five or six languages other than his native tongue.[16] And Northampton and Cecil both spoke Spanish.

One topic that was not broached in the chamber was the future of those English Catholics who had remained in the country, resisting diaspora. James was increasingly restive at what he considered the clandestine strength of the Catholic community, which he himself had unintentionally done something to nurture by making the crypto-Catholic Northampton Warden of the Cinque Ports, calling him pawkily 'the tame duck' – that is, a decoy for flushing out other Catholics. The earl surely made sympathetic murmurings on the subject to the Spaniards, for Philip III regarded it as extremely important, but these covert opinions were offset by the attitude of the Commons, where any relaxation of statute and its enforcement was regarded with abhorrence. When James planned tougher action he took care to have it laid before the House, and in May he had wanted Cecil to give consideration to a bill against recusants who sent their children abroad for a Catholic education. After only four sessions of the peace conference a bill requiring the execution of statutes against Jesuits, priests, recusants and anyone else was introduced into the Lords. The only spoken opposition came from Lord Montagu, and he was silenced by arrest and imprisonment in the Tower. (His loyalties could be discerned from his provocative middle name – Maria.) The bill went to the Commons, was revised and after passage through both Houses it received the royal assent on 4 July.[17] To the French ambassador, Beaumont, James made soothing noises to be conveyed to Henri IV, but also intended for Spanish and Venetian consumption.

Meanwhile, all Tassis could do was work quietly while a secular priest and a layman were taken and executed in Warwickshire. They were victims of the penal code but also zealous magistrates; before this de Velasco had been moderately hopeful that his attempts to lighten the burden of the Catholic laity by promising pensions to key individuals, notably the King and Cecil, might be successful. The Venetian ambassador had wind of this open-handed policy, underwritten by Philip III, and he thought that Tassis was giving out presents daily. By the end of July the channel for at least promises – the Countess of Suffolk – was claiming that a hefty *douceur* would get the laity freedom from the laws for twenty-one years, and certainly the Constable arrived with very large funds and the discretion to use them. He sailed from Gravelines in an English ship, arriving in Dover with a large retinue and a large supply of ice.

Among those chosen to wait on him in the port was Edward, Lord Wotton, a crypto-papist who did the same office on the Constable's departure and received 30,000 reales. Much more intriguingly, the King's men were also sent, including William Shakespeare in scarlet livery, who – judging from the famous scene in *King Lear* – prowled out of the town while the Spanish gathered themselves for the journey by road and water to London. When they came up the Thames from Gravesend on 10 August in grandly decorated barges, the city and court flocked to every available boat on the river and vantage point on the banks. In one of the barges were Cecil, Nottingham, Suffolk and Queen Anne, masked to watch the spectacle. Landing at the stairs of Somerset House, the Constable was met by the King's bodyguard and those of his own suite and servants who had arrived by road. Then he entered the palace and, passing through two anterooms, came to the splendid Presence Chamber with its tapestries, embroidered canopy and throne emblazoned with the royal arms. Although there was no king to occupy it, de Velasco was met here by court officials chosen to serve him during his stay, including the increasingly familiar actors – grooms of the chamber. De Velasco's meticulous accounts list a payment of 4,700 reales to boatmen, musicians and actors, but the idea of the King's men performing a play at Somerset House for the Spaniard is surely a myth.[18]

The total amount shown in the accounts kept for Philip III and the Spanish Treasury is 400,000 Spanish ducats, the equivalent of 4,560,000 'reales of the Netherlands', or some £104,000. To provide English currency Philip III used the well-known Genoese bankers Ottavio and Vincenzio Centuriani.[19] The money directed by the King went in the first instance to the latter, in Brussels, who drew the necessary bills on London merchants who must have included men like Baptist Hickes. Not all the money came to London, for de Velasco spent large sums on presentation gifts, despite his eventual hesitation over the treaty submitted to his consideration. Even so, he acknowledged that he would sign it because His Most Catholic Majesty wanted a peace and possibly already, like Queen Anne, nurtured the idea of a wedding between Prince Henry and the young Infanta. As de Velasco ruefully remarked, if the Pope remained silent it was because 'nothing can be done in the matter of religion'. With an austere realism he commented that it was 'not possible to be worse off than we are at present'.[20]

If Robert Cecil (then Lord Cranborne) accepted a Spanish pension at this time, there is no mention of it in the Constable's accounts.[21] Indeed, the Spanish had no particular reason for offering one, since in the negotiations he resisted without pyrotechnics most of their claims while blunting others. Under the terms of the peace James would not levy troops to fight in the Low Countries, though no barrier was placed on volunteers. British ships would also now co-operate with Spaniards in breaking blockades, and British merchants would be free to trade their goods in Spain. In a separate accord it was agreed that such men (and other Britons) would not be harried in Spain on grounds of religion, providing they avoided any possible public scandal (like Britons today in Saudi Arabia) and behaved in a seemly fashion if entering a church or on meeting a religious procession. There were omissions: nothing was said on the Spanish unwillingness to allow British traders entry to their colonies, and the Spaniards wanted the Dutch cautionary towns returned despite British treaty commitments to the Estates-General.[22] Even so the main provisions, once established, made de Velasco's visit primarily ceremonial, and the ratification was arranged while James was in London. Having allowed Cecil and the commissioners to shoulder the burden of the detailed exchanges during the summer, James reluctantly quit his hunting to arrive in London on 14 August, finally meeting the Constable in a private audience on the 16th.

On Sunday 19 August the Earl of Southampton took a company of fifty gentlemen to Somerset House to escort the commissioners (except a bedridden Aremberg) to Whitehall. From there James led them and the court to the Chapel Royal, apparently at Spanish insistence, for a ceremony invoking divine sanction for the peace. Cecil handed a copy of the treaty to de Velasco, and then read aloud the oath by which James and Prince Henry, holding Bibles, swore to observe its terms – it was known as the Treaty of London. Later a banquet was held in the Audience Chamber at Whitehall, with the Earls of Pembroke and Southampton acting as gentleman ushers. The entry of the dignitaries was followed by a standing grace, and then ritual cleansing, with James washing his hands (nothing more than normal) and Buckhurst presenting him with a towel. The Queen received her towel from Nottingham, and then Prince Henry and the Constable washed from another basin.

Seating for the guests was railed off from those admitted merely to watch, and to a background of music James's first gesture from the throne under the canopy of state was to present the Constable with a branch of oranges (from Theobalds or Beddington?) and a melon. The Constable kissed the King's hand and then divided the melon into three, presenting one portion himself to Anne. Toasts and pledges followed including one made by de Velasco drinking from an agate cup, set with diamonds and rubies, bought in Antwerp for 120,000 reales (£2,750). This was then presented to James. The present to Anne was a markedly less expensive crystal cup or goblet bought in Brussels for 4,000 reales, but she also got three diamond pendants bought in London for £3,000 to make up for this. Jewellers and dealers in expensive curiosities and works of art had been summoned to Somerset House to display their wares, and the Constable and his suite had bought numerous items.[23] The visitors also ventured out to the Royal Exchange, and though they might have expected some hostility they even boldly went one day to the notorious Bartholomew Fair – a year later, and they might have been engulfed by a riot.

Among the recipients of Spanish gifts were the Countess of Suffolk; the Countess of Bedford; the Countess of Rutland; and the Earls of Southampton and Pembroke. Cecil's diamond ring was augmented by other jewels valued at over £5,000 which he shared with the Earls of Devonshire and Northampton.[24] All this was balanced by the presents he had to give, most probably acquired from Alexander Prescott, who did a substantial amount of work for him that year. James's presents to the Spaniards were determinedly extravagant – this was a gesture he had never made before to a foreign embassy, least of all one from the most powerful nation in the world, and with a rush of blood to the head he was prompted to raid the Jewel-House. This sovereign generosity meant that de Velasco and his fellow-envoys received gold items weighing 290 ounces and gilt plate weighing nearly 29,000 ounces. The Constable's startling booty of five gold items included the astonishing basin and ewer designed (it is believed) by Holbein for Henry VIII's queen, Jane Seymour, and a medieval enamelled cup of gold weighing $68\frac{1}{4}$ ounces, now called the Royal Gold Cup of the kings of France and England.[25] Despite alterations – one at least intentional – which have spoiled the noble proportions of a unique piece made in France in about 1380, the cup can still be admired, since it was acquired in the late nineteenth century by the British Museum.[26]

With the end of the war and formalities, James said his adieus to the bedridden de Velasco and Aremberg at 6 a.m. on Tuesday morning. He then galloped off with a hunting party, since there was nothing else requiring his presence in London. The Constable and his party left London on Friday 25 August with their honour escort, travelling via Rochester and Sitting-bourne to Dover. From there de Velasco wrote a letter of thanks to James (as well he might, considering the booty he was taking). Since the matter of recusancy fines had not been settled, he included a request that Catholics should be tried by judges who were *graviores ac prudentiores*.[27] Tassis, having said his farewells to the Constable, returned to London, remaining as resident ambassador until the following summer when Don Pedro de Zúñiga took his place. The problem now was who would represent England in Spain for the ceremony of ratifi-cation there. Buckhurst and Cecil could not be spared, and it had to be someone of great dignity and importance. With the exclusion by James of the 2nd Duke of Lennox the inevitable choice was the ageing Earl of Nottingham. This was going to be expensive and the Lord Treasurer appealed to Cecil to persuade his Howard friend to be more moderate in his demands. But curtailing the size of the embassy when so many clamoured to go was difficult, though events abroad might have done it for him. English non-diplomatic interest in the treaty was primarily for the trade concessions, and early in 1605 merchants and mariners reported renewed harrying by the Inquisition. After a preparatory visit to Spain by Thomas Wilson, one of Cecil's most dutiful agents, Nottingham de-parted and by his own account achieved a great diplomatic success. This was contradicted in secret letters from Sir Charles Cornwallis, the new English resident ambassador in Spain, to his mentor Northampton. Although Cornwallis was from a prominent recusant family, he attacked Spanish atti-tudes and the behaviour of Nottingham. The use of these stories by Northampton to undermine the old man's credit with James was apparently not much resisted by Cecil.[28] If a Howard party existed, it was a fragile creation.

Nottingham's expansive attempts to nurture the tiny seed of Anglo–Spanish amity at Valladolid were hardly likely to dispel tough anti-Spanish feelings in England. The Treaty of London was far from popular there so, trying to generate some enthusiasm for it, the government commissioned a pamphlet to grind out its merits from Robert Treswell, Somerset Herald. He tried to convince, picturing the Spanish as refulgent with goodwill. But there was contrary evidence too: both Salisbury and Cornwallis had to intervene personally to secure the freedom of Adrian Thibault, brother-in-law of Peter Van Lore, royal jeweller and money-lender. Nor was peace on the Continent going to be easily achieved and held when both the Dutch and the Archdukes recruited Englishmen for their armies. In an attempt to curtail this Salisbury had a law passed making it a felony to serve any foreign prince without first taking the oath of allegiance at the port of embarkation. But still impoverished younger brothers like Sir Charles Percy had to do something, and when he was mooted as a possible colonel of the English regiment, it dissipated much of the effort he had put into repairing his relations with Cecil and the Crown after his involvement in the Essex treason.[29]

∾ 10 ∾

On the great matter of the Union of Scotland and England, it was naturally James who took the initiative, Cecil with others acting as his diligent aide. The theme of peace abroad, which bore fruit in the Somerset House Conference after the trenchant diplomacy of the Secretary of State, was paralleled by the pursuit of peace and unity in Britain, stressing the need for a union of hearts and minds. The Borders were an immediate area of concern after the succession because of a spasm of plundering in the West March by the anarchic Grahams and Armstrongs. But when they had been suppressed by troops sent from Berwick by James when on his way south, the garrison, as the town had glumly anticipated, became redundant. It was the sovereign's will that the English and Scots should be one people with one currency to encourage trade and hence peaceful amalgamation. Why then did the arrival of the Scots in London, along with the royal family, cause such a rapid surge of English discontent, shading into hatred? – and, within a very short time, a pained regret for the passing of the Elizabethan age.

It was principally the arrival at court of what the English tended to regard loftily as rapacious clansmen of an only superficial civility that caused the friction. James was now by generous consent King of England, a nation naturally superior to Scotland, and it seemed that the somewhat dubious majesty of the man was undermined by his companions. They spoke the King's incomprehensible language and threatened to monopolize royal favour. It was the accent that led to English discomfort and derision, for as early as 1562 the ushers at Richard Mulcaster's Merchant Taylors' School were criticized because 'being northern men born, they had not taught the children to speak distinctly or to pronounce their words as they ought.'[1] Yet the English perception of the newcomers tendentiously exaggerated their numbers and the extent of their power, and there was no 'flood of Scots' into England or its government. A handful did join the English Privy Council without a reciprocal arrangement for Scotland. Sir George Home (later Earl of Dunbar) was for a time Chancellor of the Exchequer and Master of the Rolls, important but not key offices which were annexed by Cecil and his Howard allies. Other important Scots were the Duke of Lennox, Sir Thomas Erskine, and a clutch of Murrays, including the Groom of the Bedchamber, John Murray.[2] Cecil's man there was Philip Herbert, later Earl of Montgomery.

A second tier of Scots had lesser court positions of moderate importance. Alexander Douglas was Keeper of the Council Chamber; Thomas Reid became Secretary of the Latin tongue; Sir William Stewart was Master of the Royal Bears, Bulls and Bandogs; David Ramsay was Clockmaker Extraordinary and Abraham Aberconway was Sadler to Prince Henry. This desire of James's for familiar faces and voices was not at all odd: what was reprehensible was that to reward his followers generally he handed out pensions and cash with such unthinking determination that he wrecked royal finances, which were soon permanently in crisis.[3] Actually, many who filled their pockets were then shunted back to Scotland, leaving the English in a state of teeth-gnashing anger. Some of this even seeped into the streets, so that in April 1604 James ordered the arrest of city gangs called 'Swaggerers' who attacked Scots in London.[4] Naturally English playwrights spotted satirical possibilities and Ben Jonson, John Marston and George Chapman had a collaborative effort, *Eastward Ho!*, staged in 1605 by the Children of the Queen's Revels at Blackfriars. Jonson later averred that it was

Sir James Murray who sparked the row about slighting references that led a prudent Marston to flee, while Jonson and Chapman had a spell in prison. Publication by William Apstey only made matters worse, and Jonson wrote a dignified letter of self-defence to Salisbury, and then to any other noble who might get them released. Chapman was more self-abasing and eventually, with the help of the Earl of Suffolk, they were freed.[5]

Purveyancing, wardship and monopolies all made the first Jacobean session of Parliament a controversial one. However, it was the matter of union as a key element in royal policy that was intended as the principal issue for debate, and so it proved, occupying 'more parliamentary time than any other subject'.[6] It was a topic with apparently divine sanction, James using the elevated language of sacred nuptials to state his belief that what God had united no man should seek to sunder: 'I am the husband, and all the whole isle is my lawful wife.'[7] As it happens, though, the belief of many historians that James's original intention was 'to secure a substantive union in 1604', and that this plan was wrecked by the burgeoning democratic process in Parliament, gives the wrong slant. What he wanted, and indeed got, was a parliamentary commission to report to the next session. An ancillary request concerned the royal style – that the 'King of England, Scotland, France and Ireland' should now be 'King of Great Britain'. This yoking together of his peoples symbolized a high conception, the new sublime tranquillity, so it is not difficult to see why later the Gunpowder Plot caused such a spell of rage and dismay. To lay the change before Parliament for ratification when he could simply declare it was a further sign of the new intended harmony that would erase the memory of the many sleights inflicted by his proud and minatory predecessor.

Or so James thought. His proposals were laid before joint conferences on 14 April, and the debate on style then went on for two weeks. Amongst others Nicholas Fuller and Sir Edwin Sandys spoke against, with Sir Francis Bacon in favour.

Sandys's argument was that an institution called to consider the affairs of England could not consider the matter of 'Great Britain', and that a change would invalidate all manner of legal mechanisms and institutions.[8] A royal attempt to stem the unwelcome discord failed to silence an increasingly confused and heated debate. Even Sir William Morrice's ingenious notion that James should be 'Emperor of Great Britain' was fleetingly aired again. On 26 April Sandys spoke against the change once more, and a committee under Bacon compiled a list of objections to the proposed change for the next conference. This became superfluous when the English judiciary agreed with the view of the Commons on the style and James was forced, as it were, to rein in. The only advance was on the commission, which became operative in June.

Apart from James, few people have given any attention to the attitude of the Scots. In fact, there was considerable tension in the headless body because the arguments used in the Commons about precedency and the poverty of Scotland incensed many. Resisting pressure from the south, the Scottish Parliament sought the maintenance of Scottish laws, the alliance with France, and objected as well to some of James's own nominations for the Scottish representation on the commission. The feeling was that these men were tainted with English attitudes and likely to be dominated by English interests.[9] The submission from the King was examined and revised, and although the Scots Act of Commission was passed on 10 July after some seven days of debate, there was a remarkable supplementary Act which excluded changes in the Kirk from the joint commissions' deliberations. The Scots had noted the performance of James at the Hampton Court Conference and were thus registering their unease. So although men like Cecil, Mar and Balmerino were working dutifully for union, there was every reason to expect resistance up to and including the Privy Councils.

To shackle it, just as the Commission was about to meet, James had the proclamation on the style read on 20 October. His view of the reuniting of the two kingdoms under one

Crown declared: ' . . . it was unreasonable that a thing which by nature was so much in effect one, should not be a unity in name'. From henceforth the one isle would be Great Britain. This was followed several weeks later by a repetition of an earlier proclamation uniting the coinage of the two countries. Since coins penetrated to the remotest corners of the realm, it is not surprising that James and Cecil gave this matter more than routine attention.[10] The first coinage had the Scottish title inserted in the legend and the armorial quartering was modified to include the lion rampant of Scotland and the Irish harp, an instrument for which Cecil had a special esteem. In denomination it followed the coinage of the late Elizabethan period in gold and silver, with Scottish currency rated at one-twelfth of its English counterpart: so, for example, a Scottish shilling was the equivalent of an English penny, and an English shilling, when marked with the numerals XII in the field on the obverse, became twelve shillings Scots north of the border.

The second coinage, which appeared in November 1604, virtually coincided with the declaration of Great Britain, and did much to publicize the new name for the kingdom. For example, the unite's inscription (this had been the sovereign) was FACIAM EOS IN GENTEM VNAM. The half-unite's inscription, also on crowns, referred to Henry VII's uniting of the roses of Lancaster and York as well as James's uniting of the two kingdoms: HENRICUS ROSAS REGNA IACOBUS. In appearance these coins, with an attempt to vary the portraiture and the treatment of the armorial reverses, were an improvement on the transitional coins. The engraving of the dies seems to have fallen to Charles Anthony, Graver of the Mint, who had edged out Nicholas Hilliard for the post, and the Under-Gravers John Dycker and a German, John Rutlinger. But for the unite and half-unite it has been suggested that the work was given informally to someone deeply familiar with the problem of portraying the King: John Acheson, his Edinburgh goldsmith, responsible for some of the fine large gold pieces of Scotland.

The ceremony for the proclamation of Great Britain was carried out in the face of sturdy opposition. Whatever its symbolic intention, it was widely scorned. In the circumstances the meeting of the Anglo-Scottish Commission in the Painted Chamber, Whitehall, could have been disastrous. That it was not was due to the care with which the commissioners had been selected, and in large part to Cecil's careful control of the meetings. Among the thirty-one Scots commissioners were Vice-Chancellor Fyvie; Balmerino and Lord Advocate Hamilton, 'to make the delegation firmly representative of the Edinburgh establishment'.[11] Excluded were London Scots like Home, Erskine and James Hay. The English commissioners numbered forty-eight and excluded, with the agreement of the Commons, Fuller, Sandys and Percival. This says much about the 'opposition' in a Jacobean Parliament.[12]

The speed and success of the Commission's deliberations indicates how much Cecil had learnt from those costive meetings at Boulogne, and from the recently completed dealings with commissioners at the Somerset House Conference. He and Fyvie organized the agenda, with all its potential mantraps, and the result was a sequence of brisk meetings that within six weeks had drawn up a document called the Instrument. Only Hoby – generally regarded as a follower of Cecil, but also secretly a French pensioner and so defending the 'Auld Alliance' – refused to sign it. The contents were actually quite modest. Border administration was to be regularized; trade agreements revised to give free trade a modest fillip; and there was to be preparation for the clarification of the legal status of trans-border nationals. Other aspects of union – the Church, laws and Parliaments – were alluded to, but only as items in the King's grand conception of a perfect union. On 6 December the air of goodwill generated in talks in committees and at private dinners was discernible in the closing meeting held before James. As far as he was concerned this was only the beginning; for some of the commissioners, secretly, it was more than enough.

Having done its work, the Commission was then dissolved,

with the expectation of a prompt follow-up. A session of Parliament was scheduled for February 1605, having been prorogued in July 1604 following the stirring difficulties of the first session. It has been variously stated that because of some bizarre lapse Cecil was responsible in a particular way for the friskiness of the members; 'that elections were neglected at this time'.[13] Possible reasons cited include overwork and an overblown confidence in a 'honeymoon' period for the new monarch and Parliament. In the view of one historian, 'the popular party of opposition was returned with a very substantial majority'.[14] This gives a much greater unity and coherence to something still amorphous – the 'popular party' was not a muscular entity but a loose grouping of ideas, principles, irritations and vanities. Furthermore, the composition of the House of Commons in 1604 had not altered for years, and Cecil's tactics for the election were the same as they had been in 1593, 1597 and 1601. He had been interventionist then, and was again. Allegations of electoral neglect, especially from a tendentious source like Francis Bacon, must be treated with scepticism, for it was so uncharacteristic of Cecil's practice. Indeed, the evidence of the last ten years of Cecil's service to Elizabeth makes the notion completely false.

In 1601, even though his rival Essex was out of the way, Cecil used his patronage to secure twenty or more seats in the House. Nor was it always necessary to ask. John Trelawney wrote to him: 'I am bold again to present you with two burgess-ships for this Parliament.' Clearly, from this we can assume that 'again' meant that the seats for West Looe had been filled that way before. Three years later, when some historians have him out of the game, Cecil in fact did a little better. There is not much direct evidence in his papers, but by looking at the mesh of patronage of certain boroughs and their MPs it is possible to sketch in Cecil's choices where previously there was only a void.[15]

Cornish boroughs were his main targets. Cornwall was a county where, as we have seen, he had had, albeit temporarily, very large landholdings, and later sales had not diminished the number of boroughs under his sway: Launceston; Lostwithiel; Penryn; St Mawes and West Looe, where the elected MPs were his friends or clients Sir Thomas Lake, Chaloner, Provis, Dudley Carleton and Sir George Harvey, at this time the Lieutenant of the Tower.[16] In fact the Secretary's patronage quite probably accounted for both seats at Penryn and both at West Looe, and his candidates were probably successful at Saltash, St Ives, Helston, East Looe, Grampound, Callington and Bossiney. It is interesting that one of his candidates was Sir Arthur Atey, once a devoted follower of the Earls of Leicester and Essex and now selected for Beer Alston. A friend of Cecil and Sir Michael Hickes, Sir Hugh Beeston, was returned for two places, Stafford and Shoreham, the latter being one of Nottingham's seats. Sir Walter Cope, antiquarian and developer, was elected for Westminster to a seat once held by Cecil, and Stamford was, of course, a family borough which elected Sir Robert Wingfield, a distant kinsman and friend.[17] Peterborough yielded a seat and probably Bewdley another, so that the Secretary's patronage garnered twenty-two places in eighteen elections. It was a sturdy total and just what one would expect for the leading exponent of election management. Indeed, the number can even be augmented by looking at MPs found seats at his urging by other patrons. Sir Thomas Edmondes received the backing of the Earl of Pembroke for Wilton, and Howard support advanced Cecil's clients at Horsham and Morpeth.

In the Elizabethan era seventeen boroughs had shown the electoral influence of the Duchy of Lancaster, with the chancellors Hesketh and Cecil taking advantage of this power source. In 1604 Cecil probably used the Duchy to place John Bowyer again in Newcastle-under-Lyme, and his kinsman Sir William Cooke at Wigan.[18] Preston returned Sir Vincent Skinner, a first cousin by marriage of Lady Mildred Cecil, and the Council of the North very probably supported Richard Percival at Richmond (surely not the Percival who spoke against union). Nine of Yorkshire's twenty-two parliamentary places seem to have been under the Council's remit, and John

Ferne's election at Boroughbridge has also been credited to that body.[19] However, as a Cecil stalwart, he could well have been the agreed choice of the Lord President Burghley and Cecil. There was a general, if extravagant, view that to refuse a nominee would be 'worse to us than death itself',[20] but towns were not always so desperately compliant and in 1605 Ludlow denied the nomination to Cecil and Lord Eure.

James had made no move to influence the elections, issuing instead a proclamation that they should be free. Unwilling to allow this to be absolute, but also uneasy about being obvious in setting aside the royal intention, Cecil simply obscured the evidence of his manipulation. By 1605 it was clear to him from the Lords how difficult management of the Commons could be, so he and the Lord Chancellor, Ellesmere, got two further prorogations delaying Parliament until November. One of the unresolved issues of the first session was free trade, and Cecil's intention was to take the initiative from men like Sandys. The Secretary disliked the exclusive coterie of rich merchants who sought to exclude others from a profitable trade, but at the same time he acknowledged the convenience to the government of trading companies: 'organisations with which the Privy Council could deal on diplomatic and financial matters, and which provided the equivalent of modern consular services for merchants abroad'.[21] His aim was to create companies that by their inclusiveness rather than exclusiveness, with modest entry conditions, were responsive and successful. Hence his restructuring in June 1605 of the Spanish Company's charter, and the appointment of one of his clients as secretary of the company.[22] There was criticism of this, but the process was transferred to the Levant Company.

The old Elizabethan monopoly company had gone into liquidation in 1603 after a disagreement about payments to the Crown. Cecil had outflanked them by retaining the company levy of an imposition on currants and then diverting the monies to the Crown. Even so, given the diplomatic difficulties that could arise from trade in the eastern Mediterranean, he thought a company to stand between the Sultan and the

Crown would be useful. So again, despite some opposition from traders, he brought a new company into being. There was a new charter with a low entry fee, and his success here was in marked contrast to efforts designed to lead to a French Company. The English cloth trade with northern France had been particularly hit by French protectionism and while negotiations went on – forming the basis for the Anglo–French commercial treaty in 1606 – Salisbury remarked on the dissipation of English efforts because there was no one voice of authority.[23] Although he maintained a critical attitude to monopolies he did favour a new company, but the bill promoted by the committee on free trade, 'to enable all his Majesty's loving subjects of England and Wales' to trade freely with Spain, Portugal and France, passed through the Commons and even the Lords.[24]

Some of the difficulties faced by the government and the Crown might have been eased if James had not chosen to reward key followers like Cecil and Sir William Knollys with titles that took them to the Lords. When Sir John Fortescue lost his seat the only councillors left in the Commons were Sir John Herbert and Sir John Stanhope, and neither had sufficient weight to maintain control over a House prismatically divided. Herbert was a useful factotum to the Secretary and Stanhope (another Cecilian) was 'not a great parliamentary leader'.[25] The result, after the mastery shown by Elizabeth in her dealings with these men, was a remarkable frothing of energy in debates, with much hostility to royal policy. The King and Cecil had therefore to try to stem it in some way and they chose the obvious route of great attention to bye-elections. Of the ninety-five MPs elected in these, one-third were royal officials or were closely connected with the government.[26] But the damage had been done and whatever the fund of latent goodwill towards James it was constantly threatened with turbulence, mostly hingeing on money. Thus the commission to compound for assarts snatched £20,000 a year for the Crown, and Exchequer officials lined their pockets by demanding substantial fees for passing the accounts of sheriffs. In 1606 the outraged Commons called before them the Mr Typper who so ardently pursued defective land titles.[27]

By that year the hectic atmosphere had been somewhat punctured by the perturbations surrounding the Gunpowder Plot, which brought so many advantages to Cecil. The relief that was generally felt at its discovery probably encouraged a government belief that the Commons would surely be more malleable. Indeed, before the second session in November 1606 Stanhope had gone to the Lords, so Herbert was briefly left as the sole representative of the Council in the Commons until Fortescue finally got into the House in a bye-election. Salisbury's need to know the tenor and temperature of the Lower House never flagged, and he achieved his objective by requiring his followers to report in great detail on its activities. Thomas Wilson, who entered Parliament in a bye-election for Newport, Isle of Wight, a seat controlled by the Earl of Southampton, had the role of 'rapporteur' thrust on him, and it required daily reports to satisfy Salisbury. Anything Wilson missed could be supplemented by other reports from Cope, Speaker Phelips and Bacon. With the connivance of the unusually able Phelips, Salisbury was in a position to cajole, nudge and even charm the Commons. Always the master of his brief, 'to eloquence he added a moderation and a spirit of conciliation, very rare in James's councilors' [sic].[28]

The marked slowing down in the advance to union has sometimes been ascribed to secret opposition by Cecil, when it can only have been James who was responsible. The reason was his passionate concern that union should spring from total commitment on both sides. The pause 'qualifies the picture of James as a man dazzled by a private vision'.[29] After the discovery of the Gunpowder Plot, exposing deep-seated national prejudices and leading to further clashes in the streets of London, there was inevitably a second deferment. Even before this, in October, the knowledgeable Venetian ambassador thought the question of union would be dropped, 'both sides displaying such obstinacy that an accommodation is impossible'.[30] In fact, amid all the hubbub the matter was edged from central consideration, although Salisbury agreed that it should be revived as soon as possible. Even so it was not until November 1606 that union was considered in detail by either Parliament, the Scots holding off until the English took up the matter again.

In the meantime the momentum that remained was partially channelled through both governments giving attention to coins, seals, flags and commerce. One of the first acts of the reign was the making of a new Great Seal ordered by warrant on 4 April to incorporate the arms of England and Scotland. Of these the most controversial and important was the projected union of the national flags and as the historian of union pointed out, the business 'was in some ways a microcosm of the overall project'.[31] National honour was at stake and the original designs by the heralds, delivered to Nottingham, were flawed in one way or another. This was not surprising when the position next to the staff was considered superior to the corresponding position in the fly. The difficulty was that an attempt was being made not simply to unite the Red Cross of St George and the White Saltire of St Andrew, but to amalgamate or interlace them. The revised union flag is now so familiar (though frequently flown incorrectly) that the early attempts appear distinctly quaint, even clumsy. It would have been interesting to see the two submissions of the Scots with their complaint of 7 August 1606, which were claimed to balance the nations equally, but unfortunately they have been lost. The flag stayed as it was devised and since amalgamation was sought, no other variation was possible, especially since the rules of heraldry state that colour may not be placed on colour, and white in heraldry, being silver, is a metal not a colour. Even so the union flag used until 1801 was controversial, and Charles I shunned it.

When, in November 1606, the English Parliament again took up the challenge of union, it had before it a specific set of proposals outlined in the Instrument of December 1604. There was no hint then that the debate would drag on over many months, turning into a nigh-on tormented resistance to the whole idea. Those who claimed to discern a Scots advantage seized in the Commission now battled to subdue it, while fearful of the possible consequences of open opposition. A real log jam of opposing views came about, with no evidence of this arising from a preconceived strategy by so-called opposition leaders. They gallantly offered a piquant clutter of views, sometimes even reversing a previously held position. For government ministers like Salisbury the campaign by these kindred spirits in the Lower House must have been as enervating as anything he had encountered in his parliamentary career, and the cumulative signs of fatigue were growing. As has been stated, the reaction to 'the Instrument is not explicable in terms of ordinary political logic, or principle'.[32] What these testy, wayward and confused men saw, with horrid clarity, was a desperate threat to the emerging, deepening English national identity. They had an authentic contempt, widely shared, for a subordinate nation, albeit one that by a grave defect in the late Queen had provided the current sovereign, in many respects a wretched specimen. Doubtless, if union had meant superiority for everything English, there would have been a sprint to finish the business.

In the event, by May 1607 James was so angrily disconcerted that he abruptly ended discussion. In so doing he effectively put paid to any chance of commercial union or naturalization being achieved through Parliament. To establish the legal status of the 'Post-Nati', James needed a helpful court case; the 'Ante-Nati', in one of his rare fits of realism, were forgotten. Although hostile and border law were abolished in June, this was only after long debate, and by that time the King seems to have been utterly disillusioned. He was not the only Scot who was bristling; those who saw him as an absolute king urged him to spend more time in his home kingdom. The project that had with resounding idealism sought amity in union had buckled, and relations on all fronts had been soured.

11

The early 1590s had seen a revival of theological arguments stifled briefly during the great military crisis of the previous decade. In particular there was renewed sparring over Calvinistic discipline with the exiled Thomas Cartwright advocating a Presbyterian system, while opposition at home to Puritanism found a voice in the Lady Margaret Professor of Divinity at Cambridge, Peter Baro, with additional support from the Master of Gonville and Caius, William Barret. In 1595 the latter caused a great stir in his sermon 'ad Clerum', which attacked the authority of Calvin. Very quickly put under pressure, he was forced to read a recantation that was also subsequently condemned 'as savouring of Popish doctrine'. His appeal was to Whitgift, who delivered his written rebuke through Dr Clayton, the Master of Magdalene. The matter did not even then subside, and it culminated in the defeat of Barret. The drawing up of the Lambeth Articles was viewed by Cambridge Calvinists as a great step, despite the simultaneous death of William Whitaker and his replacement as Regius Professor by Dr John Overall, markedly less sympathetic to Calvinism.

Baro himself angered the Puritans by a sermon during which he criticized the Lambeth Articles. Elizabeth also disliked them and it was Cecil who conveyed her thoughts to Whitgift.[1] Burghley and a clutch of academics and divines, including Overall and Lancelot Andrewes, also disapproved of them. The Lord Treasurer weighed in to support Baro, who could have been forced out of his university post, but a timely resignation simply brought him to London, where he died in April 1599. His imposing funeral was – significantly – provided by Bancroft. At this time Robert Cecil's religious beliefs were still influenced by his father, who felt a general satisfaction with the Elizabethan settlement and was willing to enforce it. Thus in practice individual moderate Puritans like Stephen Egerton, popular minister of St Anne Blackfriars from 1598, were shielded from prosecution by the church authorities.[2] Egerton, whose book *A Brief Method of Catechizing* went through an enviable forty-four editions in fifty years, was one of those instrumental in the presentation of the Millenary Petition to James.

Although it does not seem to have carried names, the Millenary Petition was regarded as representing the opinions of some one thousand ministers and others. Seeking reform within the established Church, it was one of several similar approaches and was presented to the King in April 1603. His attitude to it was mirrored by Whitgift, who complained to Cecil in September 1603 about petitioners, while he praised the 'godlie care and great favour towards us' of the minister. In November it was Bishop Matthew of Durham's impression that Cecil actually favoured some reforms in church discipline, but it will not have been the minister who suggested to James a conference at Hampton Court between representatives of the bishops and the Puritans. It was much more likely to have been the King's chaplain, Patrick Galloway, and his patron, the Earl of Mar, who knew James's appetite for theological debate, with its scorching swapping of quotations.[3]

The conference took place in the royal presence in January 1604, after the Christmas festivities, with the ideas of the Petition nudged out of the forefront of discussion topics. It was convened on the 12th with a very puzzling quartet of Puritans, of whom the radical Henry Jacob was later to remark that they were 'not of their choosing, nor nomination'.[4] Dr John Reynolds, Laurence Chaderton, John Knewstub and Thomas Sparke had most probably been nominated at court before receiving their formal summons from the Privy Council, and there was even the suspicion that the bishops had meddled to effect the choice of those ranged against them. If so, they had done it to some purpose: Reynolds, their foreman, was an 'extreme moderate'; Knewstub, once a Dudley protégé, was well known in his home county of Suffolk, where he was rector of Cockfield, but carried little weight outside it; Laurence Chaderton, once a Cambridge Ramist and Master of Emmanuel College, was moving away from Presbyterianism; and Thomas Sparke, rector of Bletchley and prebendary of Lincoln, had just been won back to conformity.[5]

Differences of opinion and emphasis in the quartet of Puritans at the conference were matched by those amongst the men ranged against them. Thomas Bilson, Bishop of Winchester and a Privy Councillor, was an old antagonist of Henry Jacob. Anthony Wood said that his sermons preached at Paul's Cross 'made great alarms against the Puritan Brethren', and in 1599 they had been published as *The effect of certain Sermons touching the full redemption of Mankind by the death and Blood of Christ Jesus*. Bilson later received the patronage of Cecil as the minister slowly nurtured an Arminian seam in his own beliefs, finding 'the middle path – somewhere between Catholicism and Zwinglianism – in the bitter theological controversy over the Sacrament'.[6] Cecil would have winced at this time at the ecstatic but luculent writing on the matter of St Catherine of Siena: '[Jesus] made of his blood a drink and his flesh a food for all those who wish it. There is no other means for man to be satisfied. He can appease his hunger and thirst only in this blood.'

Recent work has identified two groups among the bishops, with those most touched by Calvinism persuaded to be milder towards Puritan nonconformity.[7] The deans also divided, so that James Montague of the Chapel Royal, touched notably by Cambridge Calvinists when first Master of Sidney Sussex College, did not himself enforce conformity until after the conference. Cecil, as chancellor of the university, seems to have required it, writing late in 1604 to his subordinates to press for strict discipline and conformity. By the following year Dr John Cowell, the Vice-Chancellor, reported optimistically to Salisbury that save for Emmanuel the prospects for it were excellent. As the minister forwarded this news to James he was complimented by Montague, who suggested that the situation of the Church might be resolved if Salisbury could be temporarily a bishop. A piquant idea – and certainly as a serious layman he had a strong interest in the principal areas of debate. The evolution of his private spiritual life over the years, and his interventions in confessional politics, were surely not immune to the cast of mind of his chaplains, among whom were Thomas Moigne, Richard Neile, Richard Meredeth and George Montaigne, lately a chaplain to Essex.

Little is known about Moigne, who studied interminably at Cambridge. Neile, whose early career was fostered by the Cecils and then by Bancroft, is much better known. The bishop and Cecil were allied from the late 1590s to 1610, with Bancroft helping to defeat Essex by putting up a troop of pikemen during the crisis. Neile helped to link the statesman and the ecclesiastic, especially 'when he gained the influential position of Clerk of the Closet in 1603'.[8] But what was Neile about when the then Archbishop Bancroft attacked the Catholic earls on the Privy Council, and Salisbury headed off any inclination on the King's part to pursue the matter?[9] By the 1630s Neile had become one of the leading Arminians, while George Montaigne (or Mountain), sometime Master of the Savoy Hospital and Bishop of London, was another.[10] So was Walter Curle, Bishop of Winchester, whose father William Curle had been Auditor to the Court of Wards and was buried in Hatfield Church; the younger Curle's career in the Church certainly advanced with Salisbury's help. It seems, then, that it is not unreasonable to identify a growing Arminian cluster around the earl, even if the extent of its influence requires more study.

Indeed, if Cecil's opinions were reflecting a wide range of subtle variations and formal meditations, the same may be said for James. It is doubtful if those summoned by Cecil,

Mar, Devonshire, Northampton and Northumberland to the Hampton Court Conference could have confidently delineated his views. After a Calvinist upbringing, and yet with a Catholic wife, as King of England he was soon defending the sign of the cross in baptism and the routine wearing of the surplice, and there was nothing much to balance this for even the very moderate Puritans, whose principal aim was 'to modify the rites and discipline of the established church'.[11] The conference began its work on 14 January 1604, in the Privy Chamber, with James conferring with the bishops and five cathedral deans in the presence of the Privy Council. On Monday the 16th came the hearing with the four Puritans, with Reynolds as their leading voice in exposition. It was he who slewed matters away from the Millenary Petition so that, for example, doctrine, given a minor place in it, was now vigorously promoted. He put first his request that 'the doctrine of the Church might be preserved in purity, according to God's word'.[12] Reform of the Prayer Book was another important item, but other Millenary complaints, such as bowing at the name of Jesus, 'were omitted and others, such as the ring in marriage and the clerical cap, were explicitly repudiated as grievances'.[13] There was also a hope for improvements in livings and the relaxation of the discipline of church courts. Nothing here was tainted by a virulent radicalism, though doubtless Bancroft and Bilson heard it with sour expressions.

The stir came when Reynolds innocently allowed the word 'presbyters' to twirl into the air. The supposedly moderating role of James disintegrated as he exorcized 'the ghost of Scottish presbyterianism', leading to his famous pithy expostulation: 'No bishop, no king'. With the Puritan bench silenced, he proclaimed his intention to make them conform 'or else I will harry them out of the land, or else do worse'. On the third day the somewhat crestfallen Puritans gave a grudging commitment to conformity, although they put in a plea for more time to adjust to this notion. James's response was more conciliatory after this, and in general he seems to have found the conference a worthwhile enterprise. For later generations one powerful argument for its worth was the decision to prepare a new translation of the Bible. This was on the suggestion of Reynolds, who later worked in the Oxford Old Testament group on Isaiah to Malachi.

Cecil was an observer of the Hampton Court Conference, and it gave him an excellent opportunity to watch his new monarch at work. He was impressed, and gave thanks to the deity for the King's 'understanding Heart'. The consolidation of the policy given royal approval, and the advocacy of the bishops, took place during spring and summer 1604. It was marked by stages, including in March the enjoining of the whole kingdom to a revised new edition of the Book of Common Prayer. Then in July James stated by proclamation the requirement of conformity before 30 November so that ministers who resisted could be ousted. Happily for Cecil, the duty to enforce this fell not on the government but on the bishops and Court of High Commission. His impatience with schismatics was political rather than theological, for they would 'break all the bonds of unity'. In April 1605 he took the same line when replying to a petition from Puritan gentry sympathizers in Leicestershire. For political reasons he regarded them and others from Northamptonshire, led by Sir Francis Hastings, as attempting a Calvinist reformation by stealth. He was beginning to modify his earlier Calvinistic bias, while others of the Privy Council could not even feign such a thing.

Representing the old nobility and the old religion were men like Northumberland, Suffolk, Northampton and Worcester, who regarded themselves as the natural hereditary councillors of the King. Conscious of their ancient lineage and frequently jealous of the 'new men' like Cecil and Bancroft, they had to be placated or subdued. At a lower level were the Scots, although an inner ring of five – Lennox, Mar, Kinloss, Sir George Home and Sir James Elphinstone – had to be included in the Privy Council, which at the time had a pronounced Cecilian tilt. His cousin Sir John Stanhope was a member; so were Nottingham and Shrewsbury, while Worces-

ter's son had married a Cecil cousin, Anne Russell. John
Herbert, his 'assistant' Secretary of State, was also a member,
but of so little weight that Cecil had to remind people to write
to him once in a while. Even someone like Devonshire, a
soldier with an independent career, was beholden to Cecil.
The denizenated Scots admitted to the Council actually had
little influence in English affairs, the exception being Home
(later Earl of Dunbar), who had more influence on shaping
border policy than anyone other than the Secretary himself.
Home was also for a time Chancellor of the Exchequer – to
the fury of the previous holder of the office, Sir John Fortescue.
Outnumbered heavily by Englishmen, theirs was a token
Scottish presence which gave them status at the English court,
and symbolized the unity of the realm intended by James.

For some Englishmen who had made great strides in their
careers under Elizabeth, the new reign with its new impulses
brought disaster. Lord Henry Howard's ample correspondence to James had already undermined Ralegh and Cobham,
and both failed to engage his confidence when he arrived in
England. Very soon, and on the slenderest evidence, they and
a little group of followers were ruined by the shadowy Main
Plot and Bye Plot of Thomas Watson. Cobham was imprisoned until shortly before his death in 1619 and Ralegh was
beheaded the year before, after his lamentable failure in South
America. The curiosity of these Plots (if such they were) is
that a swordsman like Sir Griffin Markham could be involved
in both and still keep his head, though not his estates, which
were confiscated and passed to Sir John Harington. Even his
prison sentence was drastically shortened, and after parole
from the Tower he was banished abroad to serve in the
English Catholic regiment fighting for the Archdukes in the
Spanish Netherlands. If Cecil used an informer to bring about
the ruin of Ralegh and Cobham it seems more likely that it
was Markham who undertook the work rather than George
Brooke, who would have been betraying a brother to their
joint brother-in-law. Allowing for possible jealousy and
rivalry, Markham's behaviour in exile suggests that he was

following a well-established pattern. He still worked for Cecil (now Salisbury) until he was driven out of the Spanish Netherlands in 1610. The colonel of the English regiment was Thomas, Baron Arundell of Wardour, a Catholic friend of Salisbury who had steady contacts with Sir Thomas Edmondes, the English ambassador in Brussels. Under their dubious commander the strength and morale of the English soldiers noticeably waned, and it was small wonder that Don Pedro de Zúñiga, the Spanish ambassador in England, opined that Arundell was serving English (or indirectly Dutch) interests.

By his phenomenal, unremitting attention to detail, his tact stiffened by flashes of steel, his *sagesse*, Robert Cecil achieved and maintained a position of remarkable pre-eminence that lasted until his death. The loss of conciliar papers for the period 1602–13 in a fire may also contribute to a focusing on him which does not do justice to his colleagues, but in any event his mastery of so many aspects of government was prodigious. He noted wryly in a letter to Puckering that the world did not always speak highly of him behind his back, and according to a recent historian he had an 'unrivalled capacity' for making enemies.[14] Just what they might be willing to do and to risk was evidenced in one of the most notorious treason plots in English history.

❧ 12 ❧

The 'Gunpowder Plot' or 'Powder Treason' has been obscured by the very things now used annually to mark the occasion – fireworks and bonfires. They flare ephemerally and then leave us in the dark about an episode that sprang from economic, social, political and theological strands that intertwined in a potentially devastating way. All the significant plotters, apart from servants swept up by the cause and three peripheral and unfortunate Jesuits, were country gentlemen like Robert Winter of Huddington, Worcestershire, 'mostly of moderate means and limited prospects'.[1] They had grown up in an atmosphere of suspicion, hatred and deprivation, seeing their Catholic fathers, uncles and brothers ground down by the anti-Catholic policies of first Burghley and then Robert Cecil. Conspiracies became the only political activity for those squeezed to the margins of late-sixteenth- and early-seventeenth-century England. Focusing their hatred on the Cecils was easier than admitting that the Queen, to whom they claimed to be loyal, allowed the policies that ruined the prospects (and estates) of Catholic landowning families. The fines on Catholics for refusing the communion of the Protestant majority were introduced in 1559, at first at the rate of one shilling a week. In 1581 this was raised to £20 a lunar month, and by 1603 there were only sixteen recusant families whose estates could meet this burden. Sir Thomas Tresham was one such and between 1581 and 1605 he was forced to pay out £8,000.[2] Those who failed to meet the financial exactions were subject to partial seizure of lands and to imprisonment. There were also other laws that placed the Catholic worshipper on the margins of English society – death for sheltering a priest; exclusion from public offices and the two universities. Hence they were 'an alienated minority' in what was slowly becoming a spiritually pluralist country, with even an intriguing tiny undercurrent of bold indifference to religion itself.

However pressing the economic disadvantage of being a Catholic, that was not the crucial reason for an act that by James's bristling calculation (always arithmetically inept) would have killed a total of thirty thousand, including himself, Queen Anne, his chief ministers, lords, judges and so on. His dismay and rage at being included is understandable when seen in the light of Stuart policy towards Catholics, first in Scotland and then in England. James VI was a Protestant king with *politique* impulses who to avoid imposing unnecessary suffering had protected Catholic nobles, with only spasmodic enforcement of conformity. One of the beneficiaries, at least until the later half of the 1590s, was the favourite George Gordon, Earl of Huntly, who conformed only under pressure from the Kirk in 1597 and was rewarded by a seat on the Scottish Privy Council in 1599. There was nothing like Elizabethan persecution and, it must be said, nothing like pure toleration either.[3] By avoiding the use of the death penalty James had given an impression that was to mislead English Catholics in a most melancholy way. He contrived the same for continental Catholics, including Pope Clement VIII.

To his Secretary James communicated his detestation of extremism: 'I will never allow in my conscience that the blood of any man shall be shed for diversity of opinions in religion.'[4] He wanted, therefore, the priests exiled 'so they may freely glut themselves upon their imagined gods', while he held their church to be 'our mother church, although clogged with many infirmities and corruptions'. This opacity in his attitude confused many on both sides of the ecumenical divide. As far as Catholic laymen were concerned, 'no compromise was possible'; indeed, the plotters never had any hopes of accommodation with James or his government in England: 'Their hope was for a Catholic England . and it always had been.'[5]

Cecil aspired to shackle the political aspirations of the divided Catholics, while allowing an elderly popish laity to worship privately, and he dealt compassionately with François Tregian, a Catholic prisoner. The new priests trained in continental seminaries who lured the young into recusancy had to be blocked, but for a time after James's succession it is immediately noticeable that the fines for recusancy fell.[6] Nor were the Catholics themselves tightly homogeneous. The pre-succession dilemma had led to a sustained division in the community following on from the Archpriest Controversy of 1598. The Appellants bitterly resented the appointment of George Blackwell, with his suspicious Jesuit and hence Spanish taint, as archpriest; and they took a huge risk in their unfolding clandestine negotiations with Cecil and Richard Bancroft, Bishop of London until his translation to Canterbury in 1604. The Appellants believed 'that the Jesuits, and those who shared their opinions, had no use for toleration given by the tainted hands of the heretics'.[7] In this they were correct, but the Jesuits themselves preferred huffing and puffing to blowing the House down (that is, up) – this activity they left to Robert Catesby and company, who were utterly dismissive of the freedom from persecution that James and Cecil had contrived, despite heavy pressure from Protestant clergy and laity.

Catesby and his fellow-conspirators had the unfathomable passion of all idealists clinging to a single violent notion; they planned an action of absolute defiance of the State. Their intention was simply that England should again be ruled by an English Catholic monarch, and history alone was not enough to dissuade them. That meant either the nine-year-old Princess Elizabeth – though they may have recoiled from the name – or, more auspiciously, Princess Mary, a mere baby of seven months. To achieve this meant a monstrous act of blood-letting by the English for the English. Neither the Archdukes nor Philip III of Spain were interested; they wanted peace and that had been achieved in 1604, so the hope nurtured over many years of Spanish assistance withered, and in so doing it left room for the emergence of a dire, defiant xenophobia, a hatred of the Scots whom it was this king's unparalleled inclination to pet and indulge. Spain may have been the enemy for fifty years, but loathing of the Scots had a far longer tradition.[8] James had, of course, fanned it into life by his singular enthusiasm for union, which had taken up so much time and produced so much rhetoric in the 1604 Parliament. Yet for all their compressed rage, all the conspirators were likely to achieve was the removal of James and his replacement by a female child. Clearly these men were not politicians of any calibre, and it was their supreme misfortune to prepare such a preposterous *coup* under the relentless scrutiny of Robert Cecil, a consummate politician to the ends of his long fingers, with a feline instinct for power over lesser creatures.

In the period after the Bye Plot Cecil had given deep thought to the Catholic threat, and late in 1604 or early the following year he seems to have devised a strategy of allowing the Catholic activists, who were constantly watched by his agents, just enough room to be consistent with safety for the inception and development of another plot. Actually, years later, the informer William Udall claimed in a letter to Sir Julius Caesar that he had told Salisbury of the plot months earlier and the earl had treated it as a joke until only a month before the intended blast. Perhaps he did, because he had long mistrusted Udall and his instability. He was also able to adopt this high-risk position because of the information he received from Lord Monteagle. By 1605 the latter was recovering some of the trust he had lost for his allegiance to Essex. His estates, like those of the Earl of Southampton, had been restored to him and in this year Cecil was supporting him in a lawsuit against the Earl of Hertford.[9] A curious rider to this is found in the story told by the poet John Donne, who said that Cecil (now Earl of Salisbury) actually challenged Hertford to a duel. Another ambivalent, strained figure was Monteagle's brother-in-law, Francis Tresham, enmeshed at the heart of the operation by the plotters. Cecil himself intended a number of things to come out of their defeat. He wanted to make his position on the Privy Council as James's leading minister impregnable; he wanted to crush Jesuit activity in England; and thirdly he aimed to sweep from power the Earl of Northumberland, who had despised him for many years. As a Percy he could flourish the multiple divisions on his eschutcheon, sneering at the modest Cecil ancestry. Indeed, he claimed on one occasion that if Percy blood and Cecil blood were poured together into a bowl, the former would decline to mingle with the latter.

The attempted *coup*, with its large projected and premeditated loss of life, was given its final momentum on 26 October 1605, after months of preliminary work and preparation by the charismatic Catesby. Monteagle was eating dinner at his house in Hoxton when he was handed the infamous anonymous note which in broad terms warned him to stay away from the opening of Parliament. This has generally been credited to a clumsy effort by Francis Tresham, whose father Sir Thomas also owned a Hoxton property. But since Monteagle knew of the plotters' activities it seems very likely that the note was concocted by Salisbury and written at his command by Thomas Phelippes, spy, forger and cryptographer. Salisbury knew his talents very well, and knew also that Phelippes was desperately keen to ingratiate himself again. In 1597, when Customer of the Petty Customs at the Port of London, he defaulted on payments to the Crown of over £11,000.[10] He had then been briefly imprisoned and his estates temporarily forfeited. Despite this perturbing dip in his fortunes he still deciphered letters and gathered information on exiled Catholics. To do this he had invented a recusant persona (Vincent) who corresponded with Hugh Owen (named as Benson). He continued this after the accession of James, and Cecil was so suspicious that Phelippes ended up in the Gatehouse. The point was not that the infamous note was meant to persuade the plotters to give up at the suggestion of Monteagle, as it appears superficially. It was concocted as tangible evidence to show James to avoid a hysterical accusation that he had been using him as bait. Salisbury gambled that nothing would deflect the seditionists – and he was right.

The government charade of bogus mystification at the meaning of the letter was maintained for James's return from hunting at Royston. When shown it he divined its meaning and on 4 November a search of the cellar extending beneath the then Parliament building revealed only the lurking presence of John Johnson (actually Guido or Guy Fawkes, a sometime professional soldier from a minor gentry family of Yorkshire), a heap of coal and kindling. The second search that night by Sir Thomas Knyvett achieved rather more, since it revealed the hidden gunpowder in a quantity that would have had a devastating effect once fired.* Presumably Salisbury wanted James to have the unique pleasure mixed with horror of uncovering the means intended for his demise. Fawkes was arrested and the following day Catesby and his cohort fled, intending to raise the country Catholics. In this, as in everything else, they failed totally and on 8 November, at Holbeche in Staffordshire, Catesby, the Wright brothers and Thomas Percy were killed, with Rokewood wounded and taken prisoner by the sheriff. Anyone even remotely suspected was rounded up by the government which, 'acting on the principle of assuming guilt until innocence was proved', achieved a memorable and crushing reverse of anti-government forces.[11] Even someone as insignificant as Shakespeare's daughter Susanna was regarded with a baleful eye for failing to appear at communion.

A somewhat rancid suspicion has since convicted Salisbury of shoddy, even shocking, dealings in the whole affair: 'Guy Fawkes was on trial for one day; the Earl of Salisbury has been on trial for three and a half centuries.'[12] True, but even after rejecting the notion that the conspiracy was a malignant fabrication by him, there is no doubting that the plot existed and its purpose was murderous. Certainly the Venetian ambassador Niccolò Molin had no hesitation in describing it as

* According to Salisbury, 'two hogshead and 32 small barrels'.

such in his reports, while Sir Henry Wotton once pointedly and knowingly declared that Salisbury created plots, as he thrived on uncovering them. Wotton's imagination did occasionally overheat and there is no evidence that Salisbury fomented the initial plan for regicide – the notion is quite grotesque, since he had worked so hard for the succession. However, once the preliminaries had been discovered there is every reason to think that he allowed the plot to develop, because it was immensely and unmistakably to his advantage. He drove it home to the hilt and the following Parliament 'laid such a foundation of good laws against Papists as might serve for a bulwark in the time to come'.[13] His responsibility for the huge propaganda advantage that accrued to the government was certainly understood by his enemies, one of whom is supposed to have hurled into the courtyard of Salisbury House on 4 December an anonymous threatening letter marking Salisbury down for assassination. But even this note is suspect, regarded as a piece of 'black propaganda' if indeed it ever existed. It has never been seen; does not exist now in his papers; and at the time voices were whispering that it was bogus.[14]

Even so, while his enemies fulminated, Salisbury developed the government policy of punishing state enemies. It was on his order that Sir Everard Digby and three others were hideously mutilated, then executed, in the churchyard of St Paul's.[15] This led to a protest that he noted and later executions were moved to secular ground. But at the time his greatest challenge was to link the Jesuits incontrovertibly with the plot, for although Fathers Garnet, Gerard and Tesimond did have foreknowledge of some vicious exploit, they had partially protected themselves (or so Catesby thought) by receiving information through confession; moreover, they still had to be captured. As it happened, Gerard and Tesimond, who had been at school with Fawkes in York, eluded Salisbury's agents and eventually fled to the Continent – Tesimond in a boat to Calais which was carrying pig carcasses. Garnet, however, was trapped several months after the storming of Holbeche at Hindlip Hall, the Worcestershire home of another brother-in-law of Monteagle, Thomas Abingdon, involved twenty years before in the Babington Plot. The famous twelve-day search of the property was undertaken by Sir Henry Bromley on the precise written instructions of Salisbury, with information so clear that the minister must have had an informer. He had never been there himself, but Monteagle had a more detailed knowledge of the formidable warren of hidden passages and angled tiny rooms that had been created by an inventive joiner.

Bromley himself knew the house from previous searches but would surely have failed again if the search instructions had not come from an expert source like Monteagle. As it was, with men and patience Bromley trapped his quarry, Nicholas Owen and Ralph Ashley, and then Garnet and Father Oldcorne lurched out of their hiding place on the eve of the execution of other conspirators. The rest and recuperation allowed them at Bromley's home was too generous to be anything other than a stalling tactic, for they were brought to the Tower only after the execution of those able to testify to their innocence. There Garnet injudiciously allowed himself to talk through a wall to his erstwhile companion while hidden listeners took notes. These were finally used to elicit from him an admission that he had more than an inkling of Catesby's intentions. Little more than this was needed at his trial, and the jury found him guilty very quickly. On 3 May Garnet was executed.

Salisbury's own defence of his annihilation of the traitors was *An Answere to Certaine scandalous Papers . . .*, which appeared with the speed of a topical Penguin Special today. This was published in January 1606; a Latin edition was produced for distribution in Europe; and since Salisbury was besieged by the requirements of his office it seems likely that it was drafted with the aid of Ben Jonson, who had already been Catholic-watching.[16] The shock of the whole affair to the King and the government was almost palpable, and as Molin wrote, the ordinary citizens were encouraged in their hatred of papists by those in high places whose principal fear seems to have been of the Jesuits. James, a selective coward for all his headlong pursuit of birds and beasts, was goaded into one of his periodic spasms against Catholics which actually went against the grain of his lurking instinct for moderation. Early in 1606, when the Parliament intended for demolition met, there was a prompt consideration of new statutes to govern policy towards priests and recusants, with Salisbury speaking in the debates and conferences. For the first time the ecclesiastical obligation of receiving the sacrament at Easter was enforced by law under pain of fines rising from £20 to £60 a year. The object was to penalize 'persons popishly affected' who nevertheless chose to go to church occasionally to maintain a façade and thus escape the penalty of the laws.

Salisbury also artfully planted a request for money at a time of morbid reflection. In a display of loyalty that actually reached to their pockets the Commons voted three subsidies and six fifteenths. By the summer, when Parliament rose, the new penal code was in place. It coincided with a heightened suspicion of the Papacy for the excommunication of the Venetian Republic. To Sir Henry Wotton, English ambassador to the Serenissima, Salisbury wrote that the provisions of the new statutes were not really new laws but 'rather explanations and directions for the better execution of former laws'. The cleansing of the realm continued with the proclamation of 10 July that ordered out of the country before 1 August all 'Jesuits, seminaries, friars, or any other priests whatsoever, regular or secular, being made by the authority of the church of Rome . . .' – nearly fifty priests held in prison were expelled abroad. Even this comparatively mild form of control was not always enforced against laymen, nor was it a policy that could be uniformly imposed across the country. So by late 1607 Zorzi Giustinian, Molin's successor, observed considerable laxity, and the following year the Bishop of Chester was told by the Council that it was the King's wish that recusants should be treated moderately. Since it has been established that during the entire reign only twenty-seven executions had a religious cause, moderation was the predominating instinct.[17] Occasionally in crisis this would be veiled so that in 1610, for example, enforcement was more rigorous. It tended to happen as well during sessions of Parliament, a political phenomenon that did not escape the attention of the new Spanish ambassador, Don Alonso de Velasco.

As might be expected, the Gunpowder Plot led to an English probing of foreign relations. Salisbury knew of (and played down) the Spanish contacts of some of the plotters, so one of the critical questions to be broached after the episode was whether any European ruler had had a hand in it. To sift the evidence he employed Levinus Munck, one of his devoted secretaries, who in spring 1606 reported that there was no proof of any foreign involvement.[18] Even so, there was something shifty about the Spanish and the Duke of Lerma resurrected the favourite diplomatic ploy of a marriage between the thoroughly Protestant-inclined Prince Henry (an admirer of Essex and Ralegh) and the Infanta, with at least some part of the Spanish Netherlands as a dowry.[19] This never advanced very far, and only Sir Charles Cornwallis, whose communications from Spain Salisbury showed to Zúñiga over many months, seems to have been fitfully enthusiastic. In fact the notion underlined in English minds how brittle was the so-called independence of the Archdukes, whose territories would revert to Spain if they remained childless (as they did).

English relations with Albrecht and Isabella were certainly more friendly than those with Spain. The Archduke wanted to increase trade with England, but there were hitches and jolts. Principally these were Dutch-ignited, for they maintained their long-established pragmatic policy of war and also covert trade. The blockade on Flemish ports continued and so interfered with English traders that Winwood was sure it would lead to a rupture. None of the plans to alleviate this tangle came to anything so trade went on, with English merchants taking risks and putting up a barrage of complaints when their business was snarled by seizure.[20]

Anglo-Flemish relations were also subject to irritations

stemming from the spying activities of both sides. There was a tang of powder, as far as the English government was concerned, about Father William Baldwin and Hugh Owen. The latter was a well-regarded servant of the Archdukes who helped to organize a counter-intelligence network and seems to have thoroughly discountenanced Salisbury in so doing. One of the latter's best conduits for information from the Spanish Netherlands was Dr William Gifford, since 1595 Dean of St Peter's in Lille.[21] In June 1606, when ordered out of the Archdukes' territory, he wrote to Sir Thomas Edmondes, ambassador in Brussels and a noted enemy of Rome, that Owen and Baldwin had laid information against him. Edmondes forwarded this letter to Salisbury and eventually money was sent to Gifford via Charles Paget, another Catholic with government links. It is worth mentioning that Salisbury also obtained information from the Papal Nuncio's secretary, Jean Xandre. His duplicity was reported to the Archduke in April 1606 by his young ambassador in London, Conrad Schetz de Grobbendonck, Baron Hoboken.[22]

Salisbury now decided to mount a campaign against Owen, long a detested adversary. Born in Plas Du in Caernarvonshire, he had been secretary to Henry, Earl of Arundel, and he fled from England in 1571 when the Ridolphi Plot was uncovered. Edmondes was ordered to seek his capture and extradition, but the Archduke would allow only a mild house arrest. Owen's response was to send an appeal to the Spanish Council of State.[23] Unable to produce the required documentary proof of his assertions, Salisbury was irked by the freedom then accorded Owen by the Archduke, with strong support from Philip III. He was allowed to travel to Madrid, returning to Brussels in 1607 with an enhanced pension.[24] If Albrecht had been free to choose, Owen and Baldwin would probably both have been bundled across the sea. As it was, the latter was eventually apprehended in Düsseldorf in 1610 and on being returned to London he was imprisoned until 1618. Then Sir Henry Wotton tried to secure an exchange of Baldwin for Molle, the tutor of Lord Roos, a prisoner of the

Roman Inquisition. He failed and the unfortunate Molle was incarcerated for thirty years, dying when he was nearly eighty-one. English antipathy to Rome was not entirely un-merited.

⤳ 13 ⤳

Elizabeth Cecil died in January 1597 and was buried with some splendour in Westminster Abbey. Three pall-bearers can be named: Sir Thomas Gorges, Sir Edward Dyer and Sir George Carew. After her death Cecil's sorrow precluded for some time any *vie intime*. He lamented her passing deeply and at a meeting with his brother-in-law, who succeeded to his father's title in March that year, both men were so stricken that they found it hard to speak. Even if the story of Cecil's hair turning silver overnight is discounted as apocryphal, he rapidly allowed himself to become a grave old man in middle age with fewer and fewer opportunities for diversions other than cards. In August 1599, for example, he was thoroughly tired and wanted to quit London for a restorative break at Theobalds, but there was some doubt about him getting permission, for 'he cannot be spared'.[1] Having quickly excluded the possibility of remarriage, a very unusual position for a man of his eminence, he had to find a way of raising a young family as a single parent just after receiving his official designation as Secretary of State. He managed it by transferring his children to servants, and by allowing them lengthy visits to relatives and friends. His heir, William, who in 1593 had had a worrying bout of chickenpox, spent his summers on a kind of infant progress, away from the many health hazards of the city. Nor did his father flinch at letting him stay with Catholic sympathizers. In September 1601 the boy went to stay with the Lumleys, who declared him to be a 'sweet' child.

Lord Lumley, a founder member of the Elizabethan Society of Antiquaries, was also a famous bibliophile, and Cecil may have hoped (albeit in vain) that some of this bookishness might cling to William, making him better company for his father, who adored books, during the winter months they spent together.

Frances Cecil, whose wet-nurse in 1593 had caused an uproar at Theobalds because of her infatuation for a young man, was later sent to stay with her widowed aunt, Lady Stourton. Evidently the genetic flaw in the Cookes was transmitted to the girl, for her deformity was subjected to treatment with various implements by one Hugh Baylye before she was presented at court. Cecil himself was acutely aware of the hurtful looks and spiteful comments that attended any physical imperfection. Fortunately the treatment seems to have been successful and in October 1599 Baylye wrote requesting his agreed fee of £100.[2] Although negotiations for her marriage to Lord Harington's son failed, she eventually married Lord Henry Clifford in 1610 and was able to dance at her wedding. Catherine, whose birth caused such travails, virtually disappears from view, although it is possible that she was still alive in 1612.

Naturally a great deal of attention was paid to William Cecil's education. When he was staying at Sherborne with his adored surrogate uncle Walter Ralegh, he may have spent time at nearby Sherborne School, refounded in 1550 by Edward VI. But his learning was principally guided by tutors who faced the additional strain of being employed by a demanding father. Cecil may well have intended to employ Aurelian Townshend in that difficult position. He sent him to Paris and then to Italy, where the young man had the misfortune to stumble into the company of Sir Anthony Sherley, lending him 200 scudi of his patron's money. This error of judgement led to a summons home, and although accident and illness delayed him in Paris, from where he appealed for funds, Townshend was paid for acting as a courier and then ignored. Cecil wanted his son to be taught by men who made impeccable choices.

At eleven William, who clearly preferred horses to books, was sent to St John's College, Cambridge. The boy took every opportunity to visit James I at Royston, presenting his compliments to the King like a seasoned courtier and then joining the hunt. Cecil could hardly rage when his dullard heir became a close friend of Prince Henry and an inseparable companion of the 3rd Earl of Essex. In 1606 William and his tutor of the moment, Edmond Casse, were with the Devereux brothers at Drayton Bassett in Staffordshire. This was the country home of Lettice Knollys, famous widow of the Earl of Leicester and a clutch of other men. Her daughter, Lady Penelope Rich, was as spirited as the old lady, and now maintained an amicable relationship with Salisbury. She wrote charmingly to him of William's close friendship with her nephews, remarking too that she thought her mother would grow young in their cheerful company.[3]

The effects of William Cecil's addiction to equine pursuits became obvious in his intellectual progress, especially when he inveigled his tutor into hunting with him. Cecil's hilarious requirement was that tutor and student should use Latin for daily discourse, even during the chase. Allegedly this was tried but proved useless. Soon after the admission that the barking of hounds obliterated all attempts at conversation in the antique tongue, the exasperated father banned his son's hunting and even forbade him to keep a hound as a pet.[4] There was a nagging rebuke for the boy on a simple matter like folding a letter: 'I have also sent you a piece of paper folded as a gentleman use . . . whereas yours are like those that come out of a grammar school.'[5] By 1607 Salisbury had to admit that his son took after his mother and was without any intellectual distinction – it was useless to keep him at Cambridge. He wrote with some acerbity to a tutor:

He cannot speak six words in Latin, out of which language I did expect you and he would not seldom have discoursed. In any part of story without book he is not able to show memory of four lines, neither is his manner of repeating anything like to those whom tutors teach to speak distinct and ornate. For his logic, a month would beget more knowledge than he hath, in one of no greater capacity. If you say his mind had affected other pleasant studies, either the mathematics, languages, or that he hath given himself to music, or any other gentleman-like quality, then I must answer you that I find no such thing. So as I conclude that either the fault is in my suffering him to be out of the University, or in your neglecting him in the University.[6]

His disappointment and exasperation were principally with those who tutored William, whose future was again a cause of reflection. It was now decided that he had to go abroad on a grand tour for truly indispensable polishing, but bearing in mind the jolts caused by Thomas Cecil so many years before, a prophylactic marriage was first necessary. In December 1608 Viscount Cranborne was married to Lady Catherine Howard, a daughter of the Earl of Suffolk, whose other daughter, the notorious Frances, was married to the young Earl of Essex. Like him Cranborne was promptly separated from his bride – this actually mattered little, since the union lasted for sixty years. Salisbury wrote ingratiatingly to Prince Henry: 'For your servant Cranborn [sic] I humbly thank your Highness for your present grace and future promises . . . I have made hold to take him from Juno and to commend him yesterday to Neptune. . . .' To the young husband he wrote mildly: 'However you may find in this letter plain-ness, and fatherly admonition, you may promise yourself that all proceeds from care and love . . . for if I may know anything you desire or want for your ease and comfort while you are abroad, be not afraid to ask it of your loving father, that prays to God to bless you.'[7] Salisbury clearly meant what he said, for the young hope of the dynasty travelled with a personal brewer, to avoid the torment of being without potable ales; several servants; Dr (later Sir) Matthew Lister; and John Finet, who in 1606 had translated from French a text with the resonant title 'The Beginning, Continuance, and Decay of Estates', and who eventually became one of Salisbury's secretaries.[8]

In spring 1610 the party was joined in France by another Salisbury employee, Robert Kirkham. Even so William Cecil did decide to ask his father for John Lanier's accomplished son Nicholas to be sent over. A singer, flautist and viol-player, this young musician was to be employed in teaching Cecil the viol during hot summer afternoons in Italy. However, this time the Lord Treasurer did not respond, most probably because he wanted soothing melodies himself during the tussles for the Great Contract which began early in the year.* In fact Cranborne might have been better advised to apply himself to his Italian studies, for when he and Lord Henry Howard, his brother-in-law, were in Venice to meet the Doge, they remained gauchely silent at the interview and Sir Henry Wotton, as was his wont, did all the talking for them. Later the Venetian terra firma gave the young aristocrat an unpleasant time, for in December 1610 he fell ill in Padua and Lister wrote to Sir Dudley Carleton that staying or removing entailed some hazard. This would have caused Wotton some palpitations, for in January 1608 Sir Julius Caesar's son, also Julius, had died in the town. The circumstances were, however, different, since he had been killed in an affray, and fortunately Cecil recovered so that his party could set out for England in February 1611.[9]

Salisbury's reluctance to part with Lanier confirms his deep attachment to music. This may have developed early, without any particular encouragement from Burghley, and the conventional view is that the older Cecil simply had no interest or liking for it. If this is correct it would be very singular, since even Walsingham had true musical tastes. The composer and organist John Bull, for example, had dealings with the Secretary of State, whose mansion at Barn Elms saw many convivial family and musical evenings. Thomas Cecil was schooled in the lute and virginal, so why not the latter instrument for Robert Cecil, who might also, it has been suggested,

* Although *a* Nicholas Lanier was paid £13. 6*s*. 8*d*. in March 1610 for carrying letters to Paris.

have played the Irish harp.[10] It is possible that as early as 1591, while he was toiling to build his court career so long inhibited by paternal discipline and Leicestrian resistance, he had in his employ an instrumentalist, Christopher Heybourne, who was probably required to train apprentice singers and instrumentalists.

In the mid-1590s several young performers joined Cecil's household. Three boys who played and sang came from Lord Burgh's household, as well as one Daniel who had formerly been in his employ. The soldier Burgh was actually much more willing to oblige Cecil than Richard Champernowne of Modbury Castle near Plymouth. He was especially incensed by the salty quip, quoted by Sir Francis Drake, that he was 'a gelder of boys for preserving their voices'. In December 1598 Cecil had a letter from Sir Percival Hart saying that the musician Henry Phillips had returned from a foray to the Low Countries and wanted a place in Hart's household. He was inclined to accept him 'for the satisfying of my own desire unto music', but delayed until he knew if Cecil himself wanted to take him on. What he did not know at the time was that Phillips had actually absconded from Cecil's employ without leave, and Hart would have sent him to London when this was revealed but for the fact that he was ill – possibly with anxiety.[11] As it was, Cecil's musical establishment, amounting to a little conservatoire, was strongest after 1603. The principal consideration was always excellence – so, for example, Innocent Lanier (who also played in the royal wind band) was paid £20 a year to tutor George Mason in voice, viol and lute. He wanted more and got it in June 1608 with a payment of some £6.[12] His place was then taken by John Cooper (that is, Giovanni Coperario), composer, musician and teacher, who received significant patronage from the earl while freelancing. In December 1609, as a token of appreciation, Salisbury gave Coperario £20.[13] Mason eventually became a court musician, as did many of those mentioned in the Cecil archive.

One of these was Cormac MacDermott (Dermode), a sighted, literate Irish harper. The earliest of the documents at

Hatfield concerning him is a petition to Cecil in December 1600 asking for a not very significant wardship of the heir of John Bysse, a Somerset yeoman.[14] From a further petition several years later it was granted, but the income was too modest. He sought to supplement it with the grant of a 'bailiwick', the office of bailiff to a village or small town, and he received Cranfield in Bedfordshire.[15] By that time he had become a part-time royal musician and was also acting as a messenger to Ireland for Cecil, who aptly named it 'land of ire'. In February 1603 he brought letters from the English headquarters in Cork to London and was paid £8 by Cecil for expenses.[16] At the end of 1604 he was back in his home country with a letter from Cecil to the Lord President of Connaught, and when he returned to London with the Earl of Clanrickarde's letters to Cecil he was again paid £8.[17] The earl was a follower of Cecil, though his wife was Frances Walsingham, relict of Sidney and Essex.[18]

MacDermott was a composer of court music, so it is unlikely that Cecil heard much of the traditional repertoire for the Irish harp. The instrument the harpist repaired for Salisbury in 1607 was almost certainly the one given to his employer a decade previously (September 1597) by the Countess of Desmond. Her intention, surely on the famous biblical precedent, was for the music of the harp to relieve Cecil's melancholy following his wife's death. Another man with a liking for what became a fashionable instrument was Sir Michael Hickes, who acquired one in 1604, and years later friends of his were searching for another.[19] The pleasure taken in the Irish harp is somewhat curious, since the men who introduced it into the grander reaches of English society were scathingly contemptuous of everything Hibernian. However, they seem to have been seduced by the long resonance of the thick brass strings.[20] The Queen, of course, played the lute, but seems to have been given a harp specially designed by the Irish recusant scholar William Bathe, who is also credited with instructing her in mnemonics.

As for MacDermott, he joined the King's Musick in 1605

and continued to play for Salisbury. Indeed, his music-making was so esteemed that when the earl travelled in his last days to Bath to seek relief for his plethora of ailments, MacDermott joined the entourage. At the earl's death the harpist was paid a fee of £10, and another payment of the same amount was made for the purchase of a harp. He continued to live close to Salisbury House for another six years.

Among other instrument dealers and makers for Salisbury to call upon were John Haan, a Dutch merchant who also traded in organs, and Thomas Dallam, of the family of organ makers. Originally from Lancashire, Dallam was one of the few masters of his craft left in London because of growing Puritan disparagement of the instrument. Salisbury knew of his skills because the organ-clock eventually sent by Elizabeth to Sultan Mehmed III to mark his accession had been the result of a collaboration. Randolph Bull supplied the clock-work, and the instrument was built by Dallam. Of great size – perhaps sixteen feet high – with striking jewelled decoration, it was ready by late 1598 and was viewed and approved by the Queen and Cecil. Then it was decided to send Dallam and some of his workers to Constantinople to rectify any flaws that appeared in the instrument during its long sea voyage, when heat, moisture and motion would assail it. One of those who went with Dallam was the energetic Rowland Buckett, a painter and interior decorator later variously employed by Cecil, most notably at Hatfield.

At first it seems extraordinary that Salisbury, a widower with a small absentee family, should embark on the hugely expensive building of a prodigy (or power) house. It stemmed from the presentation of Theobalds in 1607 to a nakedly covetous James. Entertaining the royal family and court was a heart-sinking expense, but for someone like Salisbury there was no escape from the duty. One of the most notorious of these occasions was in late July 1606, recorded by Sir John Harington with an unsparing and delicious acerbity. James, Queen Anne, Prince Henry and the court all descended on

Salisbury in order to entertain over four days the Queen's brother, King Christian IV of Denmark. The visit did have a private purpose since it was meant to dispel Anne's severe depression following the birth and death of yet another baby, Princess Sophia, whose tomb was commissioned by Salisbury from Maximilien Colt. The Danish King was a man with a gloom-dissipating sense of humour – so robust, as it proved, that he inflamed the temper of the Earl of Notthingham's young wife by impugning her virtue, compounding this by the gesture of horns which suggested that the old Lord Admiral was a cuckold. The overseas guest himself had a large appetite for women, food and drink, and the decline of the masque devised by Ben Jonson and Inigo Jones into a Bacchic rout rather than the eulogy intended has focused attention on this. Yet Christian had more in common with his host than Harington's withering description suggests. Well educated and a great lover of music, he drew to Denmark singers and instrumentalists from all over Europe.[21] His court musicians included at various times the viol-player Daniel Norcombe, who later moved to Brussels; John Dowland, the greatest northern European lutenist of his day; and Thomas Cutting, so greatly missed by Lady Arabella Stuart when he went abroad.

Until 1605, when a tiny measure of fiscal realism flared briefly in James, he had spoken of rebuilding ruined Ampthill in Bedfordshire. When this was put aside the pressure on Salisbury to hand over Theobalds for Hatfield became irresistible. It may be that he was not overwhelmingly dismayed despite his filial piety. The earl's proposal, when it was made, was eagerly taken up. On 15 April, before the deed of conveyance to exchange the two estates was signed, Salisbury wrote to Sir Thomas Lake: 'I must confess to you that I have borrowed one day's retreat from London, whither I am now returning this morning, having looked upon Hatfield also, where it pleased my Lord Chamberlain, my Lord of Worcester, and my Lord of Southampton to be contented to take the pains to view upon what part of the ground I should place my habitation.' No notion here that the old royal palace of the Bishops of Ely at Hatfield, which, with seventeen other manors, passed to him, should be expanded or simply renovated.

On 22 May, in the great gallery at Theobalds, an entertainment was given to mark the transfer of the property to royal ownership. *The Genius*, again by Jonson and his collaborator, Jones (whom he cheerfully pilloried as 'Ninny-go'), had a text that expressed some of the lingering reluctance that Salisbury affected as he parted with the grandest item of his patrimony. To measure up to it in every respect the building at Hatfield had to be on a grand scale, a monumental statement of his position in brick, wood and stone. Moreover, since the Howard clan were builders and improvers on a large scale, the King's leading minister could not allow his prestige to fall athwart of theirs. There was also perhaps an unspoken, even unacknowledged rivalry with his half-brother Burghley, the builder of Wimbledon with its glamorous Italianate garden.

Simon Basil and Montagu (Mountain) Jennings also visited the site at some time between April and August when clearing and digging began. Comments on the architect have therefore sometimes expressed surprise that Basil was not chosen as the principal designer for the grand new house. The commission was given instead to Robert Liming (or Lyminge), a carpenter who steps thereby from obscurity to semi-obscurity. However, the fact that he is known to have been employed at Theobalds may genuinely suggest why he was preferred to other more prominent figures known to Salisbury, who would have been equally guided by their employer's wishes. Thoroughly familiar with Theobalds, he was required to emulate it and Hatfield became a homage not simply to Elizabeth through its vaguely 'E' form, but also to Burghley, whose passion for building has been noted. Nor was there anything particularly unusual about such a commission going to a carpenter – Hill Hall at Theydon Mount had been designed by Sir Thomas Smith with the advice of the London carpenter Richard Kirby. It was to happen again soon when Francis Carter became the principal architect to the executors of Thomas

170

Sutton's will for the alterations begun in 1613 to the Charterhouse in London. Liming and Carter were further alike in that they both used routine classical ornament as employed in the Low Countries: 'strapwork, cartouches, banded and tapered pilasters, masks, jewels and so on . . .'.[22]

What became a huge building operation, usefully employing skilled and unskilled men, was bound to stutter sometimes in its deployment of resources. This is especially true during the early years of building, when Hatfield was only one of four sites competing for finance. By spring 1609 the awesome cost was beginning to terrorize Salisbury's closest advisers, and even his own confidence was shaken. But after intense consideration tedious plans for retrenchment were put aside, and the tempo of the work picked up again. Credit for the general efficiency with which the site was supplied with all its many wants must go to the indefatigable Thomas Wilson, so that only once did Liming pen a complaint about the shortage of materials. This was in autumn 1610 when more stone was needed for the south front, a part of the building that has long fascinated architectural historians. Conjecture (perhaps wishful thinking) has fathered it on Inigo Jones, who did ride to Hatfield with Wilson, and a payment to Jones of £10 noted in the accounts of Roger Houghton, Salisbury's Receiver-General, teasingly notes that it was 'for drawing of some architecture'. The clock-tower (damaged by fire in the summer of 1988) is also hesitantly attributed to him.

Interior decoration was sufficiently advanced to allow a royal visit in July 1611, shortly after Salisbury's stay from 10 to 14 May. Homage to James is evident in the statue of the King by Colt placed in a large half-domed niche above the fireplace in what is now the King James drawing-room. Carved from Caen stone (still imported today), it was painted to look like copper, but has since darkened to match the columns of the fireplace. The shafts of these, Doric below and Corinthian above, were of tuche, a black slate that also matched the horizontal panels. In another fireplace in what is now the library, Salisbury was commemorated in a fine mosaic portrait. In it he is wearing his robes for a Knight of the Order of the Garter, which he had joined in May 1606. Unusually, the image shows him wearing a sword when the conventional props for his portrait were his wand of office and the silver bell acquired with such a precise effort twenty years before the oil portrait on which the mosaic was based.

The painter was John de Critz, brother-in-law of Colt, whose bill for his work was £4. The picture, one of four routine copies, was sent to the English ambassador in Venice, Sir Henry Wotton, who commissioned Venetian mosaic workers to produce the copy. In April 1609 he wrote from Venice that the finished work was ready and, regarded as a present for Cranborne, it was put on a ship called the *Thomas* which sailed out of London. Captain Edmund Gardiner sailed with his cargo almost immediately, despite a local difficulty with the Venetians about trading regulations, which Wotton smoothed away. When it reached London it was presumably stored in Salisbury's yard and warehouse depot in Redcross Street in the parish of St Giles, Cripplegate, and was installed at Hatfield in 1611. Writing of the mosaic, Wotton recalled the workman's 'special suite and remembrance that it may be set in his true light and at a little more height for the eye than a coloured picture would require'.

Wotton had a true appreciation of Italian late Renaissance painting as well. As an enthusiastic connoisseur he was able to buy pictures for Salisbury, though there was an element of risk in this because Italian art was far in advance of the native (and even immigrant) work. Thus in 1608, when Wotton sent several works from Venice, it is noticeable that he included viewing notes in his letter. A portrait of a doge, 'done truly and roughly alla Venetiana', he recommended should 'be set at some distance from the sight'.[23] To a man raised among Burghley's collection of portraits, and used to the finesse and finish of Hilliard, this was probably necessary advice. However, if Philip II of Spain could be a passionate collector of Titian in the late sixteenth century, Wotton was surely correct to risk sending Salisbury a painting thought then to be a

172

collaboration between Titian and Palma Giovane. Even so, Salisbury was sometimes uneasy with problematic attributions and interpreting an aesthetic he did not fully comprehend. Lacking the sublime confidence of a true connoisseur, he would sometimes turn for a second opinion to the Earl of Arundel. The Italian nexus between the two men actually went beyond paintings to family employees, for Giacomo Verzelini, son of the famous decorative glass manufacturer, was a dependant of Salisbury, while his brother Francesco became Arundel's Italian secretary.[24]

Carvers and gilders had a heavy workload in the house, particularly in the Marble Hall and on the Grand Staircase, where John de Beeke and Rowland Buckett excelled themselves. The latter also used his brush on Salisbury's bed (in which the earl never slept more than eight nights), chair and stools, before doing friezes, ceiling pendants and the imported organ bought from Haan for over £1,000. This hugely expensive instrument seems to have been kept and maintained by Dallam until it could be properly housed. In 1611, when Buckett was painting the case, Dallam tuned the pipes, a task for which he was paid 40 shillings a year. Buckett also worked in the chapel, gilding everything in sight and producing a clutch of devotional pictures for the gallery. The most obvious are the series representing saints; less easily seen today are an Annunciation and one of angelic presentation before the shepherds. Since these pictures are saturated with Catholic overtones, a number of intriguing questions are raised. Was the painter free to choose his subjects? Do the pictures hint at Salisbury's drift towards Arminianism? There was also a big picture of Christ and the Apostles, so he commissioned such sacred topics from a journeyman painter who was very well rewarded for his efforts, being paid £577 for work done between January and November 1611.[25] This encouragement of a native painter fumbling his way towards a baroque style and scale, having barely encountered an imported Italian Renaissance, was generous indeed, when Wotton would have been delighted to obtain infinitely finer works in Italy.

The richness of the chapel's decoration was heightened by the painted glass, the east window being the product of several hands, including in later times William Warrington, who in the nineteenth century replaced a panel destroyed in the 1835 fire: 'Elisha and the Widow's Son', qualitatively inferior to the expert eye.[26] The Abraham panel shows Flemish influence and can be assigned to one Martin van Benthem. But the greater part of the window was done by a Frenchman and Richard Butler. In January 1609 the bustling Wilson agreed with his countryman terms of employment on the work – 6s. 4d. a square foot, with completion by the following Whitsun. Evidently his labours were appreciated, for soon Butler was working on the chapel windows at Salisbury House.[27]

The earl did not hesitate to destroy anything that interfered with his grand vision. There had been elaborate gardens at Hatfield, but now they were swept away. To expand he needed to buy more land from his own copyholders at £10 an acre, a procedure that went on after his death.[28] The famous English passion for gardening was growing (Gerard's *Herbal* appeared in 1597) and remodelling by the Cecils was becoming a family tradition. Soon after inheriting Theobalds Robert Cecil had commissioned Montagu Jennings to create a watercourse. Now in September 1609 Jennings and Robert Bell, the London merchant who had already imported Caen stone for the house, drew up plans for the garden, using one Bartholomew as a consultant. Salisbury then chose to call in another gardener, Thomas Chaundler, who had responsibility for the east garden, while John Tradescant became the earl's plant-buyer in the Spanish Netherlands and France at a salary of £50 a year.[29]

Before his European buying trip in autumn 1610, Tradescant probably worked on the establishment of the kitchen garden; then, late in October, he was given an advance of £10 to buy vines in the Spanish Netherlands. These were a supplement (obviously a different variety) to the gift of 30,000 such plants from Madame de la Boderie, wife of the French ambassador. With two Frenchmen, Pierre Collin and Jean

Vallet, being sent by Queen Marie de Médicis to tend the vines, as well as 500 fruit trees, Salisbury might have had a vintage if the effort had been made. The vines themselves were planted in two enclosures, probably hedged with privet and sweet briar, on the north side of the River Lea, but sloping south. However, he does not seem to have bothered with wine-making; apparently he drank little of it (or ale), taking only the occasional glass for a vague medicinal or digestive purpose. He did, however, like to eat grapes and early cherries, a preference that caused some concern later to his doctor, Mayerne. He had a particular liking for the muscat grape (used to provide communion wine for the aristocracy; others got claret), so the vines were imported.

Back from his trip, Tradescant was sent to Cranborne, and early in November was paid £2. 2s. 10d. for tree-planting.[30] By 1611 he was again at Hatfield, where problems and confusion had arisen from too many gardeners spoiling the plot. Chaundler's plan for waterworks was given over to Simon Sturtevant in January, but after nearly a year Thomas Wilson boldly intervened and engaged Salomon de Caux to scrutinize and refine the hydraulics. De Caux, a Frenchman who had travelled in Italy and had been employed in Brussels from 1605 to 1610 by the Archdukes, had come to England to be employed first by Queen Anne and then Prince Henry, for whom he had laid out the gardens at Richmond Palace.[31] Viewing the work done at Hatfield, he advised that it should be scrapped, and with perhaps a sigh Salisbury sacked both Chaundler and Sturtevant.[32]

Now it was old Mountain Jennings who was required to finish the east garden to plans by de Caux and Liming. Surrounded by heat-retaining brick walls and divided into two halves, it was laid out in a formal manner, with paths made from pulverized bricks and grassy knots bordered by Salisbury's favourite flower, the scented pink.[33] Closest to the house was a terrace with decorated rails and stairs leading down to the main garden with its quaint carved wooden lions, painted and gilded to match heraldic lions on the roof. De

Caux's design for the new fountain was suitably heroic in scale, with a massive marble basin costing £70 made by the Dutch stonemason Gheeraert Janssen (anglicized as Garret Johnson). On the basin's artificial rock stood a metal statue cast by another carver, Garret Christmas, and painted by Buckett to look like copper. Christmas went on to a successful collaboration with Thomas Middleton on mayoral pageants, and he was also a regular woodcarver and decorator for the Royal Navy after his appointment by the Lord Admiral Nottingham.[34] De Caux seems to have done little else in the garden, and after he had dedicated his book *La Perspective avec la raisons des ombres et miroirs* to Prince Henry in 1612, his patron's premature death, following that of Salisbury, sent him back to Europe to spend the years until his own death in 1626 in Germany and France.[35]

De Caux's speciality was the use of water, and at Hatfield it issued from the centrepiece to make a little stream that was corrected a number of times. One of the charming decorative ideas for this was probably inspired by French examples. Late in September 1611 Tradescant was sent off to Flanders (Spanish Netherlands) to buy plants and baskets, his expenses being covered by bills of exchange arranged by Peter Van Lore.[36] Then he moved to France to buy exotics in Paris, including orange trees at 10s. each. From there he made his way to Rouen, where he paid £12 for eight boxes of marine shells to be placed with coloured pebbles on the bottom of the stream.[37] They had all been put in place by the following May as Salisbury was dying of a portmanteau of diseases; Cecil-Hatfield, as he had intended to call it, became part of the great inheritance of the 2nd earl.

Given the expense and complexity of the Hatfield scheme, it induces a kind of awe that Salisbury also undertook commercial building in London. His principal effort was the redevelopment of the area immediately to the west of Salisbury House. Within two years of Ralegh's brutal ejection from

Durham House Cecil had secured a slice down the east side of the estate on which to enlarge his town residence. He then proceeded to acquire control of part of the Strand frontage of Durham House, including the dilapidated stables and gate-house. In 1607 he bought out Dudley Carleton's interest in an eighty-year lease. The cardinal error of the latter's excursion into public life was first to attach himself to the Earl of Northumberland and then to lease the vault to the Gunpowder plotters for storage. After a few anxious weeks of incarceration he took himself off to the Chilterns on his release, 'to take away the scent of powder'. He managed, however, to maintain his precious contact with Sir Walter Cope, and in 1607 he was still casting about for Salisbury's favour. Hence the lease sale, after which he was offered employment on a diplomatic excursion to Florence, which could hardly have been less felicitously timed – he had recently married the daughter of Sir Henry Savile.

In 1608, in pursuit of his plan for the Strand site, Salisbury obtained full possession of the Durham House lease for £1,200, paid to Sir Tobie Matthew, the late Bishop of Durham's recusant son. A year later he extracted from the incumbent a lease of the courtyard behind the frontage, securing his title in 1610 by an Act that transferred this area to him in perpetuity for a rent of £40 a year. In some compensatory fashion he had new drains to the river connected to Durham House and the bishop got new stables in St Martin's Lane. This additional frontage was required for the large commercial development, a luxury enclosed mart of very small shops. It was intended to rival Sir Thomas Gresham's famous Royal Exchange in the City, and one of Salisbury's most trusted associates had a hand in the planning.[38] Inigo Jones may also have had at least some involvement in the initial plans, which show signs of being a collaborative effort, with Salisbury too giving it powerful attention since it was such a speculative venture. The man in charge of building operations was Simon Basil.

This project, begun on 10 June 1608, was officially opened

by James on 11 April the following year. This was an astonishing sustained effort, with work unusually continuing through the winter months, perhaps to outflank any real protests from city traders who found a voice in the Lord Mayor of London. Much of the credit for successfully organizing manpower and materials should go to Wilson, who by living in Salisbury House could give the project unremitting attention. With some 250 men working on the site at peak periods such dedication was necessary; what emerged was basically brick, though to dignify the Strand front stone from a variety of sources was used, including some recycled from the monastic ruins of St Augustine's, Canterbury. To the chagrin of local people, who objected to the further destruction wrought by his agents, Salisbury was able to exploit this bribe from his sometime sister-in-law by marriage, the wife of Lord Cobham.[39]

The formal opening of the Exchange on 10 April was a court occasion, with the royal family as principal guests. Marc' Antonio Correr, the Venetian diplomat, observed the spectacle and the gifts given to them: a cabinet for James, a silver plaque of the Annunciation for the Catholic Queen, and horse trappings for Prince Henry: 'Nor was there anyone of the Suite who did not receive at the very least a gold ring.' They were also given presents, costing Salisbury £96, of exotic rare goods from India and China, the shop-holders wanting to impress potential rich clients. The so-called China Houses were shops that sold oriental silks and porcelain, and they became fashionable haunts of assignation. The taste for porcelain items became something of a mania, and not simply a metropolitan whim either. A surprising amount of late Ming porcelain of the Wan Li blue-and-white kind has been found, for example, in Exeter.[40] An inventory of the apothecary Thomas Baskerville lists porcelain in 1596, and it was seen in South Devon as early as 1587 when Drake captured the *San Felipe*. In 1609 the East India Company had to allow guests at a dinner to take home the items they had been served from.

As usual it was Ben Jonson and Inigo Jones who devised the

entertainment for Salisbury's guests; it cost about £90.[41] The King's primary task in the festivities was to name the building, and he was not swayed by suggestions from Thomas Wilson, who had mulled the matter over with his employer. It was named resoundingly (if temporarily) 'Britain's Burse'; soon the obvious 'New Exchange' took hold. Work on the building went on for some time after the ceremony, and access was made easier by paving part of the Strand – a great boon to all pedestrians when the thoroughfare was generally synonymous with a bog. Inside the paving was black and white marble, a favourite combination for Salisbury, though adequate supplies were difficult to find. Some of the windows were special armorial affairs, made and installed by Richard Butler, the leading artist in glass of his time who lived in the glazier's quarter in Southwark. He was later active in embellishing Thomas Sutton's foundation at the Charterhouse, being paid then 40s. for an armorial glass in the chapel, as well as producing four smaller shields. Two shields with Sutton's Arms in the windows of the hall even survived German bombing.[42]

Rowland Buckett also worked on the Burse, painting Wilson's office, where insurance was to be sold.[43] The son of a shoemaker and the grandson of an immigrant from near Heidelberg, he could achieve sumptuous painted effects hinted at in the chimneypiece he repaired and altered in 1626 in what is now called the Great Chamber of the Charterhouse. The emblematic paintings set in cartouches in the lower section of the chimney are generally attributed to him, 'and his name has been found at the back of the oval panel'.[44] It was something of a virtuoso performance, even for an artist with a wide range of skills, and was recognized as such by the Governors with their payment of £50. Buckett would undertake most things, like making gilded leather hangings for Althorp. Perhaps these were made to replace the nine 'Hercules' tapestries sold by Lady Elizabeth Carey (née Spencer), an early manifestation of the family habit of selling the old to underwrite new acquisitions. The tapestries measured 512 ells

(1 ell = approximately 2 feet) and they cost Salisbury £375, which he gladly paid, having a great liking for such items. Buckett also produced illuminated manuscripts and coloured maps for his employer who, like Burghley, was a dedicated collector. A document at Hatfield records a payment to Buckett of £2 on 20 June 1608 for such colouring of a book of 'Plotts and mapps of the description of Ireland' – actually John Norden's manuscript 'A discription of Ireland', which was dedicated to Salisbury and is now in the Public Record Office.[45] Buckett's Cecil connections went into the next generation, for in the 1630s he lived in a substantial house on the west side of St Martin's Lane in the development first undertaken by Salisbury.[46]

When Thomas Wilson came back to London from his European tour of duty for Salisbury, he was elected MP for Newtown, Isle of Wight, in a 1605 bye-election. This seat fell under the patronage of the Earl of Southampton as Captain of the island. The offering of it to Salisbury with a grateful flourish chimed with the fact that Southampton's son had been born in March, and he wanted the King and Salisbury to be the boy's sponsors. Wilson's other post was to manage the quotidian affairs of the Exchange, a task made easier by having his house built on a fragment of land next door. Eight yards in depth and seven in breadth, it was later sublet to the antiquarian Sir Robert Cotton. The regulations for the market make clear its pretensions: ordinary perishable goods were excluded, and only high-class merchandisers sought to sell perfumes, hats, silks, confectionery, books, jewels and so on. In summer the individual shops were to be open from 6 a.m. to 8 p.m., in winter from 7 a.m. to 7 p.m. Despite the quest for an air of civility and refinement, the robust activities of less welcome Londoners could intrude. There was fighting (sometimes even swords were drawn), ball games were played and dogs unleashed. The animals were a noisy and noisome bane of London life then as now, and since the streets thronged with them many parishes wisely employed a dog-killer. The slaughter would grow particularly hot in plague years when dogs, like cats, rabbits and pigeons, were suspected of spreading the disease.[47] Infringement of the rules of the Exchange could be subdued by corporal punishment; thieves (and the temptations were many) were put in the stocks.

❦ 14 ❦

It is hard to imagine that Cecil ever acted spontaneously in his entire life. Private and public policy was always meticulously scrutinized; control was the secret engine of his being. This certainly included his children, who were cherished but still regarded as exploitable. This exploitation was manifested in apparently neutral conditions, so that for example in 1603, on James I's birthday, William Cecil was presented to Queen Anne, who cheerfully took him in her arms, kissed him twice and gave him a jewel. The boy was unwittingly a kind of envoy for his father, whom the Queen seems to have regarded with an unease tempered by self-interest. Since James was a male chauvinist homosexual his gruff tenderness was reserved for young men, and he was quite content that his wife should be excluded from power as long as she was royally diverted. Births and miscarriages helped, as did the expensive and ephemeral masques that delighted her, but bored him.

It was part of Cecil's duty to Anne that he should provide the funds to make these entertainments as lavish as possible in terms of numbers of performers, costumes and scenery. He also had a hand in the organization of Anne's private financial affairs, arranging for her a jointure of some £6,300 a year and holding the keepership of several estates that brought in her income. With a place on her council he also acted as her high bailiff and steward, although their contacts at first appear to have stemmed from self-interest rather than warm inclination – hence the softening presence, on occasions, of William.

There is a faint suggestion in a quip made by the older Cecil years later to Jane Drummond that he found Anne a shade ridiculous, his comment being that she preferred looking at her paintings to talking to people; loved 'nobody but dead pictures'. To this Anne is supposed to have retorted that she found more contentment in them than did her husband's minister in 'his great employments'. In fact she did collect pictures and had them expensively framed in walnut.[1] What is missing in both comments is the tone. Was she scornful, and was he simply teasing lightly? Or was he making a genuine comment infused with some surprise? If the latter, then the reason may be that her grasp of English was inadequate and her accent the cause of mirth.

Further, what is to be made of an apparently insignificant gesture by Salisbury to his queen in 1611? In this case the timing and the cost are particularly notable: it was in the aftermath of the débâcle over the 'Great Contract', and the green velvet hangings which he bought from the embroiderer Mr Shaw cost £1,094. 10s.[2] This was simply a staggering price, suggesting either esteem or gratitude (had she tempered James's irritation and dismay that his minister had failed in Parliament?), or that Salisbury suddenly thought her worth cultivating in case she ever achieved a position like Queen Marie de Médicis in France.

Even so, in terms of the court and power Anne was more usually regarded as a majestic nonentity. Prince Henry was much more important, and increasingly so as he approached manhood. Salisbury paid as much careful attention to the boy as he did to the Queen, and the notion that Henry disliked him is not borne out by written evidence. In fact, for toiling energy and sobriety Salisbury and the prince make a more logical pair than the real royal father and son. The French ambassador was probably mistaken, although it should be borne in mind that the heir to the throne greatly admired Ralegh, and the relationship of Henry and Salisbury depended on acceptance and deference rather than unalloyed liking. At the beginning of the reign Cecil was well placed to build an initial contact through the prince's governor, Sir Thomas Chaloner. Once connected with the Cecils and Essex, he had slipped away from the latter's orbit in 1599 to be more firmly yoked to the Secretary of State, who sent him to Scotland. Coming again to England in 1603 in the King's suite, Chaloner took charge of a small group of aristocratic boys selected as suitable companions for the prince, including Robert Devereux, 3rd Earl of Essex, now removed from Eton, and William Cecil.

The tutor to Prince Henry was Adam Newton, later secretary of his household, and Salisbury's relaxed correspondence with him and the prince suggests that the French ambassador had erred in his assessment. Salisbury eventually saw to it that Henry was given state papers, including reports from ambassadors when appropriate. In 1607, for example, he sent one of the political libels of Robert Persons, and at the same time thanked the prince for a horse he had sent as a gift.[3] When the minister sent Henry a horse, knowing the young man shared this passion with William Cecil, he received a letter of thanks that included a quip about the animal's stature, 'which though he be little, yet he wants no mettle as all little things have'.[4] Riding back from Royston to London on one occasion, Salisbury suddenly realized he had failed to say his farewells to Henry. His note of apology said that the unintended slight had been punished by the loss of a garter which chilled his knee[5] – dutiful, and with a surprising lightness of touch. So by the time of his installation as Prince of Wales in 1610 Henry was happy to leave the ceremonial arrangements to Salisbury, who had also to promote the collection of the simultaneous feudal levy. While Cranborne had been recalled to England from France to hold the King's train at the ceremony on 4 June, it was the Lord Treasurer who read the Letters Patent of creation in the great chamber of the Palace of Westminster before the crowned King, the members of both Houses of Parliament, other officers of State and foreign ambassadors.[6] Afterwards the Prince of Wales dined alone in state in Whitehall while a forty-part choir sang

Tallis's sublime anthem 'Spem in Alium' in the English version.

Not surprisingly, the question of a marriage for Prince Henry became a thin seam to be worked after 1606 as Salisbury made English foreign policy less nakedly anti-Spanish. This bemused Zúñiga, who learned of Salisbury's inquiries about a marriage to an infanta from Robert Taylor. The meddling Countess of Suffolk, who helped only to confuse the ambassador, even suggested that a marriage alliance might be made with Savoy. The advantages of this were apparently that it would allow the diminution of persecution of Catholic recusants, and that after the swerve towards Savoy the real negotiations could begin with Spain. This would offset the revival of Franco–Dutch relations, which Salisbury regarded with no great pleasure.[7] Money too played a part in these convoluted dealings and in 1607 Philip III allowed a payment of 50,000 escudos to Salisbury, with the promise of another 50,000 if the marriages then being discussed actually happened. The payment, equalling £12,506, 'was certainly made by the summer of 1608'.[8] By this time Salisbury was also Lord Treasurer following the apoplectic demise of Dorset at the Council table, and it was a suitably princely sum, even a scandalous one by the not very exacting standards of the day. No wonder the recipient was frantically anxious for it and his dealings with the Spanish Embassy to remain secret. Zúñiga, writing to his king, was fairly hopeful that 'all this money has succeeded in hooding this little man, so that he acts with less hostile intent in every way'.[9] Acceptance gave Salisbury a fall-back resource as he embarked on the building of Hatfield on such a confident scale. Indeed, it has been estimated that Spanish funds underwrote 'half the total cost of the building'.[10] The sprawling use of gold leaf in the decoration of the house and chapel seems pointedly appropriate.

Salisbury's appointment as Lord Treasurer, to be held in tandem with the Secretaryship, was an indication of the monarch's relaxed attitude. For the first and only time in English history the two most significant offices of State were held by one man. Salisbury's own explanation of this startling conjunction, in a letter to Sir Henry Wotton, has a wry, self-deprecating tone: he says that he had not sought the office and had been chosen because 'some experience might make me more able than any new man, and the condition of my fortune (if not my honesty) divert me from the errors of corruption'.[11] The entertainment to celebrate the appointment was given between 5 and 11 May in the library at Salisbury House. As usual Jonson and Jones devised it, with the designs probably painted by Louis Dauphin. Salisbury's fee for the office was £1 a day and £15 for livery, an amount that might just have paid for his hose or gloves. Thus, when Henry was given his Cymric dignity, Salisbury, who was something of a dandy, spent £79. 10s. on the embroidery alone of a suit and cloak.[12] With his dedication to princely conspicuous consumption, the office of Lord Treasurer had to be milked, and it could be done electively or passively. The patronage wielded by the Lord Treasurer in organizing Crown finances was paramount in the Exchequer offices, receiverships of the counties and customerships of the ports. Preferment without some genteel reward for the Lord Treasurer was deeply unlikely. Thomas Bellott would have known this when he sought a place in the Customs of Ireland after an unhappy period in the King's service. Contracts with the various farmers of Customs and taxes fell under Salisbury's supervision and most of those involved were his creditors, so it does not seem unduly suspicious to regard this financial intimacy as dangerously suspect. Of £42,500 formally borrowed from twenty-one of London's leading merchants and money-lenders, over half that sum (£23,400) came from Customs farmers.[13]

Salisbury's consolidation of his position caused continual ripples around him. Expectations and loans were raised, phrases polished and anxieties renewed. One of the first to react was Sir Thomas Edmondes, with a gift and a request to his London representative William Trumball to find out 'what inclination there is to favour me in any sort'. In truth the answer was 'not much', because as Levinus Munck had made clear, Salisbury was not inclined to give up the office of Secretary. According to Munck Sir Thomas Smith would look to Irish affairs, Sir Thomas Lake would have the unenviable task of trailing after James, and Munck himself would deal with foreign correspondence. In November 1608 Sir Walter Cope praised Munck's integrity, and a little later there was a rumour (which proved false) that he would be appointed ambassador to the United Provinces.[14] Edmondes clearly wanted to return to London, to a position that would allow him to exploit his diplomatic experience. He wrote to Salisbury directly and Trumball was primed to state his case to Munck and the Lord Chancellor; the notion that he might end up in Paris as a replacement for Salisbury's friend Sir George Carew (d.1605) was not welcome. Not long after the earl became Lord Treasurer Edmondes took comfort from a speech by him at the installation of Sir Thomas Smith as a Master of the Court of Requests, but eventually he had to accept further service abroad. Realistically it was the French Embassy or nothing, with a possible hint of advancement when finally recalled.

Salisbury had a passion for power that never dimmed and would tolerate only subordinates whose independence was governed by personal loyalty. His unfaltering loyalty was to the sovereign, and despite James's sometimes bizarre behaviour it remained intact. Yet an English Secretary would hardly find that the King's treatment of his Scottish Secretary induced unflustered confidence. James Elphinstone, Lord Balmerino, was brought low by a curious episode occasioned by a letter from James to Pope Clement VIII in 1599. This was now published to embarrass the King by Cardinal Bellarmine, the leading Catholic controversialist. The phrasing of the letter suggested a royal flirtation with Catholicism, and it helped to undermine his public reputation even if he disavowed its contents. The unfortunate Balmerino was imprisoned, being held responsible for the King's signature – which, James recalled, nearly a decade after the signing, had been made without his reading the text. Balmerino's examination in the Star Chamber in 1608 by English Privy Councillors was undertaken after Salisbury had been briefed by his grandniece Honora Denny's husband, Sir James Hay. The list of questions was actually prepared by the King and Salisbury, who fabricated an angry tone and ended with a denunciation of Balmerino. The latter's insouciance before this had been marked, according to the story told by Horace Walpole. On the journey from the Tower he had stopped the coach at Charing Cross to buy what he, a Scot, called honey-blobs (gooseberries). Now, correctly assessing his predicament, he boldly confessed his guilt, and James was relieved at being saved even greater embarrassment by an action contrived between the two Secretaries.

If the charade was to have any conviction, the penalty for Balmerino would have to be execution. In fact his punishment was mild, so that it was clear to the few who cared about such bogus operations that not even James believed the trumped-up charge. It is therefore possible to admire the slippery ingenuity of Salisbury, or to frown at such activity. The absurdity of it all was underlined when James made a laboured joke to Salisbury about the mishaps that had befallen a number of European secretaries, ending by asking him (no doubt with a smirk) what would become of him as Lord Treasurer if as Secretary he proved to be a rogue. If there was any advantage to Salisbury in the political ruin of Balmerino, he seems to have nudged it aside in his own mind with worries about his own future. He remarked on a number of occasions on the fate of Empson and Dudley a century before, and since money had been instrumental in their downfall it was clearly possible that it might lead to his. A stranglehold on power, making his presence indispensable and successfully increasing royal revenues, would reduce that distressing possibility.

The parlous state of royal finances was always a potent concern to James's ministers, and had been so since the inception of his reign. During the summer after his appointment to succeed Dorset, Salisbury was out of London, leaving

Sir Julius Caesar, now Chancellor of the Exchequer, to prepare a scheme for raising more money. In July the two men together had a series of meetings with their officials, and even sought policy suggestions which Caesar edited into a wide-ranging survey of the King's estates. These highlighted the fact that deficit financing was a disturbing reality, with James unable and unwilling (whatever his protestations) to check his liberality. A few examples of this will suffice: a free gift of over £2,000 to Sir Edward Grevill; spending on Prince Henry's household, which in 1604–5 was £3,660, had gone up to over £35,000 a mere six years later; in the first four years of his reign James had distributed £68,000 in gifts, £30,000 in pensions and £174,000 in debts owed to the Crown. By 1610 the annual expenditure on fees and annuities to royal servants and courtiers was £80,000.[15] Personal extravagance meant that he spent over £7,000 on his own robes.[16] His hunting pursuits added to the burden, since the number of keepers of the buckhounds rose from nine to thirty-eight. The cost rose from £640 in 1604 to nearly double that five years later. Between 1603 and 1612 James spent £185,000 on jewels.[17] No wonder that several years before gossip noted 'much raking and scraping on all sides'.

The rolling crisis was tackled first by Dorset and then by Salisbury with a variety of measures to reduce the Crown debt and cover deficits. Since the Crown was expected to fund ordinary expenditure from Customs, feudal revenues and the Crown landholdings, these were the principal areas for ministerial scrutiny. As far as the Great Farm was concerned it covered Customs on all imports and exports, with only a handful of lucrative exceptions. The advantage of the scheme was that the farmers provided James with a set income of £112,400, and as they enriched themselves they could offer loans (albeit at 10 per cent interest). As the patron of the group that had been outmanoeuvred for the Great Farm, the Earl of Northampton, with his unsubdued reforming instincts, tried for several years to reverse the decision in favour of the Garway–Jones syndicate. In 1607 there was an unruly outburst from Sir John Swinnerton with an accusation of fraud, and he boosted his offer in a bid that John Chamberlain thought would oust Salisbury's patentees: £100,000 in a fine and £4,000 more in rent. He failed but James benefited, since Salisbury's privileged group raised their rent to £120,000.[18] In December 1611 Swinnerton had the bull-headed temerity to try again as the farm came up for renewal, offering the same fine and a yearly rent of £120,000. This did not endear him to a beleaguered Salisbury in the period after the struggle for the Great Contract and he was summoned by the Lord Treasurer, who in a rare burst of anger told him he would never get the farm, whatever the efforts of friends like Northampton. The relationship between Salisbury and the earl was irredeemably tainted. No wonder that when Salisbury was dead Northampton viciously commented to Rochester on 'the death of the little man, for which so many rejoice'.

Dorset and his successor also sought additional revenues from a method validated by the courts in the Bate's Case of 1606. In the words of Fleming, principal judge of the Exchequer Court in allowing impositions, [they] 'are duties or sums of money newly imposed by the King without Parliament upon merchandise for the augmentation of his revenues'. Bate had created the test case by refusing to pay the imposition on currants imported from the eastern Mediterranean. The judgement was of great importance to the Crown because although the imposition on the dried fruit was negligible in terms of the money so raised, the principle was established that gave the government a free hand. Salisbury did not immediately plunge into this. As usual he prepared his ground carefully with a series of meetings with merchants. On 6 June he had a conference to discuss which items might be subject to impositions and which not. Several days later he, Caesar and the barons of the Exchequer went to the Custom House of London. There Salisbury made 'an excellent speech to prove that impositions might lawfully be imposed', and despite some voices raised against the measure, the merchants allowed that this was so. Caesar almost trembled with excitement as he considered this historic breakthrough. On 28 July letters patent authorizing the new impositions received the Great Seal, and by Michaelmas the collection began.

With Crown lands Salisbury could realistically contemplate a number of strategies to boost revenue: surveys, followed by the imposition of an economic rent; raised entry fines; the sale of small and isolated holdings; the sale of timber, and as a large estate would usually raise a substantial amount, that could be considered a last resort. Some of these methods had already been followed from the beginning of the reign, although an Act of Entail had tried to stem the sale of important landholdings. However, when Salisbury found that mills held by the Crown were expensive to repair he had them put on sale, as were small properties acquired from the dissolution of chantries. Efforts were also made to boost the fines and rents of copyholders, and surveys of Crown lands could produce startling results. In Yorkshire rent payments rose from £3,291 to £11,449 a year.[19] Exploitation of woodland was stepped up, and Salisbury initiated the commission on assarts on which he sat with the Lord Chancellor Ellesmere among others. The idea was to achieve an acceptable formula for payment and to give security of tenure to those holding assarted lands – deforested lands occupied without legal title. A novel scheme such as this might well have been discussed in the Commons, yet it was never raised there at its inception and, not surprisingly, was regarded by some with a heavy frown.

Selling Crown lands of consequence was done only with the utmost reluctance, but the breaching of the earlier entail act had taken place. To reduce the likelihood of a further haemorrhage a new entail was passed in May 1609. At the same time Salisbury was taking an avid interest in the sale of woods and stands of timber within them. Like most of his contemporaries he looked upon forests generally as wasteland aching for exploitation, a view that explains why today England and Ireland have less forest than any country in Europe except the Netherlands. Disafforestation was therefore proposed for those forests in which James never hunted because of their distance

191

from a royal residence, yet only Knaresborough in Yorkshire seems to have been affected by the attention given to them.[20] Royal disapproval and local disaffection reined Salisbury in; but his influence on the better exploitation of forest resources was felt in the Forest of Dean, where the wood sold to the owners of the farm of the royal ironworks was more expensive from 1611, and quantities were increased. The following year enclosures in Wiltshire in the Chippenham and Blackmore forests were made, and this disafforestation by stealth was used to 'enhance the value of the grazing rights leased to the farmer of the herbage and pannage'.[21] This shift to grazing provoked rumbles of opposition, just as Salisbury's efforts had done in Brigstock Park, part of Rockingham Forest, early in the reign.

By 1609 the money-raising ingenuity of the Lord Treasurer was being inexorably prodded into areas he might have preferred to leave unexplored. Such was the proposal to collect the feudal aid that was due with the granting of a knighthood to Prince Henry at his Investiture as Prince of Wales. This was almost defiant of Salisbury because the feudal aid had long fallen into desuetude, and had not even been considered since the reign of Henry VII. All the King's tenants, whatever their tenures, were liable to pay the levy, and commissioners for its collection wrote to their deputies in the counties of the King's gracious willingness to accept compositions to avoid the necessity of probing tenures and valuations. Those liable in the counties did not view it at all blithely, and despite Salisbury's preparations it was not collected without much arm-twisting and persistent complaints. Whether it was worth it to collect a paltry £21,000 is open to doubt.

Some economic historians remain critical of Dorset (whose family name, Sackville, was at the time cheerfully converted by observers to 'Fill-sack') and Salisbury in the matter of royal debt reduction, so to bring down the total from some £735,000 at the beginning of 1606 to about £280,000 in 1610 is not regarded as particularly impressive.[22] For four years before 1610 the Lord Treasurer had over £1,185,000 to apply to the seething problem from the various measures just outlined. But these measures dealt only with the results; they did not dispel the causes of the inexorably rising debt: cumulative ordinary deficits.[23] By early 1610, therefore, Salisbury had in mind an approach to Parliament that would save the ship of State from being wrecked – an imaginative programme of fiscal reform widely known since as the Great Contract.

15

It has been shown that Salisbury made sustained efforts to raise royal revenue to meet increasing royal expenses. Their limitations meant that by the beginning of 1610 there was a debt of some £280,000 that was certain to rise. There was also an annual deficit of £50,000 which would rise with the establishment of Prince Henry's separate household, and abroad the eruption of the Jülich-Cleves succession crisis. What Salisbury now wanted, as the fading initiatives of the past failed to meet critical needs, was a large supply, one unprecedented in peacetime, of £600,000, to be used to pay off the debt, with the remainder put aside as a defence contingency fund. In addition, he wanted £200,000 a year as support for the King's ordinary needs. This was not intended as an extraordinary payment for one or two years – it was meant to be permanent, as James had implacable objections to any proposal for what he saw as niggardly cuts in his liberality. His view was naturally echoed by such as Northampton, whose commonplace pronouncement was that as long as the monarchy existed the Commons would have to maintain it.

The attitude of the Commons was much less deferential. There was an underswell of feeling among some members that if they were expected to respond to this novel appeal, the King would at least have to abate the grievances uncoiling out of wardship and purveyance. Moreover, they were early stirred by a parliamentary controversy over Dr John Cowell's book *The Interpreter*, an apparently innocent law dictionary which contained a short passage about the King as an absolute monarch 'whose powers were not limited by any human laws'.[1] Published several years before, it only now caused a scandal instigated by John Hoskins, a common lawyer, who drew it into the public domain as Salisbury embarked on the perils of a new grand scheme for royal finances. The House of Lords, on the other hand, saw little in it and Bancroft, a close friend of Cowell, to whom the book had been dedicated, defended man and text.[2] So at first did Salisbury, until a sudden reversal occasioned by James. He was so concerned about his finances that 'he expressed his dislike of Cowell's doctrines that the King could legislate or levy taxes without the consent of Parliament'. Above all, he was highly sensitive to the royal power and prerogative discussed in the book being openly scrutinized; Salisbury had to agree, and declared: ' . . . there are some things in the book very idle'.[3] It was this that caused the split between the Lord Treasurer and the Archbishop, and the Commons dropped the case against Cowell only when the book was suppressed.

Salisbury did not envisage reciprocity in his appeal for funds, and it is important to stress that his presentation – first to the House of Lords on 14 February 1610, and the following day to a conference of the Lords and Commons – did not set out a seamless measure called the 'Great Contract'. His tone was careful, low-key, and perhaps he did mean James to surrender purveyance, 'but he said nothing about either purveyance or wardship'.[4] He spoke instead of 'any reasonable request for the public good' – a notion broad enough to mean anything, which so mesmerized the Commons that Salisbury's insinuating mode floundered. Since he was asking, at first without figures, for a great deal of money, a brisk submission of the bare facts might ultimately have proved more useful. But the Commons declined to meet the problem in an open-handed way, setting aside supply, and on support seeking a link with the elimination of grievances. The personnel of the Commons naturally meant a concentration on purveyance and wardship, and so on 19 February the House committee for grievances included their abolition in their ten points of 'retribution'. Despite Sir Julius Caesar's Commons speech stating the sums of money involved, he did not manage on Salisbury's behalf to dispel the self-generating notion that the Lord Treasurer intended a contract, when in fact he had no such idea. The leading voice of the committee was Sir Edwin Sandys, who seems to have found it utterly inconceivable that Salisbury should seek huge sums without a serious intention to reform grievances, especially wardship.

On 24 February the Lord Treasurer spoke in the Lords. Ever attentive to him, they had no expectation that wardship would be slated for abolition, especially since many regarded bargaining with the Commons on such matters as repugnant. Salisbury himself indicated how lamentably unsatisfactory it was to yoke together 'retribution and contribution'. If he felt it to be 'altogether unfit', others in the Lords showed an even stronger disinclination to go in that direction, 'for that were to bargain'. Naturally James regarded the matter in the same light, but such stern attitudinizing would lead nowhere, so Salisbury became a little more flexible. When the petition of the Commons on wardship was presented, he told them again the necessities of the King's finances and now offered reforms on peripheral matters, with purveyance top of the list for abolition.[5] On wardship he offered reforms, but no suggestion that it might be heading for oblivion.[6] Indeed, with the single-minded devotion to the Crown that marked his every move, the reforms he proposed would (and eventually did) benefit the King more than his subjects. Meanwhile the Commons seem to have been poleaxed by the figures, and his flourish with 'matters of ease' was ignored. Finally, after a debate, the Commons laid before the Lords their agreement to meet supply eventually, but with the proviso that support depended on the King's attitude on the proposal to do away with hated wardship. When the petition for abolition went to James he was under pressure, and after pained reflection he gave way. The news of this was conveyed to a conference of the two Houses on 12 March by Northampton, who seems to have shied away from the content of the message he had to deliver.

Like an old pike, wardship had risen from the murky bottom of the pond, but the Commons offer of 26 March, a dole of £100,000 a year for the abolition of feudal tenures, was distinctly lean – so skeletal, because it substituted one impoverished scheme for another, ignoring the way revenue from wardships might be increased in the future, that after the ruminations of the Easter recess Salisbury starkly required an additional £200,000. Suddenly realizing the likely true long-term cost of proceeding on royal terms, the House balked – they could not contemplate 'excessive and exorbitant demands'. Having snagged his umpteenth cast on a low bough Salisbury came back on 4 May with an expostulation meant to camouflage his fumbling; although he had asked for £200,000, this did not mean he would not take less. At this point, however, when the contemptible notion of bargaining had been admitted, he stalled, and days later came the news of the assassination of Henri IV.

This had financial effects in England, as well as political ramifications in France. It meant that payment of French debts to the English Crown faded as a possibility, especially when Queen Marie de Médicis had to buy the loyalty of the aristocracy during the minority of her son Louis XIII. But if he hoped to conjure agreement from the Commons in the wake of the horror felt, Salisbury miscalculated. He did raise a loan of £100,000 from the City of London, but the waters were further muddied for him by a crisis over impositions, and the challenge threatened further losses to James's pocket. By the end of May it fell to Salisbury to try to revivify the whole matter by a joint conference, one of his favourite strategies. Yet even the revisions now offered, and the tactical retreat of James on impositions, failed to win over an aloof and defiant Commons. Salisbury saw the end of the session approaching and still no advance – not even an agreement on supply. On 11 June he suggested putting everything on hold until the reopening of Parliament in the autumn, with an urgent grant of supply. The rasp in his speech becomes plainer. After two days of debate the Commons declined even this. Had the equable minister exploded with incandescent rage at this stubborn, insulting resistance, who could have blamed him?

A sturdy class reluctance to do anything that might increase taxation on the wealthiest men in society, haggling over figures and other business, all delayed the provision of supply. Salisbury's top figure had another sliver removed, so that on 26 June he asked for £40,000 to be allocated to cover wardship and purveyance, plus an additional tranche of £140,000. However, after the debate on impositions which had begun three days before and went on until 3 July, a vote on supply was eventually taken.[7] Even then it proved a hideous disappointment, for Salisbury's calculations were that the King needed three or four subsidies, and the House agreed one with only one fifteenth. This contrasted odiously with the swift passage of a bill against impositions which actually expired in the Lords. When the committee of the two Houses reported wide divisions in their deliberations it was not surprising that James declared he would prorogue the session on 20 July.

In fact the prorogation was delayed until the 23rd and in a late flurry of activity, after five months of discussions, an agreement was hatched. The Commons thought they were about to lose the abolition of wardship, so to snatch it from oblivion they offered £180,000, and with James digging in his heels even raised this to £200,000. It was, of course, a provisional agreement and there were still aspects of the contract that needed attention and clarification. Thus the Commons were pressing that officers of courts who lost their jobs and income as a result of legislation should be compensated by the King. Since Salisbury was one of them this was understandable, and strangely late he seems to have recognized the probable cost while the officials lived. Considering this whole sketching out of an agreement had cost the King most during the negotiations, this oversight (if such it was) was not helpful. The worry increased when there was a rumour that £40,000 would initially be allocated to compensation. Even if this figure proved excessive, the £200,000 was still not enough to cover the deficit of £130,000 and the loss of £80,000 from the abolition of wardship and purveyance.[8]

The two Houses seem to have ended the session in a state of euphoria. As usual this was followed by a stale sense of anticlimax and a rueful reflection in court and country that all was not well. At court there had long been opposition, principled and opportunistic, to a scheme that would of necessity lead to changes both there and in government. A Cecilian like Prince Henry's governor Sir Thomas Chaloner could still shake his head at shackles being placed on the King's liberality, which 'is not so much discommendable as a little sparing'.[9] Important men in the Privy Council, like Ellesmere and Northampton, also opposed what emerged. The former recognized the horrendous state of royal finances, but in private he was unwilling to support the terms Salisbury was pressing. Nor was he keen to make the speech desired by the Lord Treasurer 'that would have given thanks for the King's consent to discuss the contract'.[10] Perhaps most importantly the Chancellor of the Exchequer, Caesar, remained sceptical about Salisbury's measures. A number of councillors saw wardship not merely as a financial mechanism profiting the government, but as 'indispensable in binding the King's greatest subjects to him'.[11] But Caesar's main thrust was at giving up so much, underpinned by history and tradition, for a real benefit amounting to no more than £85,000. His alternative was at once conservative and optimistic: if wardship, purveyance, recovery of assarts, a drive to uncover defective titles and stricter enforcement of the penal laws aimed at recusants could all be better administered, then James could be made solvent with barely a dent in his prerogative.

Caesar's thoughts were expressed in the famous memorandum dated 17 August, which has often been cited as a treacherous effort to bury the contract and politically maim Salisbury. A number of matters make its preparation and content very intriguing. Nothing in Caesar's rise from son of an Italian immigrant (albeit a well-placed court physician) to a Master of Requests and then Chancellor suggests that he was a man ready to challenge a superior. Perhaps, aware of conciliar resistance, he decided to risk an unprecedented boldness, but what if Salisbury's own commitment dipped significantly at this point? As has been pointed out, 'he probably continued to share many of the misgivings expressed by others'.[12] The contract was as much, if not more, a strategy fabricated by the Commons as it was a procedure for fiscal well-being wrought by the Lord Treasurer. His particular concern about personal compensation for the abolition of the Court of Wards may not have been of overwhelming significance, but the suggestion that he would not have suffered materially glides over some suggestive facts concerning his private finances.[13] During the time he was cajoling Parliament for royal finances he was heavily involved in the activities surrounding Charles Brooke. In April 1610 this kinsman of the earl made his will in the latter's favour, providing Salisbury dealt with the monstrous debts that assailed Brooke, whose profligacy had taken a savage toll of the family fortune. For Salisbury to do this when his hefty investment in the New Exchange was only bringing a slow return, and the cost of Hatfield, as well as the major alterations and refurbishment of Cranborne, was enormous, suggests powerfully that any real (even if temporary) disjunction of his income could spell calamity. The work at Cranborne alone between 1608 and 1612 cost over £3,000. By the summer of 1611 Salisbury's debts were over £50,000, with interest payments at 10 per cent. No wonder his aides, men like Houghton and Daccombe, were horrified.[14]

Ironically, the person most immediately taken with the proposal cobbled in those hurried last days of the Parliament was James. He hoped it betokened a 'better relationship between the Crown and the Lower House', as he said to the Master of the Wardrobe, Sir Roger Aston. So what or who persuaded James during the later summer that the Contract was so flawed that royal revision was necessary? The best candidate is Sir Robert Carr, whom historians have been quick to dismiss as a feather-brained ephebe. If Salisbury himself was pondering the quality of the provisional agreement, Carr, who was not an enemy, could well have felt emboldened to present the case against it, thus striking a chord with James's deeper instincts. But Carr's antipathy to the scheme was only one strand in James's thinking, because to preserve the 'love and obedience' of the Commons there could be no simple regal annihilation of the Contract. Moreover, Salisbury's realism would have noted that what Caesar envisaged in its place was merely a set of palliatives. King and minister had to hold back from destroying something that had taken on a wayward life of its own – until, that is, there was a hint of a possible replacement for it. Their self-control was rewarded (if that is the word) by the soundings taken in the country by MPs who had returned to their constituencies.

Until recently little weight would have been attached to such an activity, since the electorate was regarded as very limited. But recent research has shown that in counties and boroughs many more men than was once reckoned had the right to vote, though not all were aware of it.[15] All of them would have had an anxious interest in the emergent scheme and how it would affect their pockets. In outlining this MPs took account of the class structure of their audience; those who would benefit principally from the abolition of wardship being wealthier (especially in land) than those who would be relieved at the abolition of purveyance. In view of the very recent disturbances in the Midlands they would no doubt have made much of the other great intention: that taxes and prices of staple foods would not rise. As might be expected, attitudes varied and there was generally a cautious unease; 'it is obvious that members took the opinions of their constituents very seriously'.[16] If this was so it explains the very high level of absenteeism when the new session began in mid-October. Indeed, by the 22nd of the month fewer than one hundred MPs had returned, about one-fifth of the total number. Scanning the empty benches the bolder spirits present guessed the reason, and their heightened reluctance to deal with the Contract was immensely exasperating to James.

Over the summer he had acted on complaints about specific grievances, notably on some impositions, at a cost to his pocket which he estimated at £30,000. This was actually less a commitment to the Contract and more in the hope of getting money, so that on 31 October he referred to his 'just Contract'. But for a week he held off until his message to the Commons on 6 November, when he demanded satisfaction on the levy (essentially the land tax sought by Salisbury), £500,000 in supply and compensation for the officers of the Court of Wards. The Contract, disliked at court, in Parliament and in the country, had by this time become irrelevant. What James was reiterating by his stated requirement was the simple fact that a monarchy had to be paid for; as far as he was concerned these elements had been implicit, if not explicit, since February. As the Contract seemed to acquire a life of its own beyond the advocacy of a tenacious minister, so its demise was free-floating. The Commons were not now prepared to ease their position under royal pressure. On 7 November virtually all the members present rejected the King's demands, a fact that does not seem to have caused him any great perturbation. He knew the requirement for money would not go and would just have to be serviced by some other means. In Parliament the collapse led Sir George More to exclaim in bewilderment: 'I will not examine the cause, because I protest I am utterly ignorant of it.' As for Salisbury, it has been widely canvassed by historians that he was fiercely dismayed at the collapse of the interim agreement. But in fact he seems to have confronted it with considerable wry aplomb and a slightly bemused, even mild reflection that he could not understand why the initiative had foundered when the King had assented to it, and the Commons had accepted it – all he could suggest was that God was offended by it in some way and it withered.

Other more earthbound reasons did exist – not least a growing spirit of contrariety in the Commons. As John More, the aide to Sir Ralph Winwood, observed, there were now in the House 'patriots that were accounted of a contrary faction to the Courtiers'.[17] Ellesmere, when he wrote a long pamphlet on the 1610 Parliament, agreed, attributing the failure to the behaviour of an arrogant and conceited group of radical, even bristling members who formed a 'rebellious corner in the right hand of the House'. He thought the pursuit of power by men like Sir Henry Neville a threat to genuine reform, 'and to the balance and harmony of the Tudor constitution'.[18] What they (and indeed Salisbury) helped to dispel was trust between the legislators and executive. For example, on 10 July Salisbury had a private meeting in Hyde Park with a clutch of MPs, including Neville.[19] The discussion was on impositions and surely also on the Contract, although with what result is not known. What is known is that in the Commons other MPs regarded the matter with a suspicious frown. James too later blamed Salisbury's methods, with their heavy reliance on conferences, a mechanism the Commons also disliked.

As far as they were concerned the problem was the fear that their representatives, when sent to meet the Lords, would be too deferential. To prevent this the spokesmen became mere messengers, something which annoyed Salisbury, whose domination of the Upper House 'did not make matters easier in conference with the Commons'.[20] On specific points, like the much-debated purveyance, there was also distrust and tension. It was such a bugbear and already subject to so much legislation that there was a frank scepticism about whether it could ultimately be abolished, with lawyers arguing that the royal household could not exist without it.[21] Even if James did act according to the law (and impositions had shown what a minefield that could be), there did not appear to be any unbreakable formula to restrain his descendants from revisiting it on the country. Indeed, the martial spirit of Prince Henry, so different from James, might inflate royal expenditure through war and purveyance would be indispensable.

Equally – if not more – important was how new revenue was to be raised. Seventeenth-century governments did not have the option of placing VAT on gold wire, tapestries or clay pipes. Instead it seemed sure that land would be the victim and this caused various attitudes of horror and shock. It was not simply how much (£200,000? Impossible!) but how. Salisbury had already provided for a land survey and there were 'probably few things to which an assembly of land-owners in 1610 was less likely to agree'.[22] They were convulsed by the thought of the King knowing what his subjects owned, and given the alacrity with which a courtier like Ralegh had been stripped of his possessions to nurture a favourite like Carr, their alarm is understandable. Even Salisbury himself felt uneasy about a land commission sizing up his estates. In fact, the failure of the Great Contract stemmed ultimately from the one overriding, universal hatred – that of paying taxes – and Salisbury was asking for a permanent tax of £200,000.

The need, of course, had not gone away, so Parliament remained for a time in session with James and Salisbury trying to wring concessions out of them. On 16 November the King had a meeting with thirty MPs in the Council Chamber to rehearse his predicament – a meeting viewed with the standard suspicion by those not called to it. He asked whether they thought he was in want, as the Lord Treasurer told them, and when Bacon began a rather veiled reply the King turned to Sir Henry Neville.[23] He acknowledged the want straightforwardly and James's next question was obvious – was it the task, then, of his subjects to assist him or not? To this Neville's reply was charged with a sting: yes, if the King's expenses arose from the needs of the Commonwealth, but no if not. Then he reminded James boldly that the Commons had voted him four subsidies and seven fifteenths, without so far a redress of grievances. James asked what they were and Neville began to list them in the familiar litany before being cut off by Sir Herbert Croft. Following up this meeting on 21 November by a letter that was read to the Commons, James tried again to win a vote of supply by agreeing to a bill which prohibited future impositions without parliamentary consent. To make it as attractive as possible he had added some minor concessions, but a consideration of them was interrupted by a debate occasioned by the meeting with Neville and colleagues. As the speeches that were made were impertinent, James, probably on the advice of the Council, had the House adjourned from the 24th to the 29th, following some criticism of his wastefulness and peculiar liberality to his countrymen. He and Carr seem to have been enraged by a comment that it was good to hear that the King of Spain frittered all his money away on 'his favourites and wanton courtiers'. Irony was not altogether wasted on the Scots.

James's tantrum was also obliquely aimed at Salisbury, whose career as chief minister was reaching its lowest point. The adjournment was a waste of time, for all that James hoped for an improvement in the mood of the House. Then his secretary, Sir Thomas Lake, acted in such a way that Salisbury and James were involved in an angry exchange of letters. On 29 November the Commons were again adjourned, even before the scheduled meeting of the few MPs staunchly waiting for business or prorogation. Sir Thomas Lake explained it to his master as the Lord Treasurer's way of silencing those in the House who wanted to petition for the expulsion of Scots from the King's entourage. The latter was hot with anger and Lake was sent to consult with the independent Sir Henry Neville on the potential perpetrators of this outrage. Salisbury, for his part, 'denied any knowledge of such intentions in the House', and said that Lake had simply misunderstood a speech.[24] On 4 December Lake was surely attempting to redeem his lost credit with Salisbury. He referred to certain obscure manoeuvrings by Carr and malicious dealings by some MPs, 'he being the instrument'. If Carr felt threatened it is curious that he should tangle with the chief minister, however beleaguered, but the intention was to press Salisbury and the Council to uncover the anti-Scots element in Parliament. A breach between the King and his Council might have given Carr an opening he could exploit to his own benefit, and it is noticeable that in March 1611 he was made Viscount Rochester. Even so, at the end of December, when the decision was finally taken to dissolve Parliament, it was done by the King in Council.[25]

Salisbury's career had now reached its nadir. The last 'little beagle' letter from the King on 6 December would not have been especially reassuring. James noted his minister's sudden, uncharacteristic bursts of irascibility in the last two sessions; he delivered a rebuke: 'I had rather write than speak it unto you.' It has been suggested that the terms constituted a blistering attack on Salisbury's strategy, but a printed text can actually distort tone through different readings, and although James was clearly angry his feelings were mainly directed against Parliament. Salisbury's greatest error was identified as expecting 'to draw honey out of gall'. So the accusation is that, rigidly adhering to a strategy of his own devising that Parliament should be kept in being, he ignored the general view held by James that it should be ended. With his royal actions endorsed by sycophants, James could luxuriate in a momentary superiority. Salisbury's rejoinder was as usual quietly dignified, and it is possible to detect a flicker of irony in his satisfaction that the King 'hath pleased so graciously (in imitation of God that chastiseth when he loveth) to show me my faults'.

'Failure is an orphan.' It has frequently been written that after the collapse of the negotiations for the Great Contract, Salisbury was a broken man on the brink of ruin. This view sees him spurned by the King and also by Parliament, suitors and other officials. But much of the so-called evidence for this woeful decline is unsatisfactory and rests on little more than contemporary gossip, itself tainted by wishful thinking. In fact Salisbury retained all his offices, even as his delicate health and body began to disintegrate under the strain and business had to be postponed because of this very evident deterioration. It was a simple fact that, having conducted the King's business for so long and in such an individual manner, he was indispensable.[26] Furthermore, suitors continued to besiege him, so clearly they knew it too, and later Bishop Goodman noted his ability to achieve what they wanted right up to his death. Even Bacon, whose career was at last prospering and who might have smelled the shroud about his cousin, continued to send polite, submissive letters. Nor were Salisbury's informal relations with the royal family sundered. In August 1611, for example, James visited the house at Cranborne, having appointed the Lord Treasurer and the Earl of Suffolk joint Lord Lieutenants of the county in June.[27]

James had no inclination to dismiss Salisbury because he was sufficiently astute to realize the difficulty of replacing a man who understood so well the convolutions of domestic and foreign affairs. He could eventually shrug off his minister's failure to make him solvent because ultimately it was of no great interest to him – in fact he 'was never more than sporadically concerned about the state of his finances'.[28] All he needed was a supply of cash. This majestic indifference reached a kind of apotheosis in February 1611 when James distributed over £30,000 to six men – four of them Scots. It really does seem appropriate to refer to 'insane bounty'.[29] James had inherited from his mother the cheerful knack of ignoring realistic restraints on his royal wishes – he was, in the exact sense, a congenital idiot. He was in the happy position of being able to indulge his grotesque whims, knowing that no one could prevent him. As yet Parliament could not muster an organized resistance to regal self-indulgence, and Salisbury simply went on toiling in his service.

The ailing Salisbury still nudged and prodded the old sources to give James an income. A new and improved set of instructions for the management of the Court of Wards was introduced in January 1611. An important reform gave relatives and friends of a ward an exclusive opportunity to claim the wardship in the month following the death of the previous tenant. Clearly, not everyone regarded Salisbury's administration of the court as onerous. At this time William Haines (or Heynes) of Chessington, a freeman of the City of London and of sufficient importance and substance to be deemed a merchant, was making his will to provide for a large, young family after his demise. Haines, a valued friend and financial adviser to the Earl of Southampton, wrote: ' . . . all my life I have seen the Earl of Salisbury . . . to be a careful protector of the said wards. . . . '

The social aspirations of the upwardly mobile could also be converted into cash benefits for the Crown. Wealthy commoners could hanker after a hereditary title, and to exploit this Salisbury promoted an exclusive scheme whereby for a payment of some £1,000, a man could obtain a baronetcy. He might have been happier if more people with an annual income of more than £1,000 had applied, but the scheme still made a useful £50,000 in three years. This was topped up by an enhancement of the annual rent for the farm of the Great Custom, as well as the revaluation of the gold coinage. Salisbury also sought old foreign debt payments, and although nothing could be expected from Queen Marie de Médicis of France, who was buying support for her regency by pouring out the thirteen million livres accumulated by Sully, James did begin to receive £40,000 annually from the Estate-General of the United Provinces. Negotiations with Savoy and Florence for the marriage of Prince Henry also had a pecuniary aspect, even though they failed. The remaining domestic option was, of course, borrowing and the Lord Treasurer nervously informed the Crown's most important creditors that only interest payments were possible. In October 1611, when the situation was exceptionally parlous, the government revived the notion of a forced loan, since the ordinary money market was proving so turgid. James may have hoped for £200,000 or more, but he received only about £116,000.

By this time it is not even certain that Salisbury, his mind fogged by pain and bodily infirmity, cared very much. Thriving gossip suggested that the office of Secretary might go to Sir Henry Neville, who had made himself a reputation as an independent-minded Parliamentarian and had been taken up by Sir Thomas Overbury and Viscount Rochester. By spring 1612, when it was becoming clear that Salisbury was ebbing fast, it was a commonplace around Whitehall that Neville was a candidate, as was Sir Thomas Lake, who had the support of the Howards.[30] John More wrote to Sir Ralph Winwood:

> My Lord Treasurer's malady doth daily increase, to the
> great discomfort of his friends and followers. He hath,
> besides an ague, a deflation of rheum upon his stomach,
> and withall difficultam respirandi; and which is worst of all
> he is melancholy and heavy-spirited; so as it is on all hands
> concluded, that his Lordship must shortly leave this world,
> or at least disburden himself of a great part of his affairs.

Government activity slowed to a negligible pace, and in
March 1612 James declined to make even a decision about
Venetian diplomatic status without Salisbury's advice.[31]

It was of course the Lord Treasurer's doctors who got most
out of him as they struggled through a host of supposed
remedies for his catalogue of ailments. Among those who
attended him were de Mayerne, a Paracelsian once expelled
from Paris but now emphatically a powerful figure in London's medical community; Atkins; Poe; Matthew Lister;
Hammond and Sergeant Goderous, as well as four surgeons
and apothecary Higgins. It is known that Thomas Baskerville,
the apothecary in Exeter whose son Nicholas became a rich
royal physician and was knighted, obtained supplies of ben-
zoin imported from Sumatra; musk from China and Tibet, as
well as china root, camphor and rhubarb from China.[32] He
and Higgins used medicinal rhubarb, which the Roman surgeon Dioscorides the Cilician described in Book III of his *De
materia medica*. This was translated by Philemon Holland in
1601 and stated that the root was valuable in disorders of the
stomach and intestines, and could also be used for asthma and
sciatica. Pliny the Elder had thought it good for weak livers,
kidney troubles and swollen spleens, as well as cramps and
convulsions.[33] Not all the many items imported by apoth-
ecaries were expensive, but if he could have bought health it
seems certain Salisbury would have – indeed, he tried. In
December 1611 when he had rheumatism in his right arm £45
was distributed, and then in the following March over £350.
In April, before the pilgrimage to Bath for the waters, the

surgeon Watson received £15 and Mayerne another £50 to add to his previous month's payment of £100.[34]

According to John Finet, writing to William Trumball, the ambassador in Brussels, the party of about sixty left London on 27 April to stay with Walter Cope in his Kensington home. The following night was spent with Lord Chandos at Ditton Park, and among those in attendance were Salisbury's chaplain Bowles; Sir Michael Hickes; a clutch of medical men; as well as the harpist Cormack MacDermott. Among the servants was a nephew of the late Thomas Bellott, also named Thomas. The extreme discomfort of the patient led to 'many stops, and shifts from his coach to his litter, and to his chair', so that they arrived on 3 May with Cope, who left his home only two days earlier.

Getting Salisbury in and out of the water, which was allowed to rise only as far as his navel, required a specially padded chair suspended from a pulley. The partial immersion did bring some respite that offered hope: ' . . . he discovered such cheerfulness of humour, riddance of pains, recovery of sleep, increase of appetite, and decrease of swellings, as made our comforts grow to the proportions of our affections, and promise ourselves a cure. . . .' But this was not to be, though during the all too brief remission the earl was able to undertake at least one pious sightseeing visit to the Abbey church, expressing the wish that if he should die in Bath he should be interred in the building so favoured by Thomas Bellott (senior). John Bowles wrote to the Bishop of Bath and Wells of the visit and noted the earl's declared intention to 'bestow some good remembrance to the finishing thereof'. Moreover, because the older Bellott (d. 1611) had spent his money on 'charitable uses and left nothing for his kinsman, my lord in church said "I give to my servant Bellott £20 a year during his natural life"'.[35]

The dying man's spiritual perturbations were strongly manifested in the eschatological drift of his conversations with Bowles. These would have been easier for everyone had not his excruciating pains returned. The much older Hickes, whose early close friendship with the great man had fallen away over the last few years (and who was soon to die himself), found these scenes of torment most disturbing, and to mask his unease and sadness he wrote to Sir Hugh Beeston, a friend of both men, inviting him to join them to fabricate some diverting conversation and play cards. He put the bait facetiously to Beeston that so ill was the Lord Treasurer that they were bound to win a few pounds, or failing that a respectable garment like an almost new velvet cloak. This was levity used to shroud sorrow. A man of the buoyant geniality of Hickes (who married late and cheerfully acquired a horde of stepchildren) must have found it very difficult to adjust to the profound physical and psychological changes in his friend. The careworn realist was now straining after extinction, having set his mind on last things in the conventional manner of the period among believers: 'My life, full of cares and miseries, desireth to be dissolved.' Such was his state of morbid self-scrutiny that he felt himself to be in a transcendental state, a not uncommon sensation for those caught in an emotional maelstrom compounded by physical pain. Rant, prayers and tears eventually left him in a kind of stupor, 'so that for a great while there was nothing but a mournful silence'.[36]

Salisbury maintained his court contacts through the Herbert brothers, the 3rd Earl of Pembroke, who had recently become a privy councillor, and the Earl of Montgomery, both of whom hovered at his bedside. At some point he was visited by Sir John Harington, the victim of a stroke, also seeking to sluice away the ravages of age, and Salisbury managed one halting quip about this meeting of what he called cripples. He had too a last encounter with Cranborne, for William Cecil, with a touching and uncharacteristic boldness, had disobeyed his father to join him in Bath. It was an encounter freighted with emotion, with Salisbury exhorting the young man to 'embrace true religion, live honestly and virtuously, loyal to thy Prince and faithful to thy wife'. Then he took the sacrament from Bowles because, as he had written in his will, it gave 'spiritual comfort and strength, even then when I shall

211

be nearest the end of this my mortal life and beginning of the other in Heaven'.

After some sixteen days in Bath and the earlier rejection by Atkins and Poe of further partial immersion, Salisbury gathered all his scattered remnants of strength and decided to return to London. On 21 May 1612 the party set out, having been recently joined by Sir John Holles and Lord Hay, whose message from the King was delivered with a diamond ring. Reaching Marlborough, Salisbury probably stayed in St Margaret's Rectory, where he died on 24 May between one and two in the afternoon. Bowles recorded the end:

. . . though sinking rapidly, he insisted on standing erect with the aid of his crutches, while prayers were being offered. How he repeated the principal parts with affection, then, lying with his head on two pillows and his body in a swing, [he] called for Dr Poe's hand, which he gripped hard, when his eyes began to settle, and he sank down without a groan, sigh or struggle.

Epilogue

> Hang mournful epitaphs, and do all rites
> That appertain unto a burial.
>
> *Much Ado About Nothing*, Act IV, Scene i

Salisbury's decaying body was placed in a coffin and transported to Hatfield for burial on 9 June. Although he had requested an inexpensive funeral his declared wish was overturned by a newly confident William Cecil, who managed to spend some £2,000, much of it on mourning drapes, though few aristocratic mourners were present.[1] The tomb for St Etheldreda's, Hatfield, a short walk from his palace, was not ready. On completion, however, it was a superb monument and survived virtually unscathed the baleful attitude to such things of Puritan iconoclasts a generation later. Planning it had begun as early as 1609 for 'If a man does not erect in this age his own tomb, ere he dies, he shall live no longer in monument than the bell rings' (*Much Ado*, Act V, Scene ii). The chosen sculptor was Maximilien Colt, who made a submission in November of that year.

Those who read devotional literature and then gave serious thought to their end and the disposal of their body often rejected plain obscurity, especially if something more extravagant was within their means. Sir Christopher Hatton's massive tomb, ascribed to another religious refugee immigrant like Colt, Richard Stevens, was perhaps the most notorious example of sepulchral ostentation, surpassing even that

213

prepared for the Earl of Leicester in St Mary's, Warwick. Unlike Hatton, neither Burghley nor his son commanded a space for themselves in one of the busiest buildings in Renaissance London. They ignored too Westminster Abbey, where both had buried wives and where the incongruously boyish figure of Robert in an apple-green suit with a lavender cloak appeared on his mother's tomb. The curiosity of Burghley's effigy in St Martin's, Stamford (Lincolnshire) is that it represents him in armour while holding his wand of office, when the man was diffident about even riding a horse. This manly style was often repeated, however inappropriate.

Armour is the significant decorative device (this time appropriate) for the tomb commissioned by the widow of the soldier Sir Francis Vere, probably from Colt. Though now dismally neglected in Westminster Abbey, shunted into dusty obscurity, it is of particular interest as an example of the two-tier arrangement also seen in Salisbury's tomb. Vere's robed effigy lies on the usual marble version of the thin flat mat that was rolled at one end under the head. This commonly repeated item illustrated the ancient custom of laying the dying on a mat placed on the ground. It symbolized humility and contrition, and re-established corporeal contact with Mother Earth at the time of death.[2] Above Vere is the slab carried on the shoulders of near life-size figures kneeling on one knee. Surely not the sons of the dead man, as has been suggested, but Caesar, Regulus, Philip of Macedon and Alexander carved in a less than pleasing striped toffee alabaster. The slab itself is of tuche, generally referred to as black marble but actually a black slate. Resting on it, again in alabaster, is a suit of armour in pieces, a sword and a shield of arms. The artistic inspiration for this was probably French or Dutch.[3] Colt, who was born about 120 miles from Breda, must have known the famous transi tomb of Count Engelbert of Nassau (d. 1525) by the well-travelled sculptor Jean Mone van Metz. Above the transis of the count and his wife he placed a slab with war trophies resting on the shoulders of four kneeling knights. Perhaps Colt sketched this for Salisbury; it is not possible to say definitely that in 1588, when Cecil made a private excursion into the southern Low Countries, he saw it for himself.

Salisbury's tomb was eventually placed in the newly built (c. 1600–10) north (or Salisbury) chapel. Free-standing, it dominates the space t. one side of the altar in what was then widely regarded as a position sought by the privileged. Like Vere's it consists of a low, polished tuche base or ground plinth, at the corners of which are four white marble kneeling matrons supporting on their shoulders a rectangular slab of tuche on which lies the white marble gisant of the earl. It is something between $63\frac{1}{2}$ and 64 inches from the top of the head to the feet, and so may be a little over life-size.[4] Salisbury is holding his painted white wand of office (a rare original?) and hence is not praying.

Colt replaced the martial figures with female allegorical representations of the Virtues. Their flowing robes were carved with a confident generosity and the arrangement of their hair is also in the Italianate manner. Only Prudence, holding a mirror and with a snake coiling round her arm, is shown bare-breasted, a most daring rendering for that time in England. Justice holds a sword in one hand and scales in the other; Wisdom wears a wreath and armour, holding half her broken column in her left hand, while the right rests on the remnant; Temperance holds two urns with one placed on the ground, the other lying athwart her flexed knee. The urn, derived from antique examples, 'served in general as a symbol of death'.[5] It has been noted that the use of the Virtues in this manner had its roots in the French royal tombs, but then they were also annexed to replace a suspect pre-Reformation iconographic vocabulary.

Salisbury is shown flat on the slab (no 'toothache' pose here), with his eyes open in the traditional North European mode. He is bare-headed and wearing at least some Garter apparel, since he was probably buried in it. The two-fringed tasselled cushions under his head may be copies of those placed in the tomb, or the two on which he expired. Below the

215

slab is the unflinching representation of a full skeleton, exactly the same size as the gisant.[6] A few teeth are missing and it lies on the usual flat mat. This mode may relate it to the skeletalized transi on the tomb of Raynout III at Vianen in east Holland rather than the shrouded figures at Breda, but such a representation also appeared on earlier English tombs such as that of Dean John Colet (d. 1519).[7] By showing here the final stage of decomposition (*pulvis*), Colt simplified his task since he could omit the shroud so often used to give discreet covering to the lower body. The skeleton of the dean nearly a century before had reflected the hope of resurrection. Now it is merely a striking funerary accessory, with the wry reflection implied that at last all bodies come to this.

This grand tomb is equally strikingly in black and white material only, a pioneering example of the style popularized later in the century.[8] The rejection of the cheerful polychrome decoration found on so many tombs is notable, and the sobriety is all the more astonishing when compared with the flagrant richness of the nearby chapel of Hatfield House. This rarefied dignity could have stemmed from a rapid evolution of the patron's taste, or more likely because he was influenced in this matter by Sir Henry Wotton, who had seen the grandest Italian sepulchral art in Florence and Venice. Nor is there any inscription, though anonymity was not intended. Is it too whimsical to suggest that having been besieged by variously accented clamour in his life, Salisbury cherished the notion of a wordless tomb?

On 4 January 1614 Simon Basil signed a note detailing Colt's requirements for the completion of the commission. At the dead man's careful direction it was supposed to cost no more than £200, but the artist's submission was for £460 – more than the cost of the chapel. In this case Salisbury would certainly have thought it money well spent. As in so many aspects of his crowded life, the great servant was himself well served.

Abbreviations in Notes and References

AB	*Art Bulletin*
AHR	*American Historical Review*
BIIIR	*Bulletin of the Institute of Historical Research*
BL	British Library
CL	*Country Life*
CM	*Coin Monthly*
CSPD	*Calendar of State Papers Domestic*
CSPF	*Calendar of State Papers Foreign*
CSPV	*Calendar of State Papers Venetian*
EM	*Early Music*
EHR	*English Historical Review*
HT	*History Today*
JBS	*Journal of British Studies*
JBSMG-P	*Journal of the British Society of Master Glass-Painters*
JEH	*Journal of English History*
JMH	*Journal of Modern History*
JSA	*Journal of the Society of Archivists*
N & Q	*Notes and Queries*
PH	*Parliamentary History*
PRO	Public Record Office
RH	*Recusant History*
RD	*Renaissance Drama*
RC	Roxburghe Club
RHS	*Royal Historical Society*
TAPS	*Transactions of the American Philosophical Society*
WS	*Walpole Society*
WSURS	*Washington State University Research Studies*

Notes and References

CHAPTER 1

1 M.C. Bradbrook, *John Webster: Citizen and Dramatist* (1980), p. 86.
2 R.B. Sharpe, *The Real War of the Theaters* (1935), p. 121.
3 Sloane MS 2063, fol. 84.
4 L.A. Knafla, *Law and Politics in Jacobean England: The Tracts of Lord Chancellor Ellesmere* (1977), p. 45.
5 P.M. Handover, *The Second Cecil, 1563–1604* (1959), p. 14.
6 A. Esler, *The Aspiring Mind of the Elizabethan Younger Generation* (1966).
7 *CSPD*, 1581–90, p. 22.
8 A. Haynes, *The White Bear: Robert Dudley, the Elizabethan Earl of Leicester* (1987), p. 152.
9 *CSPD*, 1584, p. 199.
10 Handover, op. cit., pp. 40–1.
11 E. Butler, *The Cecils* (1964), p. 81.
12 Ibid., p. 89.
13 *CSPF*, II (1588), 281.
14 Ibid., 297.
15 D. Yahya, *Morocco in the 16th Century* (1981), pp. 135–6.
16 Butler, op. cit., p. 99.
17 A. Young, *Tudor and Jacobean Tournaments* (1987), p. 174.
18 W. Dunkel, *William Lambarde, English Jurist* (1965), p. 133.

CHAPTER 2

1 J. Winton, *Sir Walter Ralegh* (1975), pp. 128–9.

2 W. Ingram, *A London Life in the Brazen Age: Francis Langley, 1548–1602* (1978), p. 97.
3 Ibid.
4 Handover, *The Second Cecil*, p. 90.
5 R.C. Barnett, *Place, Profit and Power: A Study of the Servants of William Cecil, Elizabethan Statesman* (James Sprunt Studies in History and Political Science), vol. 51, p. 100.
6 Ingram, op. cit., p. 98.
7 Handover, op. cit., p. 89 (his name is given here as Bradbent).
8 Ingram, op. cit., p 101.
9 Ibid., p. 102.
10 Ibid., p. 103.
11 Ibid., p. 200.
12 Barnett, op. cit., pp. 149–50.
13 L. Stone, *An Elizabethan, Sir Horatio Palavicino* (1956), p. 249.
14 P.M. Handover, *Arabella Stuart* (1957), p. 95.
15 M. Edmond, *Hilliard and Oliver: The Lives and Works of Two Great Miniaturists* (1983), p. 116.
16 Ibid., p. 118.
17 A.G.R. Smith, *Servant of the Cecils: The Life of Sir Michael Hickes* (1977), pp. 98–9.
18 Ibid., pp. 99–100.
19 Harleian MS 6998, fols 97ff.

CHAPTER 3

1 Butler, *The Cecils*, p. 99.
2 Bradbrook, *John Webster*, p. 75.
3 Ibid.
4 R.E. Schreiber, *The Political Career of Sir Robert Naunton, 1589–1635* (1981), *RHS*, p. 3.
5 Harleian MS 871, fols 20–4.
6 Ibid., fols 50–1.
7 W.B. Devereux, *Lives and Letters of the Devereux, 1540–1646*, vol. 1 (1853), pp. 282–3.
8 A. Cecil, *A Life of Robert Cecil, First Earl of Salisbury* (1915) pp. 80–1.
9 Ibid.
10 T. Birch (ed.), *Memoirs of the Reign of Queen Elizabeth*, vol. 1

(1754), p. 165.
11 J.S. Cockburn, *A History of English Assizes, 1558–1714* (1972), p. 223.
12 Ibid., p. 224.
13 F.A. Inderwick, *The Inner Temple*, vol. 1 (1896), pp. 161–2.
14 F.M.G. Evans, *The Principal Secretary of State* (1923), p. 54.

CHAPTER 4

1 P. Johnson, *Elizabeth I* (1974), p. 333.
2 J. Stevenson (ed.), *Unton Correspondence* (1847), p. 237.
3 Bradbrook, *John Webster*, p. 82.
4 Schreiber, *Political Career of Sir Robert Naunton*, p. 4.
5 R.W. Kenny, *Elizabeth's Admiral: The Political Career of Charles Howard, Earl of Nottingham, 1536–1624* (1970), p. 199.
6 A.L. Rowse, *Simon Forman, Sex and Society in Shakespeare's Age*, (1974), p. 198.
7 Kenny, op. cit., p. 201.
8 Ingram, *A London Life*, p. 133.
9 Ibid., p. 134.
10 Ibid., p. 136.
11 Butler, *The Cecils*, p. 105.
12 Dunkel, *William Lambarde*, pp. 161–2.
13 Ingram, op. cit., p. 161.
14 A. Haynes, 'The Islands Voyage, 1597', *HT*, XXV, 10 (1975), 689–96.
15 Kenny, op. cit., p. 164.
16 L. Stone, *Family and Fortune: Studies in Aristocratic Finance in the Sixteenth and Seventeenth Centuries* (1973), p. 4.
17 J. Neale, *The Elizabethan House of Commons* (1949), p. 313.
18 *CSPD*, 1597–8, pp. 29–30.

CHAPTER 5

1 Johnson, *Elizabeth I*, p. 385.
2 A.L. Rowse, *The Expansion of Elizabethan England* (1955), p. 121.
3 *CSPD*, 1598–1601, pp. 88–9.
4 Handover, *The Second Cecil*, p. 183.

5 S.J. Watts, *From Border to Middle Shire* (1975), p. 81.
6 R.R. Reid, *Tudor Studies* (ed. R.W. Seton Watson) (1924), p. 228.
7 A. Collins (ed.), *Letters and Memorials of State* (Sidney Papers), vol. II (1746), p. 129.
8 G.P.V. Akrigg, *Shakespeare and the Earl of Southampton* (1968), p. 97.
9 L.L. Peck, *Northampton: Patronage and Policy at the Court of James I* (1982), pp. 17–18.
10 P.W. Hasler (ed.), *History of Parliament, 1558–1603*, vol. II, p. 479.
11 Sharpe, *Real War of the Theaters*, p. 21.
12 Johnson, op. cit., p. 408.
13 Ibid., p. 378.
14 Edmond, *Hilliard and Oliver*, p. 94.
15 S. Freedman, *Poor Penelope* (1983), p. 146.
16 HMC, Salisbury (Cecil) MS, vol. XI, p. 77.
17 Akrigg, op. cit., p. 152.

CHAPTER 6

1 Smith, *Servant of the Cecils*, p. 135.
2 Ibid., p. 134.
3 Stone, *Family and Fortune*, p. 4.
4 A.L. Rowse, 'Alltyrynys and the Cecils', *EHR*, LXXV (1960), 54–76.
5 B.W. Beckingsale, *Burghley: Tudor Statesman* (1967), p. 265.
6 Haynes, *The White Bear*, pp. 101–2.
7 J.B. Lingard, *The Houses of Robert Cecil, 1595–1612* (unpublished MA Report, Courtauld Institute, London University, 1981), p. 15.
8 Stone, op. cit., p. 33.
9 Lingard, op. cit., pp. 23–4.
10 Peck, *Northampton*, pp. 73–4.
11 My thanks to Julia Merritt for details here.
12 Ibid.
13 Ibid.
14 Edmond, *Hilliard and Oliver*, pp. 159–60.
15 Ibid., p. 168.
16 Ibid., p. 123.
17 Ibid., p. 48.
18 Ibid., p. 73.

19 Ibid., p. 143.
20 Butler, *The Cecils*, p. 121.
21 Purchasing a formula house in Dulwich does not constitute a profound interest in architecture and its principles.
22 R.P. Sorlien (ed.), *The Diary of John Manningham* (1976), p. 311.
23 Lingard, op. cit., p. 7.
24 Beckingsale, op. cit., p. 261.
25 C. Williams (ed.), *Thomas Platter's Travels, 1599* (1937), p. 173.
26 D. Hudson, *Holland House in Kensington* (1967), p. 3.
27 Stone, op. cit., p. 29.
28 Ibid., p. 34.
29 Ibid.
30 Lingard, op. cit., p. 32.
31 Ibid., pp. 39–40.
32 A. Oswald, *Country Houses of Dorset* (1959), p. 27.
33 Ibid.
34 Ibid., p. 125.
35 Lingard, op. cit., p. 40.
36 R.J.W. Evans, *Rudolf II and His World: A Study in Intellectual History, 1576–1612* (1973), pp. 185–6.
37 Stone, op. cit., p. 35.
38 Ibid., p. 36.
39 B. Sharp, *In Contempt of All Authority: Rural Artisans and Riot in the West of England, 1586–1660* (1980), p. 171.
40 Stone, op. cit., p. 38.
41 Ibid., p. 39.
42 A.L. Rowse, *Ralegh and the Throckmortons* (1962), p. 274.
43 Stone, op. cit., p. 36.
44 J. Thirsk, *Economic Policy and Projects: The Development of a Consumer Society in Early Modern England* (1978), p. 89.
45 Stone, op. cit., pp. 13–14.
46 Ibid.
47 R. Ashton, *The City and the Court, 1603–1643* (1979), pp. 20–1.
48 Ibid.
49 Ibid., p. 21.
50 Ibid., pp. 24–5.
51 Stone, op. cit., p. 40.
52 K.R. Andrews, 'Caribbean Rivalry and the Anglo–Spanish Peace', *History*, LIX (1974), 7.
53 Ibid., 8.

54 F. Braudel, *The Mediterranean and the Mediterranean World in the Age of Philip II* (1973), vol. II, p. 867.
55 K.R. Andrews, 'Sir Robert Cecil and Mediterranean Plunder', *EHR*, LXXXVII (1972), 579.
56 Ibid., 529.
57 Sir J. Neale, *Queen Elizabeth* (1934), p. 362.

CHAPTER 7

1 For details of Leicester's policy and problems see Haynes, *The White Bear*, chaps 18–20.
2 Stowe MS 179, fol. 2.
3 Haynes, op. cit., p. 189.
4 Stowe MS 179, fols 6–7.
5 L. Fox (ed.), *English Historical Scholarship in the 16th and 17th Centuries* (1956), pp. 21–2.
6 C. Roberts, *Schemes and Undertakings* (1985), p. 17.
7 Ibid., pp. 19–20.
8 HMC, Salisbury (Cecil) MS, vol. X, pp. 93–4; 155–6.
9 A.G.R. Smith, 'The Secretariats of the Cecils, *c.* 1580–1612', *EHR*, LXXXIII (1968), 497.
10 J. Goldberg, *James I and the Politics of Literature* (1983), pp. 70–1.
11 P. Croft, 'Parliamentary Preparations, September 1605: Robert Cecil, Earl of Salisbury on Free Trade and Monopolies', *PH*, 6, 1 (1987), p. 127.
12 Johnson, *Elizabeth I*, p. 417.
13 Sharpe, *Real War of the Theaters*, p. 215.
14 M. Nicholls, 'Sir Charles Percy', *RH*, 18, 3 (1987), 240.
15 Sharpe, op. cit., p. 216.
16 Ibid., p. 217.
17 W.M. Mitchell, *The Rise of the Revolutionary Party in the English House of Commons, 1603–1629* (1957), p. 13.

CHAPTER 8

1 A. Cherry, *Princes, Poets and Patrons* (1987), p. 75.
2 D. Norbrook, *Poetry and Politics in the English Renaissance* (1984), p. 197.

3 D.H. Willson, *King James VI and I* (1965), p. 135.
4 Ibid., p. 108.
5 D. Scarisbrick, 'Anne of Denmark's Jewellery: The Old and the New', *Apollo*, CXXIII, April 1986, 228.
6 Ibid.
7 Ibid.
8 Ibid.
9 M. Edmond, 'Limners and Picturemakers', *WS*, vol. 47 (1978–80), p. 79.
10 Scarisbrick, op. cit., 229.
11 J. Wormald, 'James VI and I: Two Kings or One?', *History* 68 (1983), 202.
12 J. Hurstfield, *The Queen's Wards* (1958), p. 300.
13 Smith, *Servant of the Cecils*, p. 113.
14 Stone *Family and Fortune*, p. 23.
15 Smith, *Servant of the Cecils*, p. 116.
16 Ibid., p. 117.
17 Stone, op. cit., p. 22.
18 Ibid.
19 Ibid.
20 Hurstfield, op. cit., pp. 306–7.
21 Ibid., pp. 308–9.
22 P. Croft, 'Wardship in the Parliament of 1604', *PH*, 2 (1983), 40.
23 Ibid.
24 Ibid., 41.
25 Ibid.
26 Ibid., 43.
27 PRO, S.P. 14/52/88.
28 Croft, op. cit., 47n, 15.
29 Ibid., 45.
30 Ibid., 46.
31 Ibid.
32 A.G.R. Smith, 'The Great Contract of 1610', *The English Commonwealth, 1547–1640: Essays in Politics and Society.* Presented to Joel Hurstfield (eds) P. Clark, A.G.R. Smith and N. Tyacke (1979), p. 115.
33 E. Lindquist, 'The Failure of the Great Contract', *JMH*, 57 (1985), 620.

CHAPTER 9

1 Evans, *Rudolf II*, p. 133.
2 Ibid., p. 77.
3 Details kindly provided in a private letter from Dr Evans.
4 Evans, op. cit., pp. 150–1.
5 D.B. Quinn, *The Elizabethans and the Irish* (1966), pp. 71–2.
6 Kenny, *Elizabeth's Admiral*, p. 265.
7 M. Lee, *James I and Henri IV* (1970), p. 20.
8 A.J. Loomie, 'Sir Robert Cecil and the Spanish Embassy', *BIHR*, XLII (1969), 56.
9 Lee, op. cit., p. 23.
10 Ibid., 26.
11 Loomie, op. cit., p. 57.
12 Ibid., 31.
13 A.J. Loomie, 'Toleration and Diplomacy', *TAPS*, ns 53, 6 (1963), 28.
14 Ibid.
15 Ibid., 30.
16 A.J. Loomie, 'Francis Fowler II, English Secretary to the Spanish Embassy, 1609–1619', *RH*, 12 (1973–4), 70.
17 Loomie, 'Toleration', op. cit., 31.
18 S. Parnell Kerr, 'The Constable Kept an Account', *N & Q*, ns IV (1957), 169.
19 Ibid., 167.
20 Loomie, 'Toleration', op. cit., 34.
21 Parnell Kerr, op. cit., 168.
22 R.W. Kenny, 'The Earl of Nottingham's Embassy to Spain in 1605', *HT*, 20, 3 (1970), 199.
23 Parnell Kerr, op. cit., 168.
24 Ibid.
25 A.J. Collins, *Jewels and Plate of Queen Elizabeth I: The Inventory of 1574* (1955), p. 136.
26 O.M. Dalton, *The Royal Gold Cup in the British Museum* (1924).
27 Parnell Kerr, op. cit., 169.
28 Kenny, *Elizabeth's Admiral*, p. 285.
29 Nicholls, op. cit., 240.

CHAPTER 10

1 J. Simon, *Education and Society in Tudor England* (1966), p. 363.
2 D.H. Willson, 'King James I and Anglo–Scottish Unity', in W.A. Aiken and B.D. Henning (eds), *Conflict in Stuart England* (1960), p. 47.
3 B. Galloway, *The Union of England and Scotland, 1603–8* (1986), p. 17.
4 Ibid., p. 18.
5 R. Miles, *Ben Jonson, His Life and Work* (1986), p. 95.
6 Galloway, op. cit., p. 19.
7 J.R. Tanner, *Constitutional Documents of the Reign of James I* (1930), p. 26.
8 Galloway, op. cit., p. 21.
9 Ibid., p. 24.
10 J. Mackay, 'From Elizabeth to Elizabeth Part 4', James I, pt 1, 1st and 2nd Period Coinages 1603–11, *CM* (1978), 41–8.
11 Galloway, op. cit., p. 63.
12 Ibid.
13 D.H. Willson, 'The Earl of Salisbury and the "Court" Party in Parliament, 1604–10', *AHR*, XXXVI (1931), 277.
14 Ibid.
15 J.K. Gruenfelder, *Influence in Early Stuart Elections, 1604–40* (1981), p. 35.
16 Ibid., pp. 35–6.
17 Ibid.
18 Ibid., p. 53 n. 7.
19 Ibid., pp. 45–6.
20 Ibid., p. 37.
21 Croft, 'Parliamentary Preparations', 127–8.
22 Ibid., 129.
23 Ibid., 128.
24 Ibid., 129.
25 Willson, 'The Earl of Salisbury', op. cit., 280.
26 Roberts, *Schemes and Undertakings*, p. 8.
27 Ibid., p. 12.
28 Willson, op. cit., 287.
29 Galloway, op. cit., p. 79.
30 *CSPV*, 1603–7, pp. 303–4.
31 Galloway, op. cit., p. 82.

32 Ibid., p. 127.

CHAPTER 11

1 A point made by Dr Nicholas Tyacke in a private letter.
2 N. Tyacke, *Anti-Calvinists: The Rise of English Arminianism, c. 1590–1640* (1987), p. 12.
3 P. Collinson, 'The Jacobean Religious Settlement: The Hampton Court Conference', in H. Tomlinson (ed.), *Before the English Civil War* (1983), p. 38.
4 Ibid.
5 F. Shriver, 'Hampton Court Re-visited: James I and the Puritans', *JEH*, 33, 1 (1982), 57.
6 J. Hurstfield, *Freedom, Corruption and Government in Elizabethan England* (1973), p. 101.
7 Tyacke, op. cit., p. 22.
8 A. Foster, 'The Function of a Bishop: The Career of Richard Neile', in R. O'Day and F. Heal (eds), *Continuity and Change: Personnel of the Church in England, 1500–1642* (1976), p. 45.
9 Loomie, 'Sir Robert Cecil', op. cit., 46.
10 Tyacke, op. cit., p. 114.
11 Ibid., pp. 22–3.
12 Ibid.
13 Ibid., 23.
14 Hurstfield, op. cit., p. 334.

CHAPTER 12

1 Hurstfield, *Freedom, Corruption and Government*, p. 333.
2 J. Wormald, 'Gunpowder, Treason and Scots', *JBS*, 24 (1985), 151.
3 Ibid., 150.
4 D. Cecil (Lord David Cecil), *The Cecils of Hatfield House* (1973), p. 231.
5 Wormald, op. cit., 153.
6 Hurstfield, op. cit., p. 98.
7 Ibid., p. 124.
8 Wormald, op. cit., 158; 160.

227

9 P. Durst, *Intended Treason* (1970), p. 33. Durst mistakenly refers to the Earl of Hertford.

10 L. Hicks, 'The Exile of Dr William Gifford from Lille in 1606', *RH*, 7, 5 (1964), 230 n. 12.

11 Wormald, op. cit., 163.

12 Hurstfield, op. cit., p. 334.

13 A. Wilson, *The History of Great Britain* (1653), p. 32.

14 M. Hotine, 'Contemporary Themes in "The Tempest"', *N & Q*, ns 34, 2 (1987), 226.

15 G.P.V. Akrigg, *Jacobean Pageant or the Court of King James I* (1962), p. 74.

16 B. de Luna, *Jonson's Romish Plot: A Study of 'Catiline' and Its Historical Context* (1967) pp. 44–5.

17 C. Cross, *Church and People* (1976), p. 166.

18 Smith, 'Secretariats', op. cit., 496.

19 Lee, *James I and Henri IV*, p. 44.

20 Ibid., p. 45.

21 Hicks, op. cit., 214.

22 Ibid., 221.

23 F. Edwards, 'The Attempt in 1608 on Hugh Owen, Intelligencer for the Archdukes in Flanders', *RH*, 17 (1984), 141.

24 Ibid.

CHAPTER 13

1 Rowse, *Ralegh*, p. 215.

2 HMC Salisbury (Cecil) MS, vol. IX, p. 383.

3 Bradbrook, *John Webster*, p. 66.

4 Cecil, *The Cecils*, p. 142.

5 Ibid.

6 Ibid.

7 R.E. Strong (Sir Roy Strong), *Henry, Prince of Wales and England's Lost Renaissance* (1986), p. 45.

8 Stone, *Family and Fortune*, p. 30.

9 L. Pearsall Smith, *Life and Letters of Sir Henry Wotton*, 2 vols (1907), vol. 2, p. 501.

10 P. Holman, 'The Harp in Stuart England: New Light on William Lawes's Harp Consorts', *EM*, 15, 2 (1987), 190.

11 HMC Salisbury (Cecil) MS, vol. VIII, p. 498.

12 R. Charteris, *John Coprario: A Thematic Catalogue of His Music* (1977), p. 16.
13 Ibid., p. 17.
14 S. Donnelly, 'An Irish Harper and Composer', *Ceol*, VIII, 1 and 2 (1985/6), 40.
15 Ibid.
16 Holman, op. cit., 188–9.
17 Ibid.
18 Ibid.
19 Smith, *Servant of the Cecils*, p. 167. It was Thomas Bellott (the younger) who sought it, and his success was due to Sir John Denham.
20 S. Donnelly, 'The Irish Harp in England, 1590–1690', *Ceol*, VII, 1 and 2 (December 1984), 54.
21 M. Stein, 'Christian IV, a "Renaissance Man"', *Apollo*, CXX (December 1984), 368; see also C. Christensen, 'From Elsinore to London', *Apollo*, CXXVIII (August 1988), 110–13.
22 A. Oswald, *The London Charterhouse* (1959), p. 33.
23 D. Howarth, *Lord Arundel and His Circle* (1985), p. 28.
24 Ibid., p. 30.
25 Stone, op. cit., p. 84.
26 A.L. Wilkinson, 'The Great East Window of the Chapel of Hatfield House', *JBSMG-P*, XII, 4 (1958–9), 245.
27 Stone, op. cit., p. 85.
28 L.M. Munbry, *The Hertfordshire Countryside* (1977), p. 151.
29 P. Leith-Ross, *The John Tradescants: Gardeners to the Rose and Lily Queen* (1984), p. 28.
30 Ibid., p. 30.
31 T.H. Clarke, 'I Am the Horn of a Rhinoceros', *Apollo*, CXXV, May (1987), 349 n. 18.
32 Stone, op. cit., p. 88.
33 Ibid., p. 89.
34 M. Heinemann, *Puritanism and Theatre* (1980), p. 122.
35 R.E. Strong (Sir Roy Strong), *The Renaissance Garden in England* (1979), p. 105.
36 Leith-Ross, op. cit., p. 31.
37 Ibid., p. 37; also Stone, op. cit., p. 90.
38 Stone, op. cit., p. 96.
39 Ibid., p. 102.
40 J.P. Allan, *Medieval and Post-Medieval Finds from Exeter* (1984), pp. 105–7.

41 S. McMullin, 'Jonson's Early Entertainments: New Information from Hatfield House', *RD*, ns I (1968), 163.
42 Oswald, op. cit., p. 34.
43 Stone, op. cit., p. 103.
44 Oswald, op. cit., p. 22.
45 R.A. Skelton and J. Summerson, 'A Description of Maps and Architectural Drawings in the Collection made by William Cecil', *RC* (1971), 10 n. 3.
46 Leith-Ross, op. cit., p. 178.
47 F.P. Wilson, *The Plague in Shakespeare's London* (1927), p. 38.

CHAPTER 14

1 Howarth, *Lord Arundel*, p. 26.
2 H. Avray Tipping, 'Hatfield House', *CL*, LXI (1927), 471.
3 J.M. Rodney, 'The Earl of Salisbury and Henry Frederick, Prince of Wales', *WSURS*, XXX (1965), 56.
4 HMC Salisbury (Cecil) MS, vol. XI, p. 84.
5 Rodney, op. cit., 60.
6 Strong, *Henry, Prince of Wales*, p. 152.
7 Loomie, 'Toleration and Diplomacy', op. cit., 43.
8 Ibid., 56.
9 Ibid., 41.
10 Stone, *Family and Fortune*, p. 58.
11 Collins, *Jewels and Plate of Elizabeth I*, p. 326.
12 Stone, op. cit., p. 29.
13 Ibid., p. 26.
14 Smith, 'Secretariats', op. cit., 493.
15 D. Thomas, 'Financial and Administrative Developments', in H. Tomlinson (ed.), *Before the English Civil War: Essays on Early Stuart Politics and Government* (1983), pp. 104–5.
16 L.M. Hill, *Bench and Bureaucracy: The Public Career of Sir Julius Caesar, 1580–1636* (1988), p. 142.
17 Thomas, op. cit., p. 105.
18 Peck, *Northampton*, p. 132.
19 Thomas, op. cit., 107.
20 Sharp, *In Contempt*, pp. 84–5.
21 Ibid., pp. 91–2.
22 R. Ashton, *Reformation and Revolution, 1558–1660* (1984), p. 201.
23 Ibid.

CHAPTER 15

1 J.P. Sommerville, *Politics and Ideology in England 1603–1640* (1986), p. 122.
2 Ibid., p. 123.
3 Ibid., p. 124.
4 Lindquist, 'Failure', op. cit., 626.
5 Smith, 'The Great Contract', op. cit., p. 112.
6 Ibid.
7 Ibid., 633–4.
8 Smith, op. cit., p. 119.
9 Lindquist, op. cit., 638.
10 Knafla, *Law and Politics*, 88–9.
11 Lindquist, op. cit., 638.
12 Smith, op. cit., p. 00.
13 Lindquist, op. cit., 641 n. 10.
14 Stone, *Family and Fortune*, p. 47.
15 D. Hirst, *The Representative of the People?* (1975); see also W. Notestein, *The House of Commons, 1604–1610* (1971).
16 Smith, op. cit., p. 123.
17 HMC Buccleuch, I, p. 102.
18 Knafla, op. cit., p. 79.
19 Roberts, op. cit., p. 15.
20 Willson, 'The Earl of Salisbury', op. cit., 291.
21 Lindquist, op. cit., 644.
22 Ibid., 645.
23 Roberts, *Schemes and Undertakings*, p. 15.
24 E. Lindquist, 'The Last Years of the First Earl of Salisbury, 1610–12', *Albion*, 18, 1 (1986), 29.
25 Ibid., 31.
26 Ibid., 33.
27 Ibid., 35.
28 Ibid., 40.
29 Hurstfield, *Freedom, Corruption and Government*, p. 187.
30 Roberts, op. cit., p. 9.
31 Lindquist, op. cit., 33 n. 44.
32 Allan, *Medieval and Post-Medieval Finds*, p. 107.
33 W. Gardener, 'Rhubarb', *HT*, XXI, 8 (1971), 585.
34 Stone, op. cit., p. 53.
35 A.E. Bush and J. Hatton, *Thomas Bellott, 1534–1611*, The Friends

of Bath Abbey (1966), p. 15.
36 Cecil, *The Cecils*, p. 157.

EPILOGUE

1 Stone, *Family and Fortune*, p. 55.
2 K. Cohen, *Metamorphosis of a Death Symbol* (1973), p. 59. Dr Cohen generously sent me additional material. See also H. s'Jacob, *Idealism and Realism: A Study of Sepulchral Symbolism* (1954), p. 53.
3 B. Kemp, *English Church Monuments* (1980), p. 77.
4 Details kindly provided by Mr Henry W. Gray of Hatfield.
5 Kemp, op. cit., p. 71.
6 See note 4 above.
7 J.W. Hurtig, 'Seventeenth Century Shroud Tombs: Classical Revival and Anglican Context', *AB*, LXIV, 2 (1982), 219.
8 Kemp, op. cit., p. 77.

Index

Brooke, William, 10th Lord Cobham, 18, 20, 49, 50
Bruce, Edward, of Kinloss, 66, 89, 146
Brussels, 32, 85, 87, 119, 123, 125, 148, 169, 175, 210
Buckett, Rowland, 168, 173, 179, 180
Burbage, Robert, 20
Burghley House (Lincs), 68, 72
Burghley, Lord, see Cecil, William (1st Lord Burghley)
Butler, Richard (glazier), 174, 179
Bye Plot, 147

Cadiz, 44, 46, 47, 48, 50
Caesar, Dr (Sir) Julius, 82, 152, 165, 189, 190, 196, 199
Calais, 19, 46–7, 54, 155
Cambridge, University of, 36, 141, 143, 144, 163–4
Carew, Sir Francis, 78
Carew, Sir George, 56, 161 ,187
Carey, George (of Cockington), 48
Carey, George, 2nd Lord Hunsdon, 50, 78, 85, 92, 93, 95
Carey, Sir John, 93
Carey, Sir Robert, 92–5
Carleton, Sir Dudley, 135, 165, 177
Carmarden, Richard, 25, 26, 48
Carr, Sir Robert, Viscount Rochester, 200–1, 204, 205, 208
Catesby, Robert, 71, 151, 154, 155, 156,
Caux, Salomon de, 175–6
Cecil, Lady Catherine, 69, 162
Cecil, Lady Dorothy (née Perrot), 20
Cecil, Lady Elizabeth (née Brooke), 20, 49, 69, 161, 214
Cecil, Lady Frances, 12, 69, 162,
Cecil, Lady Mildred (née Cooke), 11, 12, 13, 14, 18, 20, 214
Cecil, Robert, Earl of Salisbury:
parents, 11; family connections, 11; physical deformity, 11–12; genetic inheritance, 12; nicknames, 12, 18, 31; education, 12–14; admitted to St John's College, Cambridge, 15; praise from Vice-Chancellor, 15; admitted to Gray's Inn, 15; travels to Paris (1584), 16; in company of Dr William Parry, 16; returns to London, 17; elected MP for Westminster, 17; execution of Parry, 17; re-elected MP (1586), 17; first

government duties, 17; joins embassy of Earl of Derby, 18; travels through Spanish Netherlands, 18; meeting with Duke of Parma, 18; meeting with Prince Maurice of Nassau, 19; returns to London, 19; death of sister Anne, 19; Armada crisis, 19; meeting with envoy of Shārif of Morocco, 19–20; courts Elizabeth Brooke, 20; death of mother, 20; possible benefits from death of Walsingham, 21; candidates for post of Secretary of State, 22; rivalry with Earl of Essex 22–3; knighted (1591), 22; joins Privy Council, 23; member of a conciliar commission, 24; commissioner dealing with captured 'Madre de Deus', 24–7; assisted by Ralegh, 26; tracks a stolen diamond, 27–9; deputizes for Burghley, 31; secret service contacts 31–2; maiden speech in Parliament, 34; growing political confidence, 35; High Steward of Cambridge University, 36; views on Lopez Conspiracy, 37–8; dealings with Essex, 39–40; power and patronage in Northern England, 42–3; preparations for Cadiz Expedition, 47–8; appointment as Secretary of State (1596), 47–8; aftermath of expedition, 49; party for Queen Elizabeth, 49; death of wife Elizabeth, 49; family mourning, 49; preparations for Islands Voyage (1597), 51; Cecil group in House of Commons, 52; envoy to King Henri IV of France, 54–5; death of father Burghley (1598), 55; Master of the Court of Wards (1599), 57; rival Essex in Ireland, 58; emergency privy council, 60; Cecil's 'mild courses', 61; useful secret service data, 63; rout of Essex rebellion, 64; speaks at trial of Essex, 64; helps Earl of Southampton, 66; secret correspondence with James VI, 66–7; provisions of Burghley's will, 68–9; Cecil's inheritance, 69; property development, 69; dealings with Nicholas Hilliard, 72–3; passion for rarities, 75–6; land purchases, 76–9; aspects of income,

237

Northampton, Earl of, *see* Howard (Lord Henry)
Northumberland, Earl of, *see* Percy (Lord Henry)
Nottingham, Earl of, *see* Howard (Charles)

Oldcorne, Fr John, S.J., 156
Oldenbarnevelt, Johan van, 116, 117
O'Neill, Hugh, Earl of Tyrone, 56, 58, 85, 114
Ostend, 18, 19, 116
Owen, Hugh, 153, 159
Oxford, Earl of, *see* de Vere (Edward)
Oxford, University of, 35, 77

Parker, William, 4th Baron Monteagle, 152–4, 156
Parliament, 79, 95, 106–10, 134, 136, 138, 139, 154, 155, 157, 158, 183, 184, 196, 197, 198, 200, 201, 202, 203, 205, 206, 207; House of Commons: 91, 106, 107, 108, 109, 120, 121, 131, 133, 134, 136, 137, 138, 140, 157, 195, 196, 197, 198, 200, 202, 203, 205; House of Lords: 53, 106, 107, 108, 109, 121, 137, 138, 195, 196, 203
Parry (ap Harry), Dr William, 16, 17
Pembroke, Earl of, *see* Herbert (William)
Percival, Richard, 133, 135
Percy, Sir Charles, 93, 127
Percy, Lord Henry, 13th Earl of Northumberland, 90, 93, 94–5, 117, 145, 146, 153, 177
Percy, Thomas, 42, 71, 154
Perez, Antonio, 36, 37, 44, 45–7
Persons, Fr Robert, S.J., 17, 65, 115, 184
Phelippes, Thomas, 36, 153
Philip II, King of Spain, 33, 36, 38, 45, 51, 55, 59, 64, 172
Philip III, King of Spain, 87, 115, 118, 119, 121, 122, 123, 151, 159, 185
plague, 36, 180–1
Platter, Thomas (Swiss writer), 75
Plymouth, 25, 48, 49, 51
Poe, Dr Leonard, 209, 212
Poems Lyrical and Pastoral (Drayton), 98
Popham, Sir John, 39, 60, 74
Portugal, 20, 21, 137
Prescott, Alexander (goldsmith), 79, 106, 125

Privy Council, 46, 49, 51, 52, 60, 63, 85, 92, 101, 115, 119, 129, 136, 144, 145, 146, 206
purveyance, 107, 110, 130, 195, 199, 203

Ralegh, Sir Walter, 24, 26, 29, 46, 50, 51, 52, 61, 82, 90, 94–5, 117, 147, 162, 176, 183, 204
Reynolds, Dr John, 142, 143, 145–6
Richard II (Shakespeare), 63
Richardot, Jean, 119, 120
Robida, Alessandro, 119, 120
Rochester, Viscount, *see* Carr
Rome, 42, 89, 96, 115
Rouen, 17, 30, 47, 86, 176
Royal Exchange, 125, 177
Royal Gold Cup, 125
Russell, Francis, 4th Earl of Bedford, 71
Rutland, Earl of, *see* Manners

Sackville, Thomas, Lord Buckhurst, 1st Earl of Dorset, 36, 60, 63, 65, 69, 79, 82, 85, 88, 93, 106, 120, 124, 126, 185, 188, 192
St Etheldreda's, Hatfield, 72, 213
St John's College, Cambridge, 13, 163
St Martin's Lane, 177, 180
St Paul's Cathedral, 93, 155
Salisbury House, London, 66, 70–1, 155, 174, 176–7, 178, 186
Sandys, Sir Edwin, 107, 130–1, 133, 136, 196
Savile, Sir Henry, 44, 177
Scotland, 97–8, 112, 113, 114, 128–9, 184
Seymour, Lord Edward, Earl of Hertford, 88, 89, 94, 95, 152
Shakespeare, William, 15, 63, 95–6, 98, 122–3, 154
Sherborne Abbey (Dorset), 57, 76, 162
Sherley, Sir Anthony, 113, 114–15, 162
ships: *Dainty*, 24; *Foresight*, 25; *Golden Dragon*, 24; *Lionness*, 82–3; *Lion's Whelp*, 48–9; *Madre de Deus* (*Dios*), 24, 34, 49; *Prudence*, 28; *Revenge*, 24; *Roebuck*, 24; *San Felipe*, 178; *Thomas*, 132; *Truelove*, 47, 52; *White Greyhound*, 83
Sidney, Sir Philip, 30, 167
Sidney, Sir Robert, 50
Skinner, Sir Vincent, 80, 135
Slavata, Vilém, 112, 114

238